SURVIVORS

SURVIVORS

What We Can Learn from How They Cope with Horrific Tragedy

GREGORY K. MOFFATT

PRAEGER

AN IMPRINT OF ABC-CLIO, LLC
Santa Barbara, California • Denver, Colorado • Oxford, England

Library of Congress Cataloging-in-Publication Data

Moffatt, Gregory K., 1961–
    Survivors : what we can learn from how they cope with horrific tragedy / Gregory K. Moffatt.
        p. cm.
    Includes bibliographical references and index.
    ISBN 978-0-313-37664-1 (alk. paper) — ISBN 978-0-313-37665-8 (ebook)
1. Psychic trauma.   2. Adjustment (Psychology)   3. Victims of violent crimes—Psychology.   4. Survival skills—Psychological aspects.   I. Title.
    BF175.5.P75M64   2010
    155.9'35—dc22   2009051214

ISBN: 978-0-313-37664-1
EISBN: 978-0-313-37665-8

14   13   12   11   10   1   2   3   4   5

This book is also available on the World Wide Web as an eBook.
Visit www.abc-clio.com for details.

Praeger
An Imprint of ABC-CLIO, LLC

ABC-CLIO, LLC
130 Cremona Drive, P.O. Box 1911
Santa Barbara, California 93116-1911

This book is printed on acid-free paper ∞
Manufactured in the United States of America

CONTENTS

PREFACE

It is only through adversity that we begin to see our true selves.

This book is, at least at this point in my professional life, the culmination of all that I am and all that is important to me—researcher, professor, psychologist, husband, and father. I know that sounds as though I might be overdramatizing a bit, but I'm not. The genesis of this book simmered in my thoughts for several years before I began writing and formally researching and, unlike my other books that I completed in about 12 months, this book took more than 10 years from beginning to end. In the beginning, it didn't start out to become what it is—a book about the meaning of life. I started out writing a clinical psychology book on trauma. As I look backwards, I can see that the evolution of my personal and professional life has led me to this point.

I have invested nearly 20 years of my career studying violent behavior. My original interest when I began my work as a fledgling PhD graduate was to learn ways to assess risk of violence among historically nonviolent individuals. I wrote articles, researched, and presented my findings to many groups ranging from businesses to law-enforcement agencies to therapists and physicians. This pursuit prompted me to write my first book, *Blind-Sided: Homicide Where It Is Least Expected*. From that study arose the question as to why people were aggressive to begin with. That led to my second book, *A Violent Heart.* In this second book I briefly addressed children and the development of aggression. By the conclusion of that work I realized aggressive children and aggression against children deserved its own book. Therefore, I wrote *Wounded Innocents and Fallen Angels.* My goal was to help therapists, physicians, parents, and others interested in child abuse and child aggression to understand child abuse and also to understand the treatment of aggression in children as well as trauma resulting from being a victim of child abuse. As I was writing this book I was also working on a parenting book that was completed just a few months after I sent my final draft of *Wounded Innocents* to my publisher. I chose to write a parenting book because during the course of writing all of my books, articles, and newspaper columns as well as through my experience as a therapist, I realized that almost nothing is as important in the prevention of aggression and the creation of productive adults as quality parents. If I could provide information to help parents avoid many of the mistakes they often make, perhaps I could save children the trauma of abuse and neglect and perhaps even save lives.

Other books on various topics followed, but even though I believe all of my books have been productive contributions to the body of research and information, I have fallen into the same trap in which psychologists have been bogged down for years. Beginning with Freud, the father of modern psychology, psychologists have focused on what is wrong with people rather than looking at what is right with them. We look for dysfunction rather than function—failures rather than successes. My book *Stone Cold Souls,* an examination of evil behavior, is the epitome of this process. Even though I have attempted to include success stories in most of my books, I have chronicled several hundred cases of vandalism, violence, abuse, and murder and only a few stories of success. The antithesis of this focus on failure is something called "positive psychology." Researchers like Dr. David G. Myers, who is well-known in the field for his work on the study of happiness, have pioneered this area of psychology by focusing on what people do right.

I have been amazed at how well some of the survivors of trauma that you will read about in this book have adjusted to life after their ordeals. They overcame incredible abuse, horrifying accidents, and terrifying assaults to become productive, healthy, highly functional people. In fact, many of the hundreds of patients I've seen over the years have displayed this same sense of resiliency. Seeing them survive unthinkable circumstances and seeing how they seemed to let their tragedies disappear in the wake as their lives moved forward has always amazed me. How did they do it and what component or components were present in their lives that allowed them to overcome? The answers to these questions were missing in my research and I wasn't certain why in some cases people successfully overcame their trauma and others did not. How is it that some children endure horrifying abuse at the hands of cruel parents and go on to become healthy adults and exceptional parents and yet other children, perhaps even suffering abuse to a lesser extent, elect a path of aggression in their adult years, even becoming serial rapists and serial sexual killers? I wanted to answer these questions and the result was this book.

In order to cope with the day-to-day sadness of murder, assault, abuse, and tragedy that I see, I have to believe that the bad guys do not always win and our futures are not predestined. This book is the result of many years of research into the successes of life. Some of the subjects in this book are people you will know of—famous people who have endured traumatizing events that have made the evening news, published their stories, or seen their stories made into movies. Other people in this book will not be known to you. They were never celebrities, rich, or famous. They simply were normal, everyday people going about the business of living when tragedy interrupted their lives and changed its course forever. During my interviews with these people, I have developed very good friendships with many of them as they allowed me to peer into their personal worlds— seeing both the good and the bad of their lives. They allowed me inside their lives because, like me, they wanted to contribute to a work that might help others overcome adversity. They are courageous, strong, and exciting people. I was not only grateful to them for their participation in this book, but I was also inspired by their stories and honored to get to know them.

I chose to interview these subjects personally because I wanted to see their lives firsthand. I did not want to rely on the sanitized versions of their stories that made the evening news or books about their experiences. Too many times, these works omit the harsh reality that even when people successfully overcome trauma, they are still affected by it and some of these effects are not very attractive. In no way do I wish to defame these people or take advantage of the honor they bestowed upon me by allowing me to come into their private worlds. However, with the good comes the bad. No one is perfect and all of our lives, whether we are victims of trauma or not, include our unpleasant and ugly qualities as well as our pretty ones.

In short, the harsh reality is that even when people overcome tragedy, they still struggle. Their lives are not perfect and trauma still haunts them all in one way or another. Therefore, you will see both sides of recovery in the stories contained in these pages.

In military training, service men and women, especially those in elite special units, are trained to assess their own injuries on the battlefield and how to survive them. There may be no medic available to save them. This training allows them to save their own lives. Their fears do not stand in the way of their survival. This is a book about people like this. During the years I worked on this book it was a pleasure to focus on success rather than tragedy. Interviews, written reports, and the other data that I used to draw the conclusions I present in these pages were palatable because I knew that instead of ending at the morgue, these stories had happy endings. These are the stories that allow me to continue to believe the best in people and to hope for something better than what the world seems to be when I watch the evening news. Writing this book changed me and inspired me. I learned that from the struggle to survive, one can experience growth—something called "posttraumatic growth." In fact, psychologist and researcher Dr. Richard Tedeschi of the University of North Carolina has found in his research that 25 percent of those who experienced trauma would not change anything if they could go back. What I hope to show in this book is that the secrets to survival are not secrets at all.

REFERENCE

Tedeschi, R. G. (2003, March). The paradox of trauma: Learning how to live well. Invited address, 26th Annual Convention of the Behavioral Sciences, University of Georgia, Athens, Georgia.

ACKNOWLEDGMENTS

With each book I write I find myself more deeply indebted to my helpers along the way. I could not write as much as I do if it were not for the gracious privilege of working at Atlanta Christian College where I have been a faculty member for more than 20 years. My deans, Dr. Dennis Glenn and Dr. Kim Macenczak, allow me to teach a reduced load and provide plenty of free time to write. Without it, I could never get it done. Thank you for being so understanding, accommodating, and for being my friends. I want to thank my father who taught me to take care of myself and I want to thank my dearest friends—Eddie, Wye, Dean, Pat, and Tommy—who taught me I don't have to do it all by myself. To my sixth-grade teacher, Mr. Rouse, who was the first person who taught me to believe in myself. Thank you to my clients, both adults and children, who through their resiliency and recovery became my teachers.

I cannot even begin to express my appreciation to the people who opened their private lives to me for this book. I interviewed many more people than the few that I've written about here. To all of them I express my gratitude. But I especially wish to thank Murray Lynn, Tammy Legg, Pius Nyakayiro, and Minna Hong, who have taught me much and have become my good friends. Your examples have extended well beyond this book for me. You have shown me something about life that I would never have seen otherwise and I am a better person because you have touched my life. I hope my presentation of your stories has honored you. That was my intent.

Thank you to Nick Hersey, my research assistant and my friend. Nick has worked with me on other books and projects and he has my complete confidence. Nick squeezed in hours of research for this book among his many other obligations as a graduate student, clinician, father, and husband. Nick, I am indebted to you for your contribution to my work and I value your friendship.

I cannot omit the contribution my family made to this book. Writing and researching involves hours away from home and even when I'm writing in my office at home, I'm unavailable to my children and my wife. When I finished my first book, my son, then only a preschooler, meekly said, "Daddy, you aren't going to write another book are you?" Since then I have worked especially hard to focus on family first and my writing second, but undoubtedly I don't always succeed. Thank you Benjamin, Kara, Megan, and Stacey for giving me space to work and for being patient with me.

Finally, to all those who struggle in life, to those who feel as though the pain of life is more than you can bear, I dedicate this work to you. May you find hope in these stories and may you realize strength within yourself that you didn't know was there. Life moves on and better times lie ahead.

1

TRAUMA AND RESILIENCY

Even his griefs are a joy long after to one that
remembers all that he wrought and endured.

—Homer (*The Odyssey*)

When I first began studying trauma and resiliency, I quickly discovered that these are interesting, but illusive subjects. The definition of "trauma" varies depending upon whom you ask. Lay people use the term to describe events that, for them, were very difficult to handle—emotionally, spiritually, or physically. Lawyers carelessly toss the word around the courtroom in order to gain jury sympathy for their clients. Clinicians use the word to describe an event that meets certain generally agreed-upon criteria in the profession, yet even in the clinical world, there is no consensus as to what makes an event traumatizing. The concept of "resilience" is even more confusing. Most of us recognize something we can call "resiliency" when we see it, but as yet no one has been able to adequately describe where this thing comes from. Can we learn it? Are people born with it? Nearly all of us have heard stories of incredible trauma and seen people survive seemingly unscathed. We have wondered to ourselves how one could endure such things. As yet, these questions have remained unanswered, but it is clear that something is operating that helps people overcome tragic circumstances. Consider the story of Cambodian journalist Dith Pran, as recounted in the 1984 film *The Killing Fields.*

Pran, a journalist, assisted *New York Times* correspondent Sydney Schanberg as he reported on American activity in Cambodia during the Vietnam conflict and the rise of the Khmer Rouge regime. Pran, who declined the opportunity to flee the pending Khmer Rouge takeover with his family, was arrested shortly after the fall of Phnom Penh. His only crime was his role as a journalist. Over the next four years he endured a forced labor camp, starvation, beatings, torture, and numerous close encounters with death. Then, after escaping from the labor camp, he was captured by one of several warring factions of the Khmer Rouge regime. Again, after months as a captive, he barely escaped with his life. He walked through jungles and over mountains until he eventually found his way to a Red Cross station on the Thai border, and later he moved to the United States. During their tumultuous reign that spanned more than two decades in Cambodia, the Khmer Rouge were responsible for the death of as many as two million people due to torture, starvation, and outright slaughter—many of these victims were elderly, women, children, and even babies. Pran lost more than 50 of his own relatives, including his father, three brothers, a sister, and their families to the killing fields. One has to wonder how anyone could cope with the horrors of war, the slaughter of friends and relatives, the grueling confines and torture of a slave labor "reeducation" camp, and the day-to-day nightmare and fear of living in tenuous circumstances in which one might be summarily executed for nothing more than one's former political affiliation, for speaking French, or for standing in the wrong place.

One of my own clients survived the killing fields of Cambodia, stealthily smuggling his family out of the country across the border into Thailand a few at a time over many weeks and under the cover of darkness. After making several such trips, his own escape from the country was thwarted. It took 10 years before he was able to join his family in America—years that he spent trying to avoid the terror that befell many of his friends and neighbors. As a clinician, I would have expected that a man who had experienced this kind of life would be resentful, depressed, or vengeful. After all, his once thriving and vibrant country was overtaken by a ruthless dictator. He was forced to leave his home, lost his family one at a time, and then, when he was about to rejoin them, a separation he thought would be only months became years. Instead, however, what I found in his character was not only a loving, peaceful person, but one who had communicated these qualities to his children and family members. In this book I will share with you the lessons we can learn from people like this—brave men and women who have endured unbelievable trauma and in many cases become better people because of it.

Some of what you will read in this book will not surprise you. People who are mature, socially competent, and mentally sound tend to cope well with trauma. One such person was Corrie ten Boom who, along with her family, hid Jews in her home in Holland during World War II and was eventually arrested. She was a mature woman of strong religious conviction prior to her arrest. Even when many of her relatives, including her sister, died in a concentration camp, Corrie maintained her faith and conviction that God would prevail. She emerged from the trauma of fear, arrest, starvation, humiliation, disease, and loss stronger than ever. We all know that the strong survive, yet what you will also see in this book is that sometimes even psychologically weak people rise to the occasion. It appears that meeting a hardship or trauma head-on forces one to "fish or cut bait" as my grandfather used to say. When one coasts through life with minimal stress, it is much easier to maintain a fragile existence. When trauma presents itself, however, such luxury does not exist. To coast means to accept defeat. Therefore, sometimes as people face their crises, they develop and hone skills they had never before been forced to use. In cases like these, we are left with many questions. Either the event was not as traumatizing as we might have supposed or these people possess some characteristics that others lack that allow them to rise above their trauma. If we can identify what these circumstances and characteristics are, we can use our knowledge to help others overcome trauma.

We do our best to cope in whatever circumstances in which we find ourselves. But, what is it that allows for two people to experience nearly identical events and yet respond completely differently? Is it something in our personalities or genetic makeup? Could it be that just as some people are naturally gifted at playing the piano, other people have an innate gift for problem solving and coping—something we'll call "resiliency"? This idea presents several problems, but most obvious among them is the fact that our genetic makeup cannot be changed. If resilience is genetic, there may be little that a clinician, teacher, pastor, or parent can do to help people overcome trauma. While genetics may play a role, there is substantial evidence that resilience is more than genetic code. This genetic argument is the exception rather than the rule and even maternal twins face their problems differently. Most of us use the tools for coping and problem solving that we have acquired through direct instruction as well as by observing others. Coping with trauma, without question, is the result of many factors including the defining of the traumatic event itself. In other words, identifying an event as traumatic and coping with the event is based, at least in part, on our social environment. How we learn to cope with problems, attribution theory, self-efficacy, and our personal experience with our struggles all combine to create a unique formula that becomes the resource on which we draw during times of crisis. We practice dealing with crisis many times each day. A traffic jam; difficulty with a roommate, coworker, spouse, or child; and conflict with a store clerk over a defective item all provide opportunity for us to practice dealing with the struggles of life. How we deal with these minor struggles provides a preview of how we will deal with larger, more important "traumas." As reasonable as this sounds, a problem exists here, as well. If what I have just said is true, how can we explain amazing resilience in children who have had little or no opportunity to practice? Once again, we are left with more questions than answers.

There are two poles of the continuum on which I will focus in this book—resiliency resides at one end while vulnerability exists on the other. Vulnerable children and adults experience relatively minor setbacks in life and sometimes are incapacitated by them. They cope with their trauma by turning their hurt inward. They use drugs, engage in self-mutilation, self-starvation, suicide attempts, or other self-destructive behaviors. The traumatic event scars their psyche and detrimentally affects their social relationships—sometimes for the rest of their lives. Other vulnerable people, instead of turning their anger and hurt inward as I've just described, turn their frustrations outward. They attack other people verbally or physically. For example, most workplace shootings, school shootings, and many domestic assaults result from this type of behavior. These people will also have difficulty in their relationships for many years, if not for the rest of their lives. Resilient people, on the other hand, not only take daily difficulties in stride, but they also cope effectively with serious trauma. They overcome the odds, so to speak, when it seems that life has dealt them a very unfair hand. These are the really amazing stories where people have endured the most severe trauma, perhaps far more than vulnerable people, and yet their trauma has only made them stronger.

So that one doesn't get a false impression of resilient people, it should be noted that regardless of how resilient a person may be, nearly everyone who experiences trauma will suffer some adverse consequences. Some of these consequences include physical symptoms—stress-related responses, heart problems, respiratory problems, allergies, and rashes. Other common symptoms of trauma are psychological responses—inability to concentrate, lack of motivation, and failure to find pleasure in ordinarily pleasurable events. Contrary to what we might think, it is not the presence or absence of symptoms, per se, that distinguishes between individuals who are resilient and those who are not. Rather it is a matter of how long these symptoms persist and how debilitating they are that distinguishes the vulnerable person from the resilient one.

As discussed in the preface, since the beginning of its life as a science, psychology has focused on dysfunctional behavior—what is wrong with people, what's missing, and pathology. This is called the "damage model." My education largely focused on the damage model. I have spent much of my professional life as a writer, clinician, and professor looking at what was wrong with people. Emerging in recent years in contrast to the damage model is something called "positive psychology"—a study of what is right with people. Instead of researching what dysfunctional people have in common, positive psychology looks for the things that healthy, highly functional people have in common. In my work with psychologically unhealthy people over the years, I've regularly come across a "victim" who should be functioning much more poorly than he or she seems to be. I have been fascinated with what I have learned from these healthy people. I am intrigued to know what factors have helped them turn their traumas into something positive that made them stronger. This is the focus of resiliency study. What I present to you in the following pages is the summation of my research. You will see that social skills, intelligence, and efficacy are important differences between those who survive and those who do not. You will also find that virtues, which have long been promoted by religious organizations—purpose/hope, perseverance, forgiveness, and gratitude—also play a role in helping people overcome trauma. But before we can begin, we must first identify what trauma is, what resiliency is, and how perspective affects one's interpretation of a traumatic event.

DEFINITIONS OF TRAUMA

Trauma, like beauty, is in the eyes of the beholder. In other words, an event is traumatic when it is interpreted as such by the one experiencing it. Some events, such as surviving a plane crash, the loss of a limb in an accident, a kidnapping, sexual assault, or observing a murder, would be traumatizing to nearly everyone. Other events may be considered traumatizing by some people, but not by others. For example, one of my former clients was the first person to come across the scene of an automobile wreck. It was late at night on a dark and rural road. When he arrived at the scene, the automobile was burning and flames were edging into the car's interior. As my client stopped to investigate, he heard anguished cries from the driver of the wrecked car who was trapped in the burning vehicle. The driver made eye contact with my client and cried for help just as the car was totally engulfed in flames. There was absolutely nothing that my client could do to help the trapped victim, but the guilt he experienced over the man's death nearly crippled him. He could not sleep, eat, or pay attention at work, and the mental image of the dying man even interrupted my client's relationship with his wife. These were the symptoms that brought him to me. Clearly, the event was traumatizing for him. Yet not everyone would have found this event to be so traumatizing. For example, emergency medical technicians (EMTs), emergency room doctors, firemen, and policemen all deal with similar situations with some regularity and are not significantly traumatized by those experiences.

A very young man with whom I was once acquainted was diagnosed with cancer. He was seemingly healthy and the father of two young and vibrant children. A normal checkup revealed problems that led to further testing. The cancer had totally consumed his internal organs. His prognosis was zero and his physicians told him he had mere days before death would claim him. One might expect that such an event would generate bitterness, resentment, anger, and a host of other emotions, but just the opposite happened. The man used his remaining days to get his affairs in order and to prepare for his death. He calmly accepted his fate and became the primary support for his grieving family members and friends. While he was sad to see his life end so suddenly, he accepted his fate with poise and courage. "I've lived a wonderful life—even though it was short" were among his final words to me. He was dead within 10 days of the diagnosis. Most of us would find it hard to face a situation like this with as much courage. More likely we would be traumatized by the news of our impending death.

No event is too small to be traumatic, especially if the victim has minimal ability to cope with the event. Children find relatively minor events extremely upsetting. For example, one of my clients, an eight-year-old boy, was exhibiting symptoms consistent with trauma. His parents brought him to see me because they had noticed his agitation, moodiness, and difficulty concentrating at school. I suspected something traumatic had happened based on these symptoms and during my intake session with the parents I searched for some event in the child's life that could have been the cause—death of a pet, illness of a friend at school, a sudden move or change in family situation. Nothing seemed unusual, but in the first session with the child, he confided to me that he worried that his parents were going to abandon him. He explained that they had argued about money a few weeks earlier and since that time he felt as though he had to be careful so that they wouldn't get upset. When I talked to his mother about the argument, it became evident that she and her husband had not argued at all. They were both frustrated with an unusual number of unexpected expenses they had experienced that month and as they negotiated how to cut costs, their frustration led them to talk louder than normal. Neither parent was angry and the situation was manageable. However, for this eight-year-old who had rarely seen his parents upset like this, the event was traumatic. He failed to properly interpret what he was seeing and he failed to put it into a proper context. These two errors led him to feel helpless and responsible. His limited experience, minimal coping skills, and misinterpretation of the meaning of the event made it difficult for him to cope.

Most adults have more coping strategies at their disposal than this, and these skills prevent minor issues from being traumatizing. For example, anyone who has ever been on the receiving end of a traffic ticket knows how humiliating, frustrating, and angering it can be. In the back of our minds we realize the ticket will cost money and time, and potentially affect our insurance rates. Once when I was preparing for a vacation trip with my family, I was ticketed for speeding. My happy mood quickly changed to irritation and humiliation when I saw the police car in my rearview mirror. As I sat along the side of the road and the officer completed the ticket, I thought it was interesting how quickly my happy mood had changed. Had the officer caused that change? Of course not. I realized it was up to me to decide whether to let the ticket ruin my vacation or not. I decided to be happy and it was amazing how quickly the knot in my stomach eased. The trauma of the ticket was forgotten. There is certainly a big difference between getting a traffic ticket and being the victim of a crime, a plane crash, or finding out one has cancer, but even though all of these events are different, the process of interpreting them is the same. In the case of my ticket, the psychological tools that helped overcome the traumatic event were effective coping and problem-solving skills, reframing of the event, and interpretation of the meaning of the event. These same tools help people overcome severe trauma—times when the stakes are much higher.

Even though I have made the argument that almost anything can be traumatic, some basic criteria are helpful. Richard Tedeschi, a researcher and professor of psychology at the University of North Carolina, has spent his career studying the effects of trauma. He proposes that traumatic events share seven common elements and three common characteristics. According to Tedeschi, traumatic events are unexpected, uncontrollable, threatening, unusual, and irreversible. Events are also traumatic if they occur at a vulnerable developmental stage and if the cause lies outside of oneself. I have adopted Tedeschi's seven criteria. When I use the word "trauma," this is what I mean. These criteria are consistent with the fact that almost anything could be traumatizing—a traffic ticket, a divorce, fire, injury, disease, kidnapping, murder of a loved one, witnessing a crime, a car accident, or a near-death experience. In all of these examples, the primary difference, other than the specifics of the events, is the interpretation and meaning assigned to the event. *Perception is everything!*

DEFINITIONS OF RESILIENCY

"Resilience" is harder to define. Jerry Moe, author and children's therapist at the Betty Ford Clinic, says that resilience is the capacity to spring back, rebound, successfully adapt in the face of adversity, and develop social competence despite exposure to stress. Others suggest that resilience is a "self-righting force within everyone that drives him/her to pursue self actualization, altruism, wisdom, and harmony with a spiritual source of strength." Even more succinctly, some argue that resiliency is "a good adaptation in the face of severe stress." Resilient people refuse to be defeated.

There are some researchers who argue that there is more than one type of resiliency. Howard, Dryden, and Johnson note three kinds of resilience: overcoming the odds type, coping in the face of sustained negative circumstances, and recovery. While a person may be resilient in regard to overcoming past experiences, he or she may be vulnerable when faced with ongoing traumatic experiences (i.e., physical abuse). On the other hand, a person might readily cope at the moment of the trauma, but find

overcoming the inevitable effects of trauma difficult or impossible. Identifying one's resiliency type clearly has many clinical ramifications. Other
theorists distinguish between resiliency and malleability. While resiliency
is the ability to recover from stressful or traumatic events, malleability,
often perceived to be synonymous with resiliency, is adjusting to changing
situations. Resilient people are "capable of returning to an original shape
or position" while malleable people are capable of being shaped or formed
and "able to adjust to changing circumstances." Both types of people handle stress and trauma, but resilient people appear to be unchanged by their
experiences while trauma causes malleable people to change in order to
adapt. This change can either be functional or dysfunctional. For example,
a resilient child who experiences abuse is able to recognize feelings, form
plans for coping, and learn from the experience. He learns from the experience and becomes stronger because of it. You will see this type of resiliency
in the story of David Pelzer in chapter 4. A malleable child who is routinely
physically abused, on the other hand, changes to accommodate the abuse.
He literally loses physical sensitivity, and laboratory tests on children like
these show that they do not feel pain nearly as quickly as children who
have not been abused. These children often forget the past quite easily,
something called "dissociation." As these children become adults, they
have almost no memory of their early years. These changes allow them to
cope, but paradoxically, each of these skills also inhibits healthy functioning later in life. On the other hand, malleability can also be healthy. For
example, a malleable child might learn how to adjust his behavior to make
abuse less likely by adjusting his schedule to ensure he was away from
home at times when abuse was more likely. He might adjust the words that
he uses or the times when he speaks to make it less likely that his abuser
will target him. In general, resilience is not better than malleability, but
resilience doesn't have the potential dysfunctional aspect of malleability.

   It is also important to make a distinction between resiliency and denial.
In some cases, it appears that a person has weathered a storm. She seems
fine, has a good attitude, and doesn't appear to be adversely affected by
the trauma. Yet under closer scrutiny, a therapist can see symptoms of
denial. When one engages in denial, the effects of trauma are ever present. Neurosis, depression, moodiness, and other symptoms will continue
to emerge as long as no reconciliation with the trauma has occurred. In
therapy, a client in denial will avoid topics in regard to the trauma with
which she has not yet dealt and she will exhibit symptoms, either mild or

severe, in her day-to-day life such as emotionalism, irritability, difficulty getting along with family or friends, difficulty sleeping, eating disruption (inability to eat or overeating), and inability to concentrate. When a subject is in denial, it is imperative that the therapist push the client (gently or firmly depending upon the client) into confronting the underlying emotions related to the trauma.

In summary, resilient individuals learn to cope with their circumstances without denying their importance and without changing themselves in dysfunctional ways. They roll with the punches but are not defeated. Finally, resilient people do not deny their trauma and they do not pretend they are unaffected by it. Addressing their feelings and difficulties immediately helps them overcome traumatic symptoms more quickly and efficiently.

HOW CAN CHILDREN FROM THE SAME FAMILY TURN OUT SO DIFFERENT?

Siblings in an abusive home may choose different paths in life. One may become a doctor while the other becomes a rapist. Most of us can think of children of our friends or family members who grew up in the same home and yet one was a model student while another was delinquent. Even children growing up in the same household approach life with differing sets of coping skills and they assign meaning to events differently. In Lenore Terr's longitudinal study of the children who were abducted on their school bus in Chowchilla, California, in 1976 and eventually buried underground and left to die, it became apparent over time that the survivors dealt with the trauma very differently. Some of these children were siblings. While there were similarities in their responses, there were also stark differences in the way these children coped with an identical event. Whenever I speak to a group on dysfunctional behavior, especially child abuse, inevitably one or more people from the audience confesses to me that they were repeatedly abused as children and yet "they turned out fine." There are several ways to respond to this phenomenon.

The first possibility is that these people really are fine. They were resilient and they overcame their trauma in a healthy, functional way. These people, although they are rare, had many of the traits addressed in later chapters in this book. Therefore, they were protected by their social environment and they had personal factors that allowed them to effectively deal with their painful circumstances.

A second possibility is that they really did not "turn out fine." They just think they did. This is a common problem among immature and disturbed individuals as well as older persons who have had many years to accommodate to dysfunctional living. The immature and emotionally disturbed individual is unable to see the effects of the event and objectively evaluate how it has negatively affected him or her. For example, a 17-year-old girl was referred to me by her physician. The girl had been raped by a relative and as a result, she developed an eating disorder. She acknowledged the eating disorder, but she denied it was a problem and she was blinded to even more serious symptoms she exhibited such as extreme emotionalism, suicidal ideation, self-mutilation, and chronic depression. She was an honor student at her high school, but her relationships with both males and females were stressed. She had been sexually violated by at least two boyfriends, but she continued to date them both. Her relationship with her parents was tumultuous and she saw herself as totally alone in the world, even though she had a very willing support system around her (parents, her church, and her counselors). She was so immature and dysfunctional that she did not recognize any of these things as problems. In her mind, the problems she experienced were the fault of others in her environment and she refused to accept any responsibility for change. There was little question that she hadn't "turned out fine."

In a similar way, older people who have lived their entire lives with dysfunctional habits, dysfunctional relationships, and dysfunctional coping skills don't know any other life. They believe they are fine because they have found ways to exist that serve them even though their existence is dysfunctional. These are among the hardest clients to work with because they often do not see any need for change. In fact, even when they do see a need for change, change is frightening because it means abandoning the very survival tools that have allowed them to cope with their trauma. For example, a client of mine was a 65-year-old woman. The youngest of three girls in her family, she had been repeatedly sexually abused by her father. Her father promised her that if she remained quiet and allowed the abuse, he would leave her sisters alone. She complied and endured the abuse throughout her teen years. Thirty-five years later she discovered that he had made the same agreement with both of the other girls. She was devastated and this revelation brought her to my office. By this time in her life, however, she had adapted to her emotional turmoil by several means. She regularly utilized denial, pretending the abuse hadn't affected her, but on a semiconscious level, the horror of her sexual trauma was never far from her mind. She was a very needy woman with few friends and a difficult marriage. Her husband (who had significant issues of his own) found it difficult to understand her moodiness and frigidity that had been a part of their marriage for more than 30 years. She was very emotional and she had difficulty accepting constructive criticism. These characteristics created problems with her employer, an insurance agency, due to the fact that she was overly eager to please nearly everyone. She was so eager for acceptance that she would ignore her assigned duties and focus on any request made by nearly anyone in her organization. Her work assigned by her boss was often left undone because of the many favors she was doing for other people. As she approached senescence, this woman had lived a life of dysfunctional relationships and dysfunctional coping skills for so many years that she knew no other way. In her mind, she was doing just fine, even though she could admit that her past caused her pain. In her mind, she was in therapy because of the revelation of her father's lie. She would likely have argued that despite his sexual abuse, she "turned out fine." Obviously she did not.

A third possibility has to do with perspective. Two individuals can experience a similar event and yet have different perspectives on the motive and meaning of the event. A father who is harsh in discipline might be perceived as rigid, cold, and uncaring by one child and yet stern, but loving, by another. The child who perceives the father in a negative way will be more likely to assume his motives are selfish and cruel while the other child would assume his motives are selfless and caring. Two sisters who came through my practice had both been molested by their father. Part of their issues related to the mother's failure to protect them. The older sister saw her mother as selfish, distant, and uncaring. She believed her mother knew about the abuse, but her failure to intervene was due to her selfishness and lack of compassion for her daughters. This perspective led the elder daughter to develop deep resentment toward her mother. The younger daughter saw her mother as a weak woman, but one who was also a victim of her husband's selfishness. Rather than resenting her mother, she pitied her and believed she was just as much of a victim as the two daughters. Once again, perspective is everything.

A fourth possibility involves personality differences. Protective personality traits that are present in resilient children may be absent in another, more vulnerable child. Numerous traits, which I will address throughout this book, have been associated with the ability to rebound from difficulty. Therefore, as children differ in their personalities we would expect differences in how they deal with traumatic events. Also related to personality differences are differences in physiology, chemical makeup of the brain, diet, sleep patterns, and activity patterns. There is no question that the way the brain produces and processes neurotransmitters has a stark effect on the way people behave. These differences contribute to differing responses to stress among children in the same household.

A final possibility has to do with social experiences. Even if personality traits of individuals are similar, they may have very different social experiences. Social experiences, like personality traits, serve as protective factors when a person is faced with trauma. No two children in a family have identical social relationships or social experiences. In fact, especially when children are close together in age, they tend to pursue very different social lives and interests. For example, some years ago I had a client who was an adult woman. She and her two younger siblings were raised in a tumultuous home. Her father physically and verbally abused her mother, and screaming and yelling were everyday occurrences. My client, being the oldest, felt responsible for her siblings even when she was only five or six years old. She did her best to shield them from the fighting. One of her strategies was to herd her siblings into a closet, close the door, and pound on the wall with a shoe to drown out the noise. The younger siblings saw this activity as a game, but to her it was stressful, frightening, and traumatic. Therefore, even though all three children grew up in the same home, they had very different experiences regarding the aggression in the home.

I often tell parents that none of my three children have the same family. Even though my wife and I have been married for over 25 years, our first child, a daughter, was born into a home with no siblings and with inexperienced, young parents. My second child, also a daughter, had a family that was older, wiser, more experienced, and she also had an older sibling. My third child, a son, had parents who were a dozen years older than when we first became parents, plus he was born into a family as the youngest of three siblings. Their differences in personality as well as differences because of our growing experience and wisdom has led each of them to grow up in families that are different in many ways from their siblings'. These differing experiences lead to differing abilities when it comes to responding to trauma. Differences in family experiences, personality, and perspective all

contribute to how people respond to the stressors they face in daily life.
The amazing thing about the following case study is not only how perfectly
it serves as an example of family systems theory, but also how it serves as
a clear example of how different members of the same system respond to
similar stressors within that system.

The Gilliard Family: A Case Study on Coping[1]

Family systems theory tells us that each part of the family system has
an effect on the other parts. The analogy often used is that a family is like
a group of people in a canoe. One person cannot move without having
some effect on the other occupants of the canoe. The more disruptive one
member's behavior, the more likely the canoe will tip and families balance their canoe by offsetting exaggerated behaviors of the other members. Imagine a person leaning way over the starboard side of the canoe.
Another member can compensate and balance the canoe by leaning way
over the port side. For each movement, a counter movement is necessary
to maintain stability. In a dysfunctional family, instead of floating down
stream, comfortably seated in the middle of the canoe, members are un-
comfortably stretched to their limits, afraid to move for fear of capsizing
the canoe. As long as no one moves, the canoe remains upright, but with
members hanging over all sides, the slightest disruption could capsize the
family system. Members are stressed, uncomfortable, and their distorted
positions lead to exaggerated behaviors. This is what happened to the
Gilliard family.

Ted, the father, was in the audience at a seminar where I was speaking and afterward he told me that his eldest daughter, 16-year-old Kelly,
had attempted suicide a few days before. I agreed to see the family and we
scheduled an appointment for a few days later. Their story was a complicated one. Kelly had attempted suicide by ingesting over-the-counter
medication and had been briefly hospitalized. The incident served as a
wake-up call to a family whose canoe was about to capsize. The suicide
attempt occurred immediately following a fight between Ted and his wife,
Maria. After the argument Ted left home, swearing never to return. Not
long after Ted stormed from the house, Kelly emerged from her room and
confessed to her mother that she had swallowed nearly all of the tablets in
an aspirin bottle. Maria rushed her daughter to the hospital and then notified Ted who had gone to his brother's home. Ted went to the hospital,

moved back home when his daughter was released, and it was just a few days later that he approached me after my seminar.

Ted and Maria had been married for 18 years. They met at their church when Maria was pregnant by the man to whom she was married at the time. She was very young, only 19, and her husband of just six months had abandoned her when he found out she was pregnant. As a friend and confidante, Ted stayed by Maria's side during her pregnancy and delivery. Not long after Maria delivered a daughter, Hanna, Ted proposed and the two were married. Two years later, they had a child of their own, Kelly. Two other children followed—Salina and Martin. At the time I saw the family, Hanna was married and living away from the family. Salina was 15 and Martin was 12.

From the opening session, distinct differences in personality and approach to the family's situation emerged. Ted was a thin man in his early forties, about six feet tall and about 170 pounds. His rough hands told of a blue-collar worker who spent most of his working hours laboring in a warehouse. He was very kind and loving, but he was also compulsively organized and very controlling. In the coming weeks, he consistently called several times each week to confirm his appointments and he tended to dominate discussions if others were not given permission or opportunity to speak. He always looked me directly in the eye; his words were very matter-of-fact; and his general approach to problems was to attack them head-on. His approach to life was to find the problem and fix it, even if he was part of the problem. For example, he told me several times, "If the problem is me, I can take it, but I want to know so I can change."

Maria was his antithesis. She was short, slightly overweight, and very reserved. She spoke only if I prodded her and even then Ted tended to interrupt and either answer for her or finish her sentences for her. Her eyes rarely left the tabletop around which the family sat during our sessions, and she provided the shortest answers possible. Often I could barely hear her meek voice, but despite her demeanor, her comments were usually candid. She started almost every comment with "I feel" and it was clear that her affect was the driving force in her decision-making. For example, in an argument over which was the shortest route to a certain store from their house, Maria validated her route by saying she "felt it was closer." This, of course, significantly irritated her analytical husband who believed feelings had nothing to do with facts.

Kelly looked much older than her 16 years and I couldn't help but feel that, more so than most adolescents, she perceived herself as an adult. Her appearance was stately and elegant, nothing like what I expected from one who had attempted suicide just a few days before. She had seen a psychiatrist a few times, but her sessions had ended two weeks before the suicide attempt. She was an honor student, very involved in her church, and well aware of all the activities that went on in her home. Kelly always sat directly across the rectangular table from me. I sat at one end and she sat at the other. This was a place that I might have expected her father to sit, but as you will see, as I got to know this family, this was the most appropriate place for her—at the head.

Salina was usually engaged as an active listener in the discussion, but she only spoke when she was asked a direct question. At 15, she looked like a typical pubescent teen. She was an average student and she seemed interested in her family situation, but from the very first session it appeared that she was tuned in only when she felt like it was necessary. Finally, Martin sat next to Kelly and spent much of the session slumped over on the table daydreaming with his chin in his hands. He clearly was disengaged for much of our time together and any conversation directed his way had to be repeated because he rarely heard what was said.

In our first session, the seating arrangement proved to be a microcosm of the power within the family. Ted, who had the most power in the family, sat to my left. Next to him was Kelly, then Salina, and then Martin. Immediately to my right was Maria, the person in the family system with the least power. I spoke first in our opening session.

"I understand there is a lot of fighting at home and Ted wants to find a way to make life more pleasant at home," I said, referring to a description I had been given by Ted prior to our meeting. "What do you all think about that?" I asked, trying not to make eye contact with anyone in particular. I wanted to see who would answer first. Kelly was the first to respond.

"We do fight a lot," she said. "So do mom and dad. I really wish that we could straighten things out."

Salina spoke next. "I know! You two fight like children," she said referring to her parents. "We are supposed to fight, but you are adults and you are supposed to act like it."

Ted very matter-of-factly agreed. "You're right. Your mother and I do fight too much. We do need to behave more like adults." He was so objective that I felt almost as if he was talking about someone else.

Maria eventually agreed with the others about the fighting, saying, "I feel like we might fight too much," but she said little else.

Kelly took charge again. "Another thing. You two let Martin get away with too much. Like the other day when he was supposed to be on restriction and he complained until you caved in. You need to make him stay home when he gets suspended [from school]."

I found it interesting that Kelly, the one who was the reason for the family attending therapy in the first place, so quickly took charge of the direction of our discussion, and nobody had yet mentioned the suicide attempt.

"What do you think, Martin?" I asked him. He tilted his head and looked surprised that I addressed him and shrugged his shoulders. "What do you think?" I asked a second time. "Do you think you should be put on restriction when you are suspended?" Kelly answered for him.

"I think when he gets suspended he should be put on restriction. He can't keep on not going to school. You have to do something."

Salina gave her opinion next and then each family member supplied an opinion—each one except Martin. Even though I asked him the question, he was the only one who didn't answer. Rather he sat in his same slumped posture staring off into space. It was obvious that Martin didn't have to answer. The family did the work for him. Eventually, I asked him the question again. This time he simply responded with "I guess so." I told Martin that I noticed that everyone answered the question except him and I found that interesting.

"Sometimes," he said, "I feel like they are all in here (he put his hands in the center of the table) and I'm out here." He put his hand on the edge of the table. A picture of this family, their problems, and more importantly, their coping skills, was beginning to emerge. For the remainder of the session, we talked about the family's problems, money issues, discipline, and finally the suicide attempt. It was obvious to me that Kelly did not intend to kill herself. Her motive was much simpler.

By the end of that first session I had a fairly clear idea of at least some of the family's issues, and we scheduled a regular appointment that we would keep for nearly six months. Over the subsequent sessions it became clear that Ted and Maria had great difficulty getting along. Their personalities were completely different, leading to many disagreements and misunderstandings. Kelly served as a surrogate parent for Martin and as a mediator for her parents' arguments. At a cursory glance, Salina appeared to be the ideal child because she never got into any trouble, but time would show that this was not the case. Martin had learned how to cope with the family problems in a way that would lead to major problems at school. Following is an examination of how each family member adjusted to circumstances in a way that he or she believed to be the most functional. These descriptions demonstrate how they had all responded to similar circumstances with very different behaviors.

Ted. Ted's mother and father divorced when he was a teenager and shortly afterward, his father committed suicide. Ted was the oldest child and was forced to take on the role of father to his siblings and, in a way, as surrogate husband to his mother, a very dependent woman who expected far more from the teenage boy than was reasonable. Ted was probably always an organized person, but I suspect that the dysfunction in his family of origin that led to his parents' divorce may have encouraged his compulsiveness. His parents' divorce, his father's suicide, and his mother's tendency to push him into a fatherly role while only in his early teens led him to become an organizer, planner, and "intellectualizer." Freud argued that one way in which we defend ourselves from threatening stimuli is to intellectualize. This means that the person removes the emotional component from the situation. "Just the facts, ma'am." Even though Ted was often aware of his feelings, something many intellectualizers are not aware of, he rarely allowed his feelings to show. It was much easier for him to deal with facts and details. One of his most common responses in therapy was, "Just tell me what to do. It won't hurt my feelings." Indeed, never in therapy did it appear that his feelings were hurt.

Intellectualizing can be helpful. Panic and hyperemotionalism can make it very difficult to function, especially in a crisis. However, when a person never acknowledges or deals with one's feelings, it can build up to a point of frustration. Intellectualizing is also frustrating to close friends and family members. Most of us have a need, at least occasionally, to see the feeling side of the people we love. Intellectualizers like Ted rarely ever let their feelings show. Ted deeply loved his wife and was totally committed to her, but he did not know how to show his affection in a way that was satisfying to her.

Ted was a mature and functional adult in most of his adult relationships, but he carried his parenting methods that he learned as a young teen into his current family. Instead of developing new and more effective adult-like parenting methods, when Ted interacted with his children, it was almost as if he were still 14 years old.

Maria. Maria had the most interesting history of the group. She had been married to Ted for nearly 20 years and most of those years had been difficult. Although he was a loving husband, he never showed affection to her. In his mind, working hard, providing a safe home, and meeting his family's needs were his way of showing affection. Their difficult marriage was laden with arguing, misunderstandings, and repeated threats to end the relationship. One evening during a private one-on-one session with Maria, I asked her if she loved her husband. I suspected that even though she loved him at some level, deep down she did not love him in the passionate way that many married people love each other.

"Of course I do," she said, as if she was trying to convince herself as much as she was trying to convince me.

"I don't know that I believe you," I told her. "Your marriage has been hard since the beginning and you have told me how unsatisfying it is in many ways. I don't doubt your commitment to Ted, but I do not think you want to admit to yourself how you really feel."

She covered her face with her hands and began to cry. "No, I don't love him," she whispered. "I want to, though."

She had spent 20 years of her life with someone that she was very unhappy with and yet she wouldn't even think of leaving him. Threats to end the marriage always came from Ted. The reason became evident when she told me more about her past.

Maria was the youngest of three children. Her oldest brother was a teenager when she was born and her sister was about two years older than she. As an infant, only 18 months of age, her alcoholic father committed suicide. Her mother suffered from a mental illness and had to be institutionalized. At that point, Maria's brother was sent to a boy's school where he remained until he graduated high school. Following graduation, he immediately joined the military. Consequently, Maria never really knew him as a sibling. After her mother's institutionalization, Maria and her sister were placed in foster care. The family with whom they lived, the Dugans, cared for the two girls like their own children, but after six years in the home, Mr. Dugan died unexpectedly. Unable to care for the two girls by herself, the children were removed from Mrs. Dugan's custody and placed in a second foster home. In this second home, the Smiths cared lovingly for both girls for the next several years. When Maria was 16, two things happened that dramatically changed her life. Her sister graduated from high school and left the Smiths' home for college. Her sister, the only person who had always been with Maria, left her. Secondly, Mr. Smith died of a heart attack. Mrs. Smith, a woman now in her seventies, was unable to care for an adolescent teen so Maria was forced to move in with a new family. This time, her new guardians were the daughter and son-in-law of the Smiths—Linda and Andrew Evans.

Linda and Andrew were unable to have children of their own and they welcomed Maria with open arms. Maria, who was already familiar with the Evans family, quickly bonded with Andrew and looked up to him as a father. Less than two years later, Maria finished high school and almost immediately married a man several years older than she. Within weeks she was pregnant and before the marriage was six months old, her husband left her. She moved back in with Linda and Andrew, who were in the process of adopting a child.

During this time, Maria met Ted at church and they began dating. Shortly after the delivery of her baby, the Evans' adoption of their own newborn came through. Maria served both as older sister to the new baby and mother to her own child. Two years later, she married Ted. In the meantime, Maria's sister conceived a child out of wedlock and later married the father. That marriage ended and she again conceived a child out of wedlock. She eventually married the father of this second child, but that marriage, like the first, quickly ended in divorce.

Every male in Maria's life had left her. Three fathers had died; her brother left for the military; her sister's husbands were gone; and her own first marriage ended in divorce. Even though Andrew remained in her life, when she returned to his home after her divorce, his interests and attention were consumed with his new baby, leaving Maria feeling isolated and ignored. Time had taught Maria that all men leave eventually. Why had she not left Ted? To use her words, he had "put up with her" for nearly 20 years and he was still around. I believe that her marriages to two much older, controlling men demonstrated her desire to have a father take care of her. Not only did she not want to lose the only person who ever stayed with her, but she also didn't want to lose another father either. Leaving never entered her mind.

Kelly. Kelly was the oldest child at home. She was bright and capable. Her coping and problem-solving skills were far superior to those of her parents and, early in her teen years, they began seeking her opinion on family matters. Both parents used Kelly as a sounding board as they voiced their frustrations about the other. Eventually Kelly took on a parental role with her siblings and she began mediating fights between her parents.

This shift in position from child to adult led to her involvement in other parental matters—money, bills, and discipline of the other two children. Kelly became *parentified*. This means the role of the parent was deferred to her. Along with the normal emotional issues and life problems that most 16-year-old girls have to deal with, Kelly also had to take on the stress of leading a family, balancing the budget, and keeping her parents' marriage together. She did her job well, but on the night her father left, the night of her suicide attempt, she had played all of her cards. She had tried to mediate their fight that evening, but none of her attempts were successful. Either consciously or unconsciously, Kelly knew that her father would come home if someone was sick. Therefore, she swallowed the bottle of aspirin. She had no intentions of dying. She took the aspirin to demonstrate to her parents that the situation was serious. Immediately after taking the aspirin, she told her mother what she had done. This was not done just to save her life. It was done to ensure that her father was quickly notified so they could get back together as quickly as possible. Her plan worked. She suffered no serious effects from the overdose and her father was back home within hours. It is also interesting to note that she selected a method of problem solving that existed in both her mother and father's family of origin. The head of both her parents' homes had committed suicide. Likewise, it is interesting that Kelly was forced into a parentified role just as her father was in his teen years.

Salina. Salina was a crafty child. She learned to function in her family system by realizing that as long as she didn't get into any trouble, people would leave her alone. Her mother tended to favor her as long as she was making reasonable grades and staying out of trouble. This gave Salina power that she often used to manipulate her mother. For example, if she wanted a new sweater, she would beg her mother until she conceded. The Gilliards had a very tight budget and money was a consistent stressor. Maria's concessions to Salina, especially when money was involved, led to arguments between Ted and Maria. Instead of addressing the fact that Salina was manipulating Maria, Ted and Maria would argue over how much money was spent. Salina was like a quiet card player, storing up trumps to play at just the right time. She had learned when and how to play her trump cards to get what she wanted.

Martin. Martin concerned me the most. He, like Salina, manipulated his parents for his own gain. If he wanted something, he would ask the parent he thought would most likely grant him permission. If permission was denied, he went to the other parent and asked the same question. For example, once he wanted to spend the night with a friend. His mother said no because he had a test the next day and his grades were falling in that class. She wanted to make sure he had time to study. However, instead of studying as he was told to do, Martin went to his father and asked for permission to spend the night with his friend. Ted, who knew little of his grade troubles and nothing of the test the next day, gave him permission. When Maria found out that Martin had gone to his friend's home against her will, instead of demanding his return, she attacked Ted for giving him permission to go. Not only was Martin not held accountable for his manipulative behavior, he wasn't even in the house when his parents argued about it. He didn't even have to listen to the argument. He could easily get what he wanted with absolutely no consequences. Both Martin and Salina manipulated their parents for their own gain, but Martin's behavior got him into trouble outside the home. When he tried to use these same methods with his teachers at school, school officials did not let him get away with such manipulative tactics and he quickly found himself in serious trouble. Salina recognized that her manipulative behavior would only work with her mother, so she had no behavior problems at school. My concern for Martin was that he would eventually find himself in trouble with the law if he continued to use his manipulative behavior patterns in settings other than at home.

Summary. As you can see, all members of this family dealt with their life stressors in different ways. Ted became an intellectualizer. Maria became overly dependent upon her husband and her fear of losing anyone, including her children, made it impossible for her to do anything that might threaten the love she received from them. Therefore, she rarely, if ever, disciplined her children. Kelly took on the role of parent, believing that if she didn't take charge, the family would collapse. She accepted the responsibility of leading the family and she dealt with the family turmoil, financial problems, and parenting problems as best she could. Martin and Salina dealt with their family turmoil by manipulating people for their own advantage. Even though all five of these people lived in the same home, they were all very different in their family backgrounds; their personalities were different; and their problem-solving methods led to very different coping behaviors.

CONCLUDING COMMENTS

No two people respond to trauma in the same way. It is frustrating to search for answers when the formula for cause and effect relationships in the social sciences is so complicated, but it is naïve to suppose that anything in our social interactions can be reduced to a simple cause-effect relationship between two variables. Often times, people critique our work in social science because it seems to them that we can never say anything with 100 percent certainty. This demonstrates an overly simplistic approach to life. Even in physics (a "hard science") there are few certainties and much variability. There are many kinds of radioactive elements, but gamma rays are a particularly dangerous radioactive ray. Gamma rays cause damage in our bodies when they ionize DNA material within the body's cells. The potential effects of radioactive exposure are well known—cancer, burns, and birth defects. What you may not know is that as gamma rays pass through the body and penetrate cells, they only ionize the DNA of some cells. For some unknown reason, some cells are affected and others are not. Some cell walls rupture as the gamma rays pass through and some do not. Some DNA is ionized and some is not. We accept this seemingly random truth in physics. Since this is true in the hard sciences, there is no reason that we should not expect differential responses in the social sciences. Just as we expect differential responses to gamma rays, we should *expect* differential cognitive and behavioral responses to traumatic events.

There is a principle in chaos theory called the "Heisenberg Uncertainty Principle." This principle reduces the "hard" science of physics to probability theory—the very foundation on which much of the research in social science is based. For example, because of "chaos" in physics, one cannot fully answer the famous question, "If a butterfly in China flapped its wings, could it affect the weather in North America?" The answer to this question cannot be answered with total certainty because there are so many variables that affect the weather. An answer could be approached, but not stated with certainty. Einstein was troubled by this principle, but he could not refute its existence. Likewise, there are so many variables that could have an effect on a person's behavior that we are reduced to probability theory. We can only approach an answer and we can only talk about what outcomes are likely. Even though we can identify many things that affect a person's behavior, we cannot say for sure what the exact outcome of any one variable in isolation would be. Just as the Heisenberg Uncertainty Principle frustrated Einstein, this same uncertainty frustrates us in the social sciences, but we cannot refute its existence.

In summary, we all face various events throughout life that are difficult. How we handle them varies by person and event. In the following pages, I will unravel some of the mysteries of resilience and trauma. While I cannot provide a formula for resilience, I will describe for you issues related to vulnerability and resilience. You will read stories that will amaze you, but even more important, you will learn about the skills that these people drew upon that helped them to overcome their difficulties. Knowledge of these skills will hopefully help us all become more resilient to the traumas that we might face and it will also help us to provide a context in which our children will be more likely to cope with their traumas, as well. What I have attempted to do in the following chapters is provide dramatic stories of those who have survived and I have highlighted one or more of the traits that they believed helped them to overcome the tragic events in their lives. Let us learn from their struggles.

NOTE

1. The names and some details have been changed to protect the identity of this family.

REFERENCES

Howard, S., Dryden, J., & Johnson, B. (1999). Childhood resilience: Review and critique of literature. *Oxford Review of Education, 25,* 307–324.

Moe, J. (2002, October). *Helping children build their strengths.* Presentation at the annual meeting of the American Association for Play Therapy, St. Louis, MO.

Perry, B. D. (1997). Incubated in terror: Neurodevelopmental factors in the "cycle of violence." In J. D. Osofsky (Ed.), *Children in a violent society* (pp. 124–129). New York: The Guilford Press, p. 124.

Richardson, G. E., & Waite, P. J. (2002). Mental health promotion through resilience and resiliency education. *International Journal of Emergency Mental Health, 4,* 65–76.

Tedeschi, R. G. (2003, March). The paradox of trauma: Learning how to live well. Invited address, 26th Annual Convention of the Behavioral Sciences, University of Georgia, Athens, GA.

Terr, L. (1976). *Too scared to cry.* New York: HarperCollins.

Thompson, C. L., & Rudolph, L. B. (1996). *Counseling children* (4th ed.). New York: Brooks/Cole Publishing Company, p. 4.

2

ARBEIT MACHT FREI: SURVIVING THE HOLOCAUST

Fire is the test of gold; adversity of strong men.

—Seneca (*Epistles*)

It was a sunny and unusually warm day in November when I arrived at the two-story brick house in Atlanta. An elegant woman met me at the door and ushered me inside. There standing in a narrow hallway waiting to greet me was a bespeckled man in his seventies. Quietly and gently, he offered me a drink and welcomed me into his home. I was nervous knowing what I was going to hear. World War II has always had a powerful effect on me, even though it ended 16 years before my birth. The drama of a world completely engulfed in war, people from every continent fighting and dying by the thousands, is almost beyond my comprehension. My wife's grandfather was a decorated war hero during World War II and for 20 years told me stories of his experiences—things he endured so I could be free. He was among the 11th Armored Division that helped liberate the inmates at Mauthausen, a concentration camp in Austria. Many times I was moved by his stories and the pictures he took of the camp as they liberated the starving and diseased inmates. As my host and I sat in a comfortable study I thought about the fact that he and my wife's grandfather could literally have crossed paths in the cold German landscape nearly 50 years earlier. I affixed a microphone to his lapel and turned on my tape recorder.

"Please tell me your story," I said as we began.

With no hesitation, he began his narrative and as I listened to his words, in my mind I could see the events that he described.

It was a cold winter night in 1942 when noise awakened Rose and Abraham Leicht from their sleep. The Hungarian secret police, collaborators with the Nazi regime, had come to arrest Abraham, a Jewish merchant and farmer in Hungary. That dark night, Abraham said good-bye to his wife and four sons. Alfred, age 12, was the oldest. Herman, Eli, and Joseph were 10, 8, and 6. The boys never saw their father again. His father and other community leaders from Bilke, a small community of about 35,000 people in eastern Hungary, were marched into the Carpathian mountains and forced to dig their own mass grave and were summarily executed. It was the beginning of the purge of the Jews in Hungary. Hitler's reign of terror reached all across Europe in large cities and tiny hamlets alike. Almost no one who lived in Europe at the time was untouched by Hitler's maniacal lust for power and his demonic passion for exterminating those whom he hated. By the end of the war, six million men, women, and children were

Murray Lynn in his home in 2009.

exterminated in concentration camps. Of those, 500,000 were Hungarian Jews. But anti-Semitic sentiment was a part of the Hungarian lifestyle long before that fateful night in 1942. Alfred Leicht recalls the bullying he suffered in primary school at the hands of racist classmates. Resentment against the Jews permeated Hungarian life and Alfred knew his teachers would not have intervened to stop the bullying by his classmates even if they had been aware of it. Consequently, today he has few pleasant memories of school.

Despite the hatred he knew in his community, his home was a different story. His parents' relationship was loving and kind and from the two of them he learned the importance of integrity, discipline, and righteousness. Honesty was "etched into his genes." A dishonest character became an intolerable trait in his later years as a businessman, and character remains an important issue for him today.

After his father's abduction and murder, the Leicht family lost their small business and they were forced to rely on their small farm for survival. For the next two years Alfred's mother worked very hard to feed her four sons and to make ends meet. "Mother was the stronger of the two," Alfred confided to me as we sat in his comfortable Atlanta home. Afternoon sunlight cast shadows across the room and his gaze was fixed on me as he recalled those days many years earlier. He remembers his mother fondly for her strength and leadership during those nightmarish and poverty stricken years. She managed their home with "grace and courage and gave us security," he said, and these traits shaped his own values.

The murder of his father, however, was only the beginning of his ordeal. Two years later, in 1944, Germany occupied Hungary and began an organized massive effort to round up the Jews. Alfred, his brothers, and his mother were among those who where taken from their homes and sent to a ghetto about 80 miles from Bilke. Confused and frightened, they tried to make sense of what was happening to them as their mother tried to create some sense of order and purpose amid the squalor of the ghetto. Three weeks after their arrival in the ghetto, train cars began to arrive. Herded like cattle into boxcars, Alfred and his family were crowded together with dozens of other frightened Jews. After the door slammed shut, they remained locked in the cattle car for three days as it lumbered across the country to its final destination. There was no food, no water, no sanitation facilities, and no bed. People were forced to relieve their bladders and bowels where they stood. Only minutes after being crowded into the cattle cars, the air became stale. Those near the exterior had more air, but there they were exposed to the cold wind of the Hungarian winter blowing through the gaps in the walls. Those in the interior of the car were warmer, but they had no air. Many people, mostly old people or very young children, died during the journey. Others "lost their minds" as they tried in vain to cope with the crowds, the filth, the cold, and their fear. Alfred is reflective as he tells me about this pivotal event. "It was like something from Dante's *Inferno*," he said.

When the train finally slowed to a stop and the doors opened, exhausted and humiliated, Alfred and his family stood among both the living and the dead. Light flooded into the car as he caught his first glimpse of Auschwitz. Barking dogs, men and women in uniform screaming orders in German, throngs of confused and frightened inmates disembarking from the hellish boxcars, smokestacks, and odors—the odor of death—all assaulted his senses. "When we saw the smoke from the smoke stacks, we knew we were doomed," he said very matter-of-factly.

On the platform, capos assisted the Gestapo in sorting the new arrivals into groups. The term "capo" comes from the Latin word meaning *head*. Capos were leaders chosen from among the inmates to help with the operation of the camp in exchange for privileges. Some capos were benevolent and only accepted this role to save their own lives. Others were cruel, sometimes even more so than the German guards themselves. One capo who was helping unload the cars whispered to Alfred.

"Tell them you are 16 years old," he beckoned.

Alfred took his advice and even though he was only 14, he fooled them. His brothers, 12, 10, and 8, weren't so lucky. They tried to convince the Germans that they were 16 years of age, but their youthful appearance betrayed them. There on the platform, only minutes after their arrival, Alfred said good-bye to his family. As he was shuttled to one line and his brothers and his mother were led away to another, Alfred recalls his mother's last words to him.

"She looked at me and called back, 'I love you son.'" Then she was gone.

Those who were to be exterminated immediately were led in one direction and those who were to survive, at least for the time being, were led in another. Alfred followed the line to a processing building where all of the prisoners' possessions were taken away. Each prisoner was then shaved, given a striped uniform, assigned a barracks, and immediately put to work. Older prisoners had their prison numbers tattooed on their fore-arms, but younger boys like Alfred were only given prison numbers on their uniforms. The Germans only tattooed those people they knew they would keep. Even though his prison uniform bore his number, prisoner number 083000, the lack of a tattoo was a constant reminder during his incarceration at Auschwitz that he might be exterminated at any moment. Alfred recalls that those prisoners who were not tattooed were destined to be gassed.

At the end of his first day, he followed fellow inmates to a large dor-mitory filled with triple-stacked bunks that were infested with lice and rodents. Excrement and vomit covered the floors and there were no bath-room facilities. Searching the crowded building, he tried in vain to find his brothers and his mother. When he explained to a fellow inmate how they had been separated, the inmate pointed out the window to a plume of smoke rising from the chimneys and said, "That's where your mother is now." He later learned that only 30 minutes after they were separated, his mother and brothers were dead, victims of the notorious gas chambers of Auschwitz.

For the next 12 months he lived at the edge of death. Inmates were pushed to the extreme both mentally and physically. Death was a daily existential nightmare and part of their lives. The fires of the furnaces never stopped. Much of the work to which he was assigned was preparing large burial areas for the mounds of human ashes taken from the ovens. Fel-low inmates died each day—some were friends and some were not. Either way, each death brought the realization that he could be next. Physically his body was tested by the daily 10–12 hour work shifts, filth, and disease. For the entire year of his incarceration at the labor camp, he had no bath, no change of clothes, and no bathroom facilities. The Germans regularly thinned the inmates, selecting for extermination those who could not work. The inmates dreaded hearing their number being called because they feared they would be sent to their deaths. When they could, they changed their names or managed to get their friends' and family members' names crossed off of extermination lists. Several times Alfred was selected for extermination, but each time he was able to slip back into the popula-tion undetected.

Nearly unbearable hunger greeted him each morning and followed him to bed at night. The hunger he had known after his father's death didn't begin to compare to the hunger in the camp. Inmates subsisted on a piece of bread and black coffee in the morning and a cup of foul-tasting soup at night. The dream of living a day without hunger loomed over the camp like a specter.

"We were programmed to perish from the time we were issued the striped suits," he said. "I dreamed about food. Hunger was the bottomless abyss. It ravaged the soul and the body. All we hoped for was to live long enough to have one last satisfying meal."

Occasionally, the inmates would hear a plane fly overhead and as it became known to the inmates that the allied forces dominated the skies, their resentment and their belief that the world had forgotten them increased. They knew the allies had to know about the camps, but no rescuers arrived, no bombs were dropped on the camps, and there was no indication that help was on the way. With each passing day, they realized their chances of surviving grew less and less. By February of 1945, Alfred and his fellow inmates could hear shelling, and the frequency of allied aircraft over the camp increased. They knew the allied army was approaching. As the close of the war grew near, the Germans tried to conceal the existence of the death camps throughout Europe, and the SS did their best to ensure that no inmates survived the camps. Auschwitz was no exception. As the Russian army neared Auschwitz, the Germans rounded up all the weak and sick inmates and immediately sent them to the gas chambers. Alfred and the other surviving inmates of Auschwitz were loaded onto train cars to be moved to another camp.

Unfortunately for the prisoners, the allies believed that the train cars contained German soldiers being evacuated from Poland. After two grueling days in the train cars, bombs from allied aircraft rained down on them. The train cars and tracks were destroyed. Many inmates, as well as some Germans, were killed. The survivors were collected and forced to walk the remaining miles to Buchenwald, one of the largest death camps in Germany. They walked in the cold and snow from sunrise to sunset and they slept where they fell at the end of the day. Each morning they arose to repeat the same grueling routine. Those who were too weak to walk were shot. Others died from starvation and exhaustion. At other times, in order to thin out their ranks, the Germans randomly fired into the crowd of skeletal Jews, killing as many as they could. During one of these shootings, Alfred was shot in the shoulder, but determined to survive, he got up and continued to march. Nearly three weeks later, and after marching several hundred miles, they entered the gates of Buchenwald.

Buchenwald, built by prisoners in 1937, was notorious for its torture and medical experimentation on prisoners. Inmates were deliberately exposed to disease, operated on without anesthesia to test pain reactions, and deliberately poisoned and burned with phosphorus so researchers could conduct experiments on treating these problems. Inmates with interesting tattoos were killed and then skinned. Their elaborately tattooed skin was tanned and then made into book covers and lampshades. After the camp was liberated, shrunken heads were found in the camp amid the piles of bodies and other human artifacts. Inmates from more than 60 countries were housed among the thousands of prisoners who passed through Buchenwald. Ironically, the first commandant of the camp was charged with the unauthorized murder of a prisoner by the SS and subsequently executed. His wife, later tried for war crimes, was well-known for her cruelty at Buchenwald. Known as the "Bitch of Buchenwald," she was among those who allegedly had gloves and other items made from human skin.

Gratefully, even before Alfred and his fellow Auschwitz inmates entered Buchenwald, a prison underground was operating in the camp. This led to an uprising that ended the camp's operation only days after he entered the camp. On the last day of its operation in a final attempt to kill as many Jews as possible, 50 of the 20,000 surviving inmates were scheduled to be executed, but when their names were called, none of them showed themselves. Camp officers, knowing the allied advance was near, quickly gave up their search for the condemned few and fled the camp. Buchenwald was the first concentration camp liberated by the allies. When American troops entered the camp, Alfred realized he had survived.

During the time of his imprisonment, he suffered dysentery, lice, grueling work conditions, psychological torture, loneliness, hopelessness, exposure to the elements, and starvation. He survived a death march of 400 miles, a gunshot wound, the allied bombing of his train, and his weight had dropped to a skeletal 65 pounds. Survivors of the camp were sent to medical facilities for treatment. In an ironic twist of fate, thousands of inmates died after the liberation. The allies, in an attempt to help the emaciated inmates, fed them solid food, not knowing that this would kill them. Alfred was so weak and sick he was sent to an American run hospital where he was given nutrients intravenously. This saved his life and he spent three weeks recovering.

After his release from the hospital, Alfred returned home. It was only then that he realized the extent of the extermination of the Jews from his

hometown. Of the approximately 1,000 Jews, made up of about 200 families who were rounded up from his village by the Germans, less than 40
survived to the end of the war.

One might have thought that his nightmare was over, but it was not. His
family was gone; his friends were dead; and even though the war was over,
Hungary still was inhospitable to the Jewish way of life. It was a lonely,
two-week train ride back to Bilke. He arrived in the late evening with no
suitcase and no possessions. The only clothes he wore were the clothes
donated by a Jewish agency from Great Britain and the United States. His
house was a two-mile walk from the station and Alfred vividly recalls seeing a light on as he approached his house. For a moment he had a ray
of hope that someone had survived—maybe a brother, he thought. He
knocked on the door and a stranger answered. Both looked at one another
with surprise.

"I thought you were all dead," the man said.

Alfred could think of nothing to say so he said, "I'm the ghost."

At that the man shut the door, momentarily wondering if he was, in
fact, a specter. He watched Alfred through a window for several minutes,
but then opened the door again and allowed him to enter. Alfred learned
that the man was a Hungarian Nazi sympathizer. He had been given the
property by the Germans for being a "good Nazi." Alfred accepted his invitation to spend the night, but privately both men realized that they might
not be safe. Alfred feared the man might kill him in the night. Who would
miss one more Jew? The man feared Alfred might kill him for collabo-
rating with the Germans and stealing his family's property. Nevertheless,
the men shared the home for two weeks until the man decided to move
out. Alfred was safe from the threat of his housemate, but now he had no
food, no money, and no way to support himself. Soon after, an uncle who
had been a soldier in the Hungarian army and who was captured by the
Russians returned home. The two shared the house for a few months, but
Alfred recognized that even though the world war was over, his war was
not. Bilke was not a safe place to live.

The Soviet Union pressed to annex part of Hungary, including Bilke
(which eventually would become part of Ukraine). Alfred decided to flee
to a neighboring country from where he thought it might be easier to get
into western Europe. He paid a man to smuggle him across the border and
he was to meet his contact in a barn at midnight for a secret crossing. As
he waited, he heard voices and saw lights. Rather than seeing his guide, he

was met by the police. The man had taken his money and turned Alfred in to the police. Alfred was arrested and taken to a small jail cell for the night. After all he had been through, he was once again unjustly imprisoned. This time he decided he would take fate into his own hands. He tore a hole in the roof of the jail cell and escaped into the darkness.

He realized he could never go home so decided to find his way to freedom alone. From 1945 to 1948, Alfred drifted. He did not know what he wanted from life and he wrestled for answers. These years he spent living in parks and on trains, traveling as a hobo across Europe, stealing food from farms to survive. Finally, he realized that even though he wasn't sure what he wanted, he knew it wasn't that lifestyle. He was taken in at a Kibbutz in Budapest and later a yeshiva in the Czech Republic that helped children orphaned by the war. There he was one of 120 boys rescued by a Jewish relief group from London whose mission was to help Jewish orphans. With their help, Alfred made his way to Ireland where he lived for a year, learned English, and then moved on to New York, where he received sponsorship to attend City University of New York. Once he was on U.S. soil, Alfred finally felt as though he had been "liberated from a continent" that had shackled him his entire life.

In 1956, he accepted a job with a firm in Georgia and relocated. Believing he would fare better with an American name, Alfred Leicht changed his name to Murray Lynn, a name he remains known by today. In the years since the war, Murray married and had three children, but for decades he left the past to itself, rarely speaking of his experiences. It was not until a life-changing event in 2001—open-heart surgery—that he decided to end his silence. Murray graciously accepted my invitation for an interview as he often does for schools, community groups, and Holocaust survivors' organizations. Because of his years of silence, it was during one of these public speeches that his wife and children heard some of his stories for the first time. Murray has moved on. He feels no hate for his captors and no vengeance for the cruelty he endured. Yet even though the Holocaust ended in 1945, in some ways memories continue to haunt him. He misses his family, especially his mother. His children were cheated of the opportunity to know their grandparents, uncles, and other relatives from Hungary. His years of willful and self-imposed silence were years spent trying to put the past behind him. Finally, he realized his past was a part of him that he could never lose, deny, or ignore.

COPING

For someone to suggest he can't cope with a situation is incorrect. Everyone copes with life's problems. Some people use exercise to cope with their daily frustrations. Others cope by focusing on their religion, family, or career goals. Some people cope with stress by drinking alcohol or using other drugs. To lie down and do nothing, allowing fate to take its course, is in itself a coping strategy. Even suicide is a form of coping. Therefore, to suggest that someone isn't coping with a situation is always untrue. Some people choose very poor coping strategies, but they are strategies just the same. The real issue is not whether or not one can cope, but rather *how* one copes—whether one uses effective and productive coping strategies or dysfunctional and ineffective strategies.

It is difficult to list all the issues that Murray had to cope with those many years ago. His father was arrested and murdered. His financial circumstances were tenuous. The world was at war. His family was displaced to a ghetto. They were crowded onto a train car for a frightening journey. He spent a year in Auschwitz with all the horrors and nightmares of a concentration camp, facing death every moment of the day. He was forced to march for weeks through the cold, nearly killed by the bombing of his train, shot, and placed in yet another concentration camp. Later his own people betrayed him a second time and he spent years trying to escape Europe. Any one of these events by itself could have been enough for some people to give up and die. Yet Murray did not because he found meaning in his existence. Surrender was no option.

MEANING

One of the most common themes among survivors is that those who have a reason to live are more likely to fight for life. Nietzsche once said, "He who has a *why* to live can bear with almost any *how*." Finding meaning in life is a distinct human need. No other species is capable of contemplating its purpose. In therapy, regardless of the presenting issues, part of the process of working toward healing is helping the client see purpose in his or her life. He must have someone or something to live for or his life becomes hopeless.

We are fortunate to have an account of the Holocaust experience from the perspective of a psychiatrist. Viktor Frankl was arrested in 1942 along with his wife and several other relatives and sent to the concentration camp

Theresienstadt. He and his relatives were eventually sent to other camps. His wife died in Bergen-Belsen and he was sent to Auschwitz, where his brother and mother were killed. He was moved several more times before 1945, when his camp was finally liberated. After his release, he wrote his short work, *Man's Search for Meaning.* He never intended it to be as widely published and read as it has been and he originally planned on penning the work anonymously, but it has been reprinted over 73 times in English and millions of copies have been sold worldwide. Frankl's basic premise is that finding meaning amid the chaos of the camps is what allowed some to survive.

People find meaning in many things—religion, families, friends, and even nature. Gordon Allport writes that "hunger, humiliation, fear and deep anger at injustice are rendered tolerable by closely guarded images of beloved persons, by religion, by a grim sense of humor, and even by glimpses of the healing beauties of nature—a tree or a sunset." Work can also provide meaning in life. For example, during his incarceration, Frankl found meaning for survival in his work. Upon his arrest, he had tried to conceal in his clothing a manuscript for a book he had written entitled *The Doctor and The Soul.* The manuscript was taken from him and destroyed when was sent to Auschwitz. While struggling to survive typhoid fever, he reconstructed the book in his mind. When he was released from his captivity he found that his relatives had all perished. His mother, brother, father, and wife were gone and many of his friends had been killed as well. A second time, he set out to reconstruct the book. This time he did it on paper. Working the book over in his mind while he was imprisoned and later working it out on paper gave his life some purpose. Perhaps even more therapeutic was the writing of *Man's Search for Meaning,* a book he wrote in only nine days that allowed him to tell his story and work out the events in his own mind. He found purpose in other forms of work, as well. He says of his work as a physician in one camp, "I knew that in a working party I would die in a short time. But if I had to die there might at least be some sense in my death." Ironically, the words over the Auschwitz entry gate, "Arbeit Macht Frei," were true for Frankl. Work did make him free.

Murray says of himself that he was always a determined child, but two things gave his life meaning in the camps. He believed that he owed it to his parents to survive. They had died, but he believed it would honor them if he lived. More important, however, was a pledge he made with other inmates. They all agreed that whoever survived would tell the story of their ordeal. They knew if no one survived the camps, the world would never know the truth. Murray says that the "most compelling reason to survive" was to be a "missionary to the world to tell of these atrocities."

"One of my most abiding memories of the Auschwitz horrors, was our solemn pledge to one another, that those of us fortunate enough to survive the savagery and existential nightmares would incessantly trumpet our message from mountains and valleys, across every continent and narrate the scope and dimensions of mankind's unspeakable unbridled hate." This would be the work that gave his life meaning.

Oddly, Murray also found meaning in the drive to find meaning. Murray told me bluntly that "insecurity drove me to do more." He was driven to prove that his life was not wasted—to prove that his existence mattered even when he was not sure of that fact himself. No matter what the issue is, man must find meaning in his existence, especially when faced with overwhelming trauma. Allport concludes that "to survive is to find meaning in the suffering. If there is a purpose in life at all, there must be a purpose in suffering and in dying. But no man can tell another what this purpose is. Each must find out for himself."

HAPPINESS

Meaning brings peace and peace is a basis for happiness. It is hard to imagine, but the survivors of trauma often say that they are happy. Happiness is a subjective state, totally dependent upon the person's perspective. In the past several years, I've traveled all over the world and during my travels and interactions with indigenous peoples I've noticed a disturbing truth about Americans. We are very hard to satisfy. Americans are among the richest people in the world. The poorest Americans are wealthier than many wealthy people in other countries. If money brought happiness then Americans should be among the happiest people on earth, but this doesn't seem to be the case. How foreign it must sound to our guests from poorer countries who hear Americans complaining about trivial issues such as the taste of the food that is provided for us. For many of them, the daily issue is whether or not they will have food—not whether or not they will have the food they like. We take it for granted that food will be provided. Therefore, we have the luxury to complain about type, quality, preparation, and convenience rather than existence of or absence of food. We have health care, leisure time, education, and recreation. We have large homes, freedom, and jobs. We have so many things that one of the fastest growing businesses in the United States is the mini-warehouse business. We need someplace to keep all of our possessions. My friend once visited a family in Japan. Eight people lived in a 400-square-foot apartment. I have more room in my home than that just to store my vehicles and lawnmower.

We seriously misuse the word "need." Walker Percy describes the stages of consumption in which the consumer moves from no need for an item, to a desire to have an item because others have it, then through other stages toward a final stage where a new item replaces the old one. This is not only an accurate portrayal of consumerism, but also an accurate portrayal of the hopeless pursuit of happiness in things. Even the best things wear out or we simply lose interest in them. Percy goes on to add that "the advantages of wealth, education, and culture is disappointing." These things are disappointing because they are weak substitutes for internalized peace.

This truth became most obvious to me several years ago while I was traveling through the arid planes of northern India. The car I was riding in struck another vehicle and totally destroyed our car. For several hours I was stranded in a tiny village in the middle of nowhere. While I was wondering if I might have to walk the 75 kilometers back to Delhi, people from the village came to investigate the accident. When they saw I was an American, they invited me to a shelter where we could get out of the 120 degree heat. The only Hindi I spoke was the few words and phrases that were in my travel book, and my newly found friends spoke no English. Despite our language barrier, we talked for several hours about our families, America, and India, mostly with gestures and by drawing pictures in the sand.

They were fascinated with how much things cost—my boots, my watch, my camera, and the cost to travel to India. By American standards, nothing that I had was very valuable—hiking boots I purchased at a discount superstore, a Timex watch, and a digital camera I bought on sale. Yet in this area of India where the average daily wage is about US $1, I realized that what I was wearing was worth more than a year's salary to them. They graciously gave me a juice box from a nearby open-air cantina and they refused to let me pay. That drink cost someone more than a half-day's pay. A shallow well with a hand pump was just a few yards from where I sat under the shelter. During my rest, I watched people carry water from that well, bathe, and water their cattle and water buffalo. Later as we walked through their village, I saw homes made from dried ox dung and grass.

Other homes were mere shelters in alleyways, under the awnings on the backside of businesses, or caves hollowed out in ancient masonry structures. There were no walls and their beds, tables, and chairs were just a few steps from the path that I walked.

In this village, people had no dental care, no health care plans, no IRAs, no health club or swimming pool, no air conditioning, no privacy, minimally sanitary water and sewage services (what they had was constructed centuries earlier), and only basic foods. Yet they seemed happy. They laughed, treated me as well as any host here in America, and they genuinely seemed satisfied with life. This is a story I've seen played out in Central America, Asia, Africa, and many other poverty-stricken places around the world. However, here in America where all of these needs are taken for granted we have higher rates of depression than almost anywhere in the world.

As the Atlanta Braves prepared to enter the World Series in 1995, a journalist was interviewing Steve Bedrosian. Bedrosian had been released by the Braves pitching roster earlier in the season. The journalist asked him if he was angry with the Braves because he was not going to the World Series.

"Not at all," he sincerely replied. "I couldn't be happier for my friends. I was one of the lucky few who got to play the game for a little while. How could I be angry?"

His response shocked the interviewer. I'm sure he expected a very different response to his loaded question. After all, here was a professional baseball player who had come within inches of playing in the World Series. One would have to wonder how he could *not* be angry. Yet at the time, Steve Bedrosian had a son who was struggling with leukemia. He was recovering and even though Bedrosian had been released by his team, he had more time to spend with his son. His lucrative career allowed him the luxury to stay home with his son without worrying about money or finding another job right away. Who can complain about getting paid to play, he went on to say, and he added that he was excited for his friends who might soon wear a World Series ring. Happiness takes on a new meaning when one realizes what one has to lose. Happiness is a frame of mind that clearly is independent of one's surroundings. Of course there are situations in which it is easier to be happy. My father used to say that money can't buy happiness, but it could buy some great substitutes. Others have joked that money can't buy happiness, but it can keep you busy while you are waiting to be happy. But even though we recognize these statements as jokes, people in our culture still pursue possessions as if they will, indeed, buy them happiness. This generation of "me-ism" has led us to believe the world owes us something. Hosen and colleagues relate some adjustment problems, including subjective well-being, to overexposure to the media, especially if it substitutes for interaction with others. "The belief in one's entitlement to happiness without effort or knowledge of human nature, these are possible (but not certain) results of mass media substitution for organic human contacts." Likewise, Buss suggests that the media presents fictitious lives that viewers misinterpret for real situations. Depression then comes from "self-perceived failures resulting in erroneous comparisons between people's lives and the lives they see depicted so glamorously in the media."

Researcher David Myers, a pioneer in this field, calls happiness an "imaginary condition." In his research, Myers has determined that people are happiest when they are with others, married, and when they are actively religious. In fact, even though mental-health practitioners tend to avoid talking about religion, the data demonstrates that religion can be a beneficial tool in recovery and regaining "happiness." According to Myers, "People of faith also tend to retain or recover greater happiness after suffering divorce, unemployment, serious illness, or bereavement." Myers dispels the myths that money buys happiness. In fact, according to Myers, as long as a person's basic needs are met, "age, gender and income give little clue to someone's happiness."

Other theorists have drawn similar conclusions. For example, Karen Horney said that happiness was a marriage between what she called the "real self" and the "ideal self." "Normal individuals, by and large, are happy with and function within the everyday world. Neurotics are unhappy with the everyday world." Adler believed that a person is happy when he recognizes the imperfections in the world, something he called "fictional finalisms," and he is content to deal with those imperfections as they arise. Diener says that goal flexibility, the ability to adapt ones expectations when adversity arises, may be the key to subjective well-being. All of these positions validate that the secret to happiness is inner peace.

A mantra I repeat at least once each week for one or more of my children is "be happy with what you have and you will never want for anything." This is a key component to resiliency and overcoming trauma. People who have suffered spinal injuries, rape, or other terrible experiences can decide to take control of life rather than let the event control them. Murray found peace in himself and that peace has allowed him to grow from his experience.

VIRTUES

Peace is also found in virtues. Murray values character because he sees its importance. For centuries many religious teachings have addressed the meaning of happiness. For example, in Christian writings, the reader is told to be "well satisfied without money if we have enough food and clothing." Similarly, those who are meek, pure in heart, peacemakers, and merciful are called "blessed," a word that is sometimes translated as happy. In these teachings, as well as the teachings in Islam, Shintoism, Buddhism, Catholicism, and Judaism, it is character and virtue that bring happiness to one's home. A look at what the research says about virtues and happiness may provide some insight into what makes people happy and, subsequently, how virtues lead to trauma recovery.

In 2002, writer William Bennett was skewered in the press because of his gambling habits. He lost somewhere around a million dollars gambling. This is not really news. Lots of people blow their money in Las Vegas, Reno, Atlantic City, and other gambling meccas. The thing that made Bennett a target for jeers and snickers was the fact that he has written extensively about virtues, including his book, *The Book of Virtues*. The popular press seem to revel in evidence of imperfection in anyone who attempts to promote virtuous living. In my own writings I have been most assaulted by reviewers, both academic and nonacademic, when I have written on the topics of character and virtue. It seems odd that people are so critical when someone suggests that we can better ourselves through virtuous living.

For years secular psychologists have ignored and even scoffed at the virtues commonly found in religious traditions. Where they did accept them, they relabeled these virtues so as not to imply any religious connotation. In recent years, however, the field has begun to see that many virtues have psychological importance in many areas, including trauma recovery. The purpose of my work here is not to promote religion, but rather to acknowledge that virtues have benefits, and to ignore the value of virtues where they can help a person recover from trauma is irresponsible and unprofessional. While studying the characteristics of survivors of trauma, I have found five common virtuous traits, one or more of which survivors have said have helped them overcome the difficulties that they faced and to live happier lives. These five traits are humility, gratitude, hope, forgiveness, and optimism.

Humility

In 2000, Tangney published in the *Journal of Social and Clinical Psychology* a research study on humility. True humility, according to Tangney, is a rich, multifaceted construct that entails an accurate assessment of one's characteristics, an ability to acknowledge limitations, and a "forgetting of the self." Tangney goes on to say that "the great writer and theologian C. S. Lewis once said that humility does not consist in handsome people trying to believe they are ugly, and clever people trying to believe they are fools . . . true humility is more like self-forgetfulness . . . it leaves people free to esteem their special talents and, with the same honesty, to esteem their neighbor's." Focus on others, rather than self, has been correlated with lessened likelihood of depression, anxiety, and phobias.

While in the camp, Murray humbled himself and chose to live because he believed it would honor his parents. Later, Murray found his meaning and purpose in his new life in America. He left behind his life in Hungary and started over. Even though Murray says that "we all came to the U.S. with hate in our hearts," it was humbling to overcome the many barriers to his new life. There were barriers because of his educational background, language barriers, and financial barriers. These were humbling, almost terrifying experiences. The humble person is more appreciative of those around him and this, according to Tangney, sets the stage for the next virtue—gratitude.

Gratitude

Even in the dismal circumstances of the concentration camp, Frankl found things for which he could be grateful. "We were grateful for the smallest of mercies," he comments. For example, even though he was starving, risking exposure to disease, and living daily with death, filth, and hopelessness, he noted that he was fortunate to work inside instead of outside. Those with such jobs were envied for their "relative luck" at not having "to wade in deep, muddy clay on a steep slope." Frankl recalls the words of a woman by whose bed he sat as she lay dying. "This young woman knew that she would die in the next few days. But when I talked to her she was cheerful in spite of this knowledge. 'I am grateful that fate has hit me so hard,' she told me. 'In my former life I was spoiled and did not take spiritual accomplishments seriously.'" Correy ten Boom, while incarcerated in a concentration camp, was grateful for lice. Because the inmates' dormitories were ridden with lice, the guards would not enter their living quarters. That gave Correy and her fellow captives freedom to practice their religion without interruption from the camp guards.

Emmons and Crumpler argue that the "ungrateful person, regularly responds to others' beneficence with resentment, hostility, or indifference." To be grateful, however, a person must see oneself as a debtor rather than one who is owed. This is a difficult concept in western cultures that promote self over others and personal interests above group interest. Gratitude is antithetical to consumerism. Consumerism suggests that you deserve something you don't have while a grateful person recognizes that he has something he doesn't deserve. Emmons and Crumpler note that many religious writings denote the importance of gratitude. For example, "the Holy Koran repeatedly asserts the necessity for gratitude and thankfulness to God throughout the chapters."

Gratitude has measurable benefits. In one study, participants in a gratitude condition felt better about their lives as a whole; they were more optimistic; they had fewer physical complaints; and they reported having made more progress toward their goals. Gratitude appears to assist in reframing. For example, one who has a brush with death, instead of resenting the near-death experience, might be grateful for surviving and being allowed a second chance at life.

Looking back over the entire experience, Murray is most grateful for the opportunity to move to the United States. He calls this his "opportunity of a lifetime." Murray is also deeply grateful for the many people who helped him survive. The man who helped him get to Ireland, the people who trained him in English, the citizens of the United States for allowing him to live and study here—the list is endless. Ungracious people wonder why they don't have more. Grateful people are surprised they have so much. The later certainly typifies Murray Lynn.

Hope

Hope is a common factor in nearly all great survival stories. Testimonies from survivors of World War II, concentration camps, prison camps in Vietnam and Korea, and many other situations demonstrate that once an inmate lost hope, he soon perished. Hope gives us focus and something to live for. Without something to hope and strive toward, life begins to lose meaning. This truth has been known for centuries. The 14th-century writer Dante, in his epic work *The Inferno,* has written across the entrance to hell, "Abandon all hope, ye who enter here." Hope provides the mental fuel to live another minute, hour or day. Frankl noted that the loss of "hope and courage can have a deadly effect."

The fear of death was ever present and Murray's goal was to live one more hour. He sought answers from God, the Bible, and men in the camp, but could not find answers in these places as to why these things had happened to him. Yet he eventually found hope in small things. He said that in the camps, their only hope was "one last satisfying meal" and that they worked simply to "survive another day." A sense of hope and future are important in creating meaning. Resilient children and adults, for example, are more likely to see future possibilities than nonresilient individuals. Frankl found that the "prisoner who had lost faith in the future—his future—was doomed." Frankl noted that part of coping with the difficulties of camps was to look beyond those circumstances for a better time ahead. Those who failed to do so became "occupied with retrospective thoughts," ruing what they had lost. Even though Murray's "future" was what he called "the next five minutes or the next hour," it allowed him to focus ahead, rather than dwelling on his dire situation and the things he had lost. Not long after his release from Auschwitz he quickly shifted his thinking into much longer-term goals. His hope and vision were for a future that was years, rather than minutes, away.

Forgiveness

Forgiveness is linked in research to many things including both psychological and physical well-being. When a person forgives, his or her perceptions of the offense and offender no longer create motivations to avoid the offender and seek revenge. The need for revenge for a wrong done consumes mental and physical energy. It also prevents reconciliation with the offender. It should come as no surprise that people are happier when they are not angry. Forgiveness promotes "relationship harmony" by reestablishing and preserving "supportive, caring relationships between victim and offender."

Murray has not found forgiveness. "I don't know if you can ever forgive—you can cleanse yourself of anger, but to forgive is something else," he explains. "I will always nurture these images. I will take them to my grave." These words do not mean he fosters resentment or anger. They only mean that his experiences were indelibly etched into his existence. He holds no grudge and he has, for the most part, left his anger behind him. At one time, he was angry at nearly everyone who was not Jewish. In the camp, even some of the Jews made him angry because of their collaboration with the Germans as capos. By letting go of his anger, he freed himself to be happier. Murray makes it clear that there is a difference between letting go of anger and forgiving. I do not see his inability to forgive as a weakness. As much as forgiveness might help, it cannot always be expected. Releasing his anger and resentment is a reasonable compromise.

Optimism

One might make the case that optimism is hope in disguise, but most researchers would count these as separate issues even though optimism might involve hope. Hope is the desire for some future event. Optimism is the explanation of current events. When a person encounters an unpleasant event, she seeks to know why. The person's causal attribution, called "explanatory style," determines how she will respond to an event. Peterson argues that optimistic people believe their plans can help them pursue their goals, and optimism provides the determination to follow through with those plans.

Even though optimism is helpful, it should not be unleashed optimism. In fact, the research demonstrates that pessimists function better than optimists in some cases. Pessimism is sometimes helpful because it prevents people from setting their expectations too high. According to Peterson, "Optimism in the form of wishful thinking can distract people." However, realistic optimists tend to report better subjective well-being. Murray described himself neither as a pessimist nor an optimist. Instead, he described himself as a realist. Indiscriminant optimism sets hopes too high, thus setting oneself up for disappointment when unrealistic expectations are not met. On the other hand, pessimists can lose hope altogether. Realists have hope but they do not negate the reality of their circumstances.

In his attempt to make sense of his ordeal—to find order in chaos— Murray sought answers from other inmates, from the Torah, and from

God. His questions about why this was happening to him and the others went unanswered. This led to a certain level of cynicism and protective pessimism, but he still describes himself as a realist rather than an optimist or pessimist. "You have to understand the Jewish mind-set," he told me. "As a self-defense, we had to be careful about getting our hopes too high." The entire history of the Jewish people has been one of ups and downs. He chose to look for the best in the situation, but he did not ignore the likelihood that he might die in the camp.

TURNING POINTS

Mark Katz, author of *On Playing a Bad Hand Well,* suggests that when people face trauma, and in the process of recovering and coping with trauma, they come to "turning points." Turning points are "specific experiences in people's lives that offer important opportunities for change." These changes, according to Katz, can "dramatically alter how we view ourselves in relation to others. In turn, it can also alter our future development." At these critical decision points, one chooses between the path that leads to dysfunction or the path that leads to survival. Traumatic events, as horrifying as they are, can serve as turning points in life.

Turning points don't just happen in the presence of trauma. They occur throughout life. They can be simple things like starting a new school, changing jobs, marriage, or having children. It is possible that the many turning points that one encounters through life actually predicate the success of dealing with trauma. This occurs when the decisions made at those turning points create a more resilient person. Practicing making decisions that lead one to a lifestyle of healthy coping produces a resilient individual. For example, as a young graduate student, I was also a runner. I ran five miles every day all year round and while I ran I literally chanted in my head the phrase, "endurance and discipline," over and over. The same type of discipline I needed to endure the heat and exhaustion I felt while I was running also gave me the strength to do the mental exercises I needed to complete my graduate degrees.

These turning points involve choice. Reflecting on the deplorable conditions of the concentration camp, Frankl acknowledges that "everything can be taken from man but one thing: the last of the human freedoms—to choose one's attitude in any given set of circumstances, to choose one's own way." According to Frankl, "The sort of person the prisoner became was the result of an inner decision, and not the result of camp influence alone." Murray chose to let his mother go on the train platform. He chose to work long days in deplorable conditions when it would have been easier to lie down and die. He chose to get up out of the snow when he had been shot on the way to Buchenwald. He chose to break out of prison in Bilke after the war and he chose to take advantages of opportunities for refugees. After being liberated from the camp, he was drifting through life. His decision to pursue life rather than an existence was critical. In his own words, he "recast" his life and decided he wanted something more. Once he set his mind to a future goal, he "knew exactly how" he would achieve those goals and he did. His decision at that turning point made the difference between living life as a rambling hobo and the new and prosperous life he found in the United States.

CONTINUED EFFECTS

Murray survived and lived a prosperous life, but he didn't remain totally unscathed. Even though he adjusted quite well to his circumstances and he has lived a very satisfying and productive life, he has carried Auschwitz with him for decades. There are three ways that we can see how Auschwitz followed Murray—denial, resentment, and abreaction.

Denial. Most obvious is the fact that Murray didn't even talk about his experiences for five decades. When he did choose to speak publicly about his experiences, his adult children and his wife were in tears with the rest of the audience. They were hearing his story for the first time. Even though Murray is a survivor, even though he is strong, he wasn't prepared to fully deal with the emotions and pain of Auschwitz until late in life. Murray told me that he didn't think it would help; he perceived it as a distraction; and it would "only open old wounds," but this is denial, a common way that clients avoid discussing painful events in therapy. In his own speeches he has often said that "it was more comfortable not to confront the ghost of the past. So, I retreated into a protective shell and pretended that the past was a mere delusion, perhaps just a dreadful nightmare." It is fascinating that the very thing that gave him hope and meaning in the camp, the pledge to be a "missionary to the world to tell of these atrocities" is something that took him nearly 50 years to accomplish.

The fact that he feels driven to discuss it today is evidence that he needed to talk about the event. Talking helps one organize, process, and make sense of an event. To address pain *is* distracting, but it is a necessary distraction. This part of trauma recovery is like a dentist drilling a cavity. It is uncomfortable addressing the problem, but if it isn't dealt with, it only gets worse. The final confirmation for me that he was denying his need to talk was the fact that he felt great catharsis when he finally began to talk about it. Since he began to talk about his experiences, he has addressed audiences at grade schools, yeshivas, and at the National Holocaust Museum in Washington, D.C. For Murray, his catharsis is not only therapeutic, but it also helps to give his experiences meaning, and he believes it serves his community.

It took open-heart surgery (he wears a pacemaker today) to make him realize that he was about to let his secrets die with him and that he would have failed his pledge to his fellow inmates. The story he tells is not just about the pain and horror of the concentration camp. His story is also one of hope and encouragement. This is the kind of narrative I want to see from my clients. It demonstrates that they not only can talk about their experiences, but that they can also bring something good from their pain.

Resentment. Even though he said he lived in "relative peace," I know he still believes there is a "missing link" being raised without mother or father, brothers, or other family because he said as much. He has always felt a void in his life—insecurity because his family was taken from him and he was robbed of his childhood. From age 14 onward, he never knew the loving nurturance of family. His children never met any of his relatives. During their childhood when they asked him why they didn't visit his family, Murray merely replied, "Because they have died." Most of us take our family heritage for granted. We knew those who came before us and our children and grandchildren know us. In Murray's case, his entire family was exterminated. He is a man with little family history and nothing to pass on to his children and grandchildren except himself. This would be painful for any of us, but it is even more painful in a lineal culture that values family heritage. Jewish traditions as well as Hungarian traditions place a heavy emphasis on children and one's family line. He is a father of three children—two daughters and a son. His daughters have not married and have no children. His son is married, but he and his wife have decided for personal reasons not to have children. Having no grandchildren is "one of life's greatest disappointments" for Murray.

While in the camp, Murray resented men and God. He felt like he had been betrayed by both, left to die by an uncaring world. He believed that the whole world turned its back on him, a fact that history has at least partially confirmed, and he believed God had broken his covenant with the Jews. He also believed that the Christian community, especially, had betrayed him. "The Christian community betrayed the teachings of its master," he said. "Christ preached love and yet the world had turned its back on the Jews."

But he does not let resentment, bitterness, or pessimism control him. Even though he admits he still harbors some level of cynicism in regard to religion, he has moved beyond hate in regard to life in general. Many of us find it difficult to forgive those who have wronged us—a lover who betrays a trust, a coworker who takes credit for an idea or work completed, or a friend who uses painful words. Letting go of the past is very difficult.

Murray assured me he held no lingering resentment toward the German people or his captors. "Hate is a cancer," Murray explained, "a pathology of the mind. You have to make peace with yourself or the past will enslave your future." Notice that he doesn't say you must make peace with your enemies. The peace that has allowed him to transcend his resentment is the realization that only he can hold his future captive. This is one difference between those who overcome and those who do not. They are willing to let go of their enemies and recover in spite of the hatred their enemies showed to them. Murray has not forgotten all that happened to him and the thought that life is unfair must occasionally cross his mind, even after all of these years. Yet he has let the majority of his bitterness go.

His mother helped him to shape his values. She was a strong disciplinarian but managed with grace and courage, and somehow was able to provide security in those uncertain times. Deep down, even at more than 70 years of age, Murray misses his mother and feels as though he was cheated out of the years he should have had with her. Even his brothers, whose faces he cannot remember, should have been a part of his life into adulthood. I suspect that he wonders what his parents would have thought of his success in life.

Even though the loss of his family led to insecurity, Murray doesn't perceive this as a bad thing. "Insecurity can have a positive impact. It drove me to do more." Here again we can see a difference between survivors and those who let trauma consume them. Murray recognizes that even though he suffered because of his family's death, he was able to grow from it. He turned a weakness into a strength.

Abreaction. I'm quite certain that Sigmund Freud would have had a great deal to say about Murray's choice to sleep on train cars after his liberation from Auschwitz. Murray told me that, compared to Auschwitz, hobo life on a train car was a "piece of cake." The trains were going in the direction he wanted to go so he climbed aboard. However, one could just as easily argue that the trauma of three days in a cattle car, especially when it was followed by the unbelievable trauma of Auschwitz, would have made the mere thought of trains so distasteful that one would choose a mud puddle over a railroad car. In therapy, this is called "abreaction"—the reliving of trauma until it is resolved. Both children and adults relive their traumas in one way or another until they reach resolution. For example, a child who has been involved in a car accident will repeatedly draw pictures of car accidents, create car accidents with models or toys, or even crash chairs or other objects together to symbolize crashing cars. Abreaction allows the individual to relive the experience, take control of it, and eventually conquer it. The repetition of the behavior exists as long as it takes to either consciously or unconsciously make peace with the traumatic experience. For Murray, this took three years. At the point in his healing when he was prepared to move beyond Auschwitz, he commented, "I knew I didn't want this." Again, even though I know that Murray meant this statement in regard to being poor, homeless, and exposed to the elements, the principle remains the same. Subconsciously, he conquered the poverty and hopelessness of the train and he was ready to do something more with his life. He was ready to beat Auschwitz rather than allowing it to beat him. With abreaction, one is not always aware *why* he is ready to move ahead. He just knows that he is.

A second example of abreaction was Murray's choice of career. He spent his life in the United States in the chemical industry. His company manufactured industrial pesticides, solvents, and many other chemicals. I find it very interesting that he chose as a career the manufacture of products that were once the very threat to his life. Again, even though the chemicals his company manufactured were not the same chemicals used at Auschwitz, the principle of abreaction remains the same. They were not the same chemicals used at Auschwitz any more than the train cars he slept on as a hobo were the same cars he rode to the labor camp. Yet he mastered both things. In fact, he became CEO of the chemical company. Symbolically, as the CEO he rose to the very height of control over the threat to his life at Auschwitz. I might have the same comments if he had worked in the food industry, the medical field, or the prison system. Just as it did with Frankl, his work made him free.

CONCLUDING COMMENTS

All trauma survivors have lingering effects, no matter how successfully they have dealt with their dilemmas. Murray is no exception. For many years he was afraid of policemen and soldiers. It took decades to overcome reactions to men in uniform. Likewise, except for his hobo years, Murray admits that for many years he could not ride trains. While he has overcome that fear, even today he still reacts to certain colors. For example, the orange symbols used on utility markers on the roadside are the exact same colors of the German armbands he saw daily in Auschwitz. Even today, 60 years later, when he sees these signs, his heart races as a conditioned response to his life in the labor camp. But he has mastered his life, and these effects do not control him. Most of us are abnormal in one way or another. The thing that separates us is not presence or absence of abnormality, but rather the depth at which our abnormalities control our lives.

More than 80 percent of the almost two million sent to Auschwitz were killed. During his incarceration, Murray's idea of the future was only "the next five minutes"—to survive another day. After the war, however, his vision extended into long-term life goals—all of which he achieved. Maslow's theory of the hierarchy of needs teaches us that when one's basic needs are unmet, it will be unlikely that we will be able to focus on what he called higher-order needs such as the need to develop relationships, the need to be seen as competent, or even the need/interest in the distant future. When faced with life-threatening circumstances, people tend to focus on their immediate needs. This was certainly the case with Murray. During his incarceration at Auschwitz, his immediate needs were physical needs—the need for shelter, clothing, food, and safety. It shouldn't surprise us then that he comments that his future was only the next "five minutes." These were the minutes that might make the difference between living and dying. Once he was freed, his health needs were met, and he was again able to focus on something other than eating; he began to focus on future events.

Many of my clients over the years, men and women whose basic needs were already met, still had a difficult time focusing on the future. Their decisions were based on immediate gratification and their moods were easily swayed by present successes or difficulties. Those humans who have the ability to see the bigger picture, the ability to set distant goals and produce means to those ends, and the ability to delay gratification for those future goals will find it easier to overcome difficult circumstances.

When Murray talks to school children, he reminds them that nothing— not circumstances or poverty—can keep them from their goals. "You can be masters of your destiny," he tells them. "You can achieve whatever your mind can conceive." In a very humble way, Murray Lynn is living up to his pledge to his fellow inmates at Auschwitz. He is, indeed, "trumpeting his message from mountains and valleys, across every continent."

Murray's parting words to me on that warm November day were these:

"The alchemy of the mind and spirit is what helps us overcome and they are powerful forces that can help us to overcome the insurmountable."

His strong self-reliance, perhaps even to a fault, helped him to survive these many years and to achieve his goals. His is an inspiring story of courage and fortitude. His attitude about his experience in Auschwitz is altruistic. "If my story can help just one person, it will be worth telling."

REFERENCES

Buss, D.M. (2000). The evolution of happiness. *American Psychologist, 55,* 15–23.

Diener, E. (2000). Subjective well-being: The science of happiness and a proposal for a national index. *American Psychologist, 55,* 34–43.

Emmons, R., & Crumpler, C.A. (2000). Gratitude as a human strength: Appraising the evidence. *Journal of Social & Clinical Psychology, 19,* 55–69.

Engler, B. (2001). *Theories of personality* (4th ed.). New York: Houghton Mifflin.

Frankl, V.E. (1984). *Man's search for meaning.* New York: Pocket Books.

Hosen, R., Solovey-Hosen, D., & Stern, L. (2002). The acquisition of beliefs that promote subjective well-being. *Journal of Instructional Psychology, 29,* 231–244, p. 233.

Katz, M. (1997). *On playing a poor hand well.* New York: W.W. Norton & Company.

McCullough, M.E. (2000). Forgiveness as a human strength: Theory, measurement, and links to well-being. *Journal of Social & Clinical Psychology, 19,* 43–55.

McWhirter, J. J., McWhirter, B. T., McWhirter, A. M., & McWhirter, E. H. (1998). *At-risk youth: A comprehensive response.* New York: Brooks/Cole Publishing Company, p. 82.

Myers, D. G. (2000). The funds, friends, and faith of happy people. *American Psychologist, 55,* 56–67.

The Nizkor Project. (2009). Buchenwald. Retrieved November 10, 2009, from www.nizkor.org/hweb/camps/buchenwald/buchenwald-01.htm, 6/2/04.

Percy, W. (1983). *Lost in the cosmos: The last self-help book.* New York: The Noonday Press.

Peterson, C. (2000). The future of optimism. *American Psychologist, 55,* 44–55.

Tangney, J. P. (2000). Humility: Theoretical perspectives, empirical findings and directions for future research. *Journal of Social & Clinical Psychology, 19,* 70–82.

ten Boom, C. (1971). *The hiding place.* Old Tappan, NJ: Fleming H. Revell Company.

3

A NEW NORMAL: SURVIVING SPINAL INJURY

Not to be cheered by praise, not to be grieved by blame,
but to know thoroughly one's own virtues or powers
are the characteristics of an excellent man.

—Satchel Paige

On my worst day, I'm in better shape than 99% of the world.

—Karen McClesky

I'm lying on a hospital bed. They've told me I've been in an accident and had surgery on my back and heart, but I don't feel anything. It is as if my lower body no longer exists. I see my toes, my legs, but I feel nothing. Lying here I pinch my inner thigh as hard as I can and I even pull at my pubic hair, grabbing it in my fists, to see if I can make myself feel pain, but I still feel nothing. I learn that Tony, my husband of 12 years, is dead. My heart is so heavy with grief that I'm numb. What an ironic thing to say when I've been told I'm paralyzed. I feel like I have to plan the funeral even though someone has told me that preparations are already underway. Time has lost its meaning for me so even though I know what day it is, I'm still confused. I worry about wearing something appropriate to the funeral, something black, because I've been in a hospital gown since I arrived. My husband is gone and I have to see him to his grave, but I don't know how I can since I'm bound to this bed.

But I'm determined to be there. I have to fulfill my role as wife and mother. Many times a day I look toward the door of my room in the ICU hoping to see Tony looking for me—coming for me to awaken me from this dream. I repeat this scene for weeks, but of course he never arrives.

My children! I worry about my children. They have never been without me. I can't really think about me and what happened in the accident. Instead, I need assurance that my children are OK. I just want to hold them, but I am also ashamed for them to see me like this. What will they think of their broken mother? Will they blame me for their father's death? Oh god, was it my fault?

It is hard when people are with me, especially my family, because I can sense something not being right . . . something not right with me. I can see their eyes widen with sadness and pity. Expressions can be very heavy in the room. Their sadness is too much to bear, but it is even harder when I'm alone. I have hours of the day to fill and yet no ability to move or do things on my own. I'm helpless. I try to trick myself into thinking that this is not reality. The thought of permanent paralysis is unreal. I think the doctors must be wrong about my prognosis. They have to be. I will be the exception. I have things I need to do—things I want to do!

A physical therapist comes in eventually and tells me I need to learn to sit in a wheelchair. It takes them several minutes to get me out of bed and into the wheelchair. How could something that used to be so simple be so difficult and painful? I'm helped into the chair and immediately my head is spinning and I'm experiencing pain like I never knew existed. My bottom and my feet are on fire, yet in a way I can't pinpoint exactly where I hurt. The sensation is foreign to me. Why can I feel this pain, but I can't walk or move my legs on my own and how can just sitting in a chair be so painful? They give me something to ease the pain, but it is still unbearable. Finally, they give me so much medication that I drift off to sleep. Finally, I experience relief.

It had been an exciting weekend snow skiing with the family in North Carolina in February 1999. Minna Hong, age 35, her husband Tony, and their two children were returning to their home in Atlanta. Life was looking up for the Hong family. Difficult first years of marriage were smoothing out and their family business was prospering. This ski trip was multipurpose. Minna and her husband were expanding their restaurant business and had driven to North Carolina to look at property so they decided to piggyback a family ski vacation onto the trip. The property was all they had hoped for; the skiing was perfect; and the family had enjoyed a much

Minna near her office at the Shepherd Spinal Center in Atlanta, Georgia in 2009.

needed vacation, but hours on the road were wearing on Tony. Minna offered to give Tony a break at the wheel and took over the responsibility of driving their SUV just outside of Anderson, South Carolina. Within mere minutes of pulling back onto the freeway her life changed forever. As she traveled southward on Interstate 85, an 18-wheeler beside her swerved toward her vehicle. Stuck in his blind spot he could not see her and there was no place for Minna to go to avoid a collision. She pulled the wheel hard to the right and then lost control. The SUV first veered right and then left again toward oncoming traffic. As the top-heavy SUV hit the grassy median, it began to roll. Minna's last memory was of the vehicle rolling over and over down the highway median. The truck driver never stopped, perhaps unaware of the tragic accident that he caused.

When she regained consciousness and opened her eyes she realized she was the only one still in the car and even though she felt like she was sitting up, she could see her legs hanging out of the window of the overturned vehicle—yet she couldn't feel them. As if through a mental fog she could hear EMS workers saying something about "one man deceased . . . two kids on the lawn . . . one serious . . ." At that moment she knew her husband was dead and she begged for information about Tony and her children as she drifted in and out of consciousness. Emergency personnel assured her everyone was fine and they pleaded with her not to move. They immobilized her, slipping a collar around her neck and easing her onto a backboard—certain signs that they suspected a spinal injury. Even so, she was deeply concerned about her family and the thought of paralysis hadn't yet registered in her mind. Shock was overtaking her and mercifully numbing both the physical pain of the accident as well as the psychological pain of what was happening to her life and the lives of her children. She remembers little of her ambulance ride to the hospital, but she clearly remembers the stone cold and frightened faces of those who saw her in the emergency room and the intensive care unit. She was a beautiful woman before the accident, but now her face was battered and bruised from the airbag and flying glass. But the look she saw on the faces of her doctors and nurses was not in response to her battered face. They knew the implications of a body limp and unresponsive from the waist down. They knew they were seeing a young woman who would never walk again.

Injuries to the spine create special problems for emergency workers. Along with the normal triage assessments, it is imperative to move the patient as little as possible. Surface injuries need to be treated. Dirt, grass, glass, and even automobile paint chips have to be irrigated from lacerations, punctures, gouges, and deep cuts. Bleeding has to be arrested including identification of internal bleeding—a task that isn't always easy and that can quickly threaten the life of the patient. Even a seat belt, the very thing that saves lives, can also cause abdominal bleeding as it exerts force on the victim during the accident. Complicating triage is the fact that spinal-injury patients may have little or no feeling in various body parts. An injury that might ordinarily create great pain might barely register with the spinal-injury patient. Compound fractures, severe internal injuries such as abdominal trauma, torn ligaments, or damaged muscle tissue may not be felt at all. Therefore, the patient cannot assist the physician in identifying injuries that may be life-threatening. The physician is dependent upon visual examination and yet even then it is not always possible to see the victim's entire body because of cervical collars and backboards. X-rays, MRIs, or CT scans assist in diagnosis. These processes involve moving the patient, which increases the risk of further damage, but even then post-traumatic swelling makes it difficult to identify the extent of injury. With traumatic spinal injury it may take days or even weeks for the physician to render a thorough and reliable diagnosis and prognosis.

Minna was rolled into the emergency room on a gurney and eased onto an examination table. She watched in disbelief as workers cut away her clothes, poked and prodded her body, and talked as if she wasn't there. "No response," was the verdict when they pinched her toes, her calves, and her thighs with forceps. She remembers little else about the emergency room. Her next clear thoughts were several hours later. She opened her eyes in a surgical recovery room. Surgeons had inserted pins into the vertebrae of her lower back to stabilize them to reduce the chance of further injury to the spinal cord. She also had a filter placed in her vena cava, a large vein near the heart. This filter, called a *Greenfield Vena Cava Filter,* is a small, six-legged, cone-shaped, wire object made of metal alloy with little hooks on the end of each leg. When a patient is immobile, as in the case of postoperative surgical patients or spinal-injury patients like Minna, a huge risk is pulmonary embolism. Blood clots form in the body and if a blood clot makes its way to the heart, a heart attack is possible as the clot blocks the flow of blood. If the clot makes it to the brain, a stroke is the result. Other organs, such as the lungs, can also be damaged by these clots that form in the lower extremities due to lack of movement. The Greenfield filter is inserted in the vena cava to capture any of these blood clots that might exist before they have a chance to move to a vital organ.

Initially, hospital personnel repeated what the emergency medical technicians (EMTs) had told Minna at the crash scene—that her husband and children were OK, but in the following days she learned the details of her accident and the truth about her husband. When she had swerved to miss the truck, the SUV lurched forward and began to roll. After nine full revolutions it finally came to rest upside down, her limp body hanging upside down suspended by her seat belt. Her husband was killed instantly when he was ejected through the sunroof of the vehicle, his body coming to rest on the median. Both of her children had also been ejected from the vehicle. Initially it was thought that nine-year-old Megan was critically injured, but in reality her only serious injury was a broken leg. Fortunately, six-year-old Kristopher escaped with only scratches and bruises. Her own injuries were devastating. She had a spinal injury low in her back at a point called a T-12/L-1. The 24 vertebrae of the spine are divided into three sections. Cervical vertebrae, annotated as "C" vertebrae, make up the first 7 from the base of the skull moving downward along the neck. Then the thoracic vertebrae, annotated as "T" vertebrae, include the next 12 vertebrae from the lower neck to below the rib cage. Finally, the lumbar vertebrae, annotated as "L" vertebrae, make up the final 5 vertebrae of the spinal column from just below the rib cage to the sacrum and coccyx (often referred to as the tail bone). Minna's spinal damage was between the 12th thoracic vertebra and the 1st lumbar vertebra—T-12/L-1.

Generally, the higher in the spine an injury occurs, the more functions that are affected and the more life-threatening the injury, especially when injuries are in the cervical vertebrae, because many vital functions, such as respiration, are controlled by nerves in areas higher in the spine. Minna's kidneys, lungs, heart, and other organs were functioning without problems. Fortunately, her spinal damage did not compromise these vital functions, but doctors were confident she would never walk again. Minna was struck with the realization that she was now a single parent; she felt responsible for her husband's death; and she would be confined to a wheelchair for the rest of her life.

Just a few days later, she attended her husband's funeral, the first funeral she had ever attended. Ironically, the funeral was just days before what would have been their 12th anniversary. Wearing a hospital gown and lying on a gurney she was wheeled into the service. It was far too painful for her to sit in a wheelchair at that point. Even on the gurney, she was in intense pain, but she refused to take any pain medication because she feared the medication would dull her senses and she wanted to be fully alert for the funeral. Still in shock from all that was happening to her and her children, she said good-bye to her husband, but she felt like he was with her. As she entered the funeral, she prayed to him for a sign and she believes she got it. That day was the first day since the accident that she was able to consume normal liquid food. She drank sweet tea—her husband's favorite—and she considered that glass of tea a sign that things would be all right. This small glimmer of hope was a first step in her psychological healing.

As her body began to heal, Minna began physical rehabilitation therapy. It is important for spinal patients to begin therapy as soon as their bodies will tolerate it. Therapy begins in small doses and simple goals—5 or 10 minutes at a time with simple movements of the arms and legs by the therapists. These movements keep the blood flowing, reduce muscle atrophy, and reduce the possibility of blood clots. When she was stable enough, Minna was moved to the Shepherd Spinal Center in Atlanta,

Georgia, for more intense rehabilitation therapy. This state-of-the-art facility is one of the world's best for treating patients with spinal cord injury
(SCI). This was the beginning of what she calls her "new normal." Once
she was admitted to Shepherd, therapists helped Minna understand the
nature of SCI. While she was aware of the meaning of paralysis, she knew
almost nothing of the physiology of SCI and its effects. Therapy was physically exhausting, frustrating, and ever present. Many times a day therapists
worked her legs, helped her in and out of her chair, and helped her learn
how to take care of herself. She had to learn personal grooming, dressing, and bathing. She had to learn how to get in and out of her chair by
herself—something called "transferring." Transferring from her chair, to
a bathtub, and back to the chair is a very complicated task. (If you think
this is a simple task, try getting into and out of a bathtub using only your
upper body muscles.) Eventually, her rehabilitation even included learning to drive. Perhaps most embarrassing for many spinal-injury patients,
Minna also had to learn bowel and bladder management. Even though she
still had some muscle control in her abdomen, it was unreliable and she
had to relearn control of her body functions. None of this is what she expected. When she first entered Shepherd Spinal Center, she thought they
were going to teach her how to walk again. Minna told me she thought
she would be "walking out of there to resume her life." When she realized
the truth that she would never walk again, she felt helpless and couldn't
see the point in doing therapy. She wanted to give up and it would have
been easy just to lie down and die, but knowing that her children needed
her and that she could not let them down forced her to continue through
weeks of therapy.

Rehabilitation from a spinal injury is a very long and painful process.
To the average person, pain is simply an inconvenient part of life. Your
pants are too tight so you loosen your belt or you feel a thorn in your leg
as you walk through the woods so you remove it. But for the spinal-injury
patient, pain management is a much more complicated process. According to Roberta Trieschmann, an expert on spinal injury, there are many
types of pain that one who has experienced spinal injury endures. Minna
described feeling a burning pain in her feet and buttocks, areas of her body
that were paralyzed, and yet she couldn't quite identify where the feeling was coming from. This is called "phantom pain." It is poorly localized
and can include pain people experience in amputated limbs or, in Minna's
case, in appendages where sensation is impossible. But even though the

body cannot physically produce pain in an amputated limb or a paralyzed body part, the pain is very real to the patient. Other pain is highly localized "somatic pain." This type of pain is what most of us experience when we hurt a body part. We know exactly where the pain is, whether it is a dull pain, sharp pain, or an ache. We often can hypothesize what to do about this kind of pain to feel better, such as adjust our sitting position or make an adjustment in our clothing. Finally, there is "visceral pain" that includes cramping, "vague and diffuse" pain. You may have experienced this kind of pain at one time or another when you have an ache in a leg, but you couldn't exactly put your finger on the place that hurts. Visceral pain includes the broader aches and pains many of us experience in our backs and legs after a long day of hard work. SCI rehabilitation involves learning to recognize each of these types of pain and learning to develop methods to cope with them. Phantom sensation, for example, is almost universally experienced by amputees. One treatment for an "itching" leg that has been amputated, for example, is to hold a mirror near the leg that still exists. This gives the reflected image that makes it appear the other leg is still there. Then, while looking at the reflection of the leg in the mirror, the patient scratches the existing leg in the approximate location where the itch exists in the phantom limb. Watching oneself scratch the nonexistent leg can sometimes ease a phantom itch. Failure to recognize pain can lead to serious health problems. While we spend much of our lives trying to avoid pain, it is pain, ironically, that helps us. Pain lets us know when something is hot, when we have exerted too much pressure on a body part, or when an area of the body needs attention. Think of trying to twist the top off of a bottled beverage. If you twist too hard and the cap doesn't come off, the pain in your hand lets you know it is time to try another method. Without pain, you might easily twist the cap until you cut your hand. Spinal-injury patients lose some or all of this warning system so they have to be especially diligent in monitoring their body parts in other ways. For example, Minna had to learn to check her skin for depressions—the sign that numbed skin was receiving too little circulation. In normal sensation, we know we need to adjust our position when our legs, buttocks, or other body parts lose circulation—the feeling that the body part has "fallen asleep." We move and circulation is restored. In spinal patients, if circulation is not restored, painful sores develop.

Patients progress at different rates through the process of learning to care for themselves, manage their pain, and cope with their limitations.

Experts in SCI note that there is variation in rehabilitation speed and efficiency depending on personality type, coping style, and even the type of treatment environment one encounters. By her hospital release date on May 30, two-and-a-half months after the accident, her house had been modified to accept her wheelchair. Her most difficult task was learning to accept her "new skin," Minna's description of learning to be comfortable looking in the mirror. Another new chapter in her life had begun. For Minna, it took two years to recover from her injuries and to learn how to adjust to her new life in a chair. She felt like a child because she had to completely relearn everything she had always known how to do, daily tasks that most of us take for granted. Even sitting was difficult and it took weeks to gradually increase the number of minutes she could sit in her wheelchair without pain or dizziness. She had to learn to do every task from a sitting position, including cooking, her favorite pastime. Dressing herself, a job that would have taken two minutes prior to the accident, could take an hour. Different types of clothing as well as different types of fasteners presented different types of problems for her, and it seemed that every day she discovered yet another challenge in movement that she had always taken for granted.

Part of adjusting to life in a wheelchair is learning to have control over one's own body. Doctors, nurses, and physical therapists are constantly touching, prodding, poking, and massaging the patient. For this reason, paraplegics may be extra sensitive to being touched without permission. One should never touch a paraplegic, the paraplegic's chair, or push the chair without first asking permission. The chair is part of the person's body and personal space. Rehabilitation can take months or even years and it involves more than the logistics of movement and pain management. Patients must also learn to cope with their emotional ups and downs of therapy, regret and resentment regarding the injury and the cause of that injury, and also the emotional struggle to find dignity in a wheelchair. Dignity is important because one is dependent upon others for even the most basic functions. Most obvious is bowel and bladder maintenance that can be humiliating to a spinal-injury victim during their first weeks of recovery. Constipation is common. Loss of bladder and bowel control is also common even in patients like Minna who still have some lower abdominal sensation because they have to relearn to control the muscles in their lower abdomens. This challenges one's idea of modesty. Spinal-injury patients must rely on others to help them change catheters, for cleaning after an accident, and for assistance in treating bowel blockage. Minna had to learn to acknowledge her emotions—hate, resentment, and especially guilt, the most difficult response of all for her. Her Korean culture made her emotional healing even more difficult because her culture teaches that one should not express emotions openly, and even to acknowledge one's feelings privately is discouraged.

Minna immigrated to the United States with her parents at age eight. At the time, the only English she knew were her ABCs and a line from the song "Proud Mary." Her third-grade teacher, Mrs. Anderson, made a difference for her. She was patient and kind, sort of a "mother figure," Minna explains. Mrs. Anderson took time with her, and Minna learned quickly about her new home in the United States. She adapted to the culture and learned the language. This ability to adapt quickly is one of the assets that helped her as she adapted to her new life in a wheelchair. After her high school graduation, she entered the University of California at Santa Barbara where she met Tony. Two years of friendship blossomed into two more years of dating before they were married after graduation. Minna's definition of happiness was the Korean tradition of family happiness. Her identity was based on her ability to be a good wife and good mother. For Korean women, their identities are closely tied to their family connections and their ability to raise children and manage a home. Men take the lead in families and it is the wife's responsibility to be obedient, subservient, and to meet the husband's needs. Yet American values had found their way into Minna's life and her early years of marriage had been difficult as she tried to be a good Korean wife while also coping with her own drive to be an individual. Prior to the accident, Minna's marriage had never been better. Their marriage had endured many stressors over the years, including her husband's gambling problem, but for the first time, things seemed to be just as she wanted them. "We got to a point where we knew that, 'OK, he's got my back.' Period," she says. Life was good for the family of four. They were making money with their restaurant business and the expansion to North Carolina meant great possibilities for the future, an exciting thought for a first-generation immigrant from Korea. After the accident, she still felt the need to maintain a facade for her family and friends. She felt pressure to pretend everything was OK and to still appear to be a good mother in control of her home, but in truth things were not OK. She had learned to take care of many of the daily household chores, cook, prepare her children for school, and keep a clean home, but despite the appearance that she seemed to be holding it together, in reality she was in deep depression. Her identity had been shattered. She was no longer a wife. The husband she loved was gone and she felt responsible, and even though she was learning to care for her family from a chair, the permanence of paralysis was devastating. Never before in her life had she been totally alone and on her own as she was now. Her life required redefinition. Prior to the accident she had to be the "good Asian wife" taking kids to soccer and school. That was gone now. Depression consumed her. She couldn't wait for her children to leave for school. As soon as they were gone, she would go to bed, stare at the ceiling, and cry. She remained there until just before her children came home. She would then "paint on a smile" and start the charade again. This continued for more than a year.

Her Korean heritage and expectations that go along with her culture created other difficulties in her recovery. Her parents tried to help where they could. At one point they even moved in with her, but after only a month, personality conflicts made it clear that the situation wasn't working. As much as her parents loved her, to this day they still have difficulty accepting her as she is. In the Korean community, a disabled person is seen as "not completely whole"—someone to be pitied. At one point, Minna's mother even told her that it was "too bad she hadn't died" because it would have been easier to handle. These words sound harsh to American ears and they certainly were painful to Minna, but this loving mother was simply expressing the depth of her pain and the truth that in the Korean community she would have been looked upon more favorably in death than in a wheelchair.

Days turned into weeks and weeks into months. Even though she had adapted to the many changes necessary for a chair-bound woman, emotionally she made no progress. One day as she lay in bed staring at the ceiling knowing what she was going to see—the ceiling and nothing else—she realized something had to change.

"I realized that the bills had to be paid," she said. "I had to get off my ass and do something." She felt like she had hit rock bottom and was "dead already."

"I had no way to go except up," she said. "If this is the worst that it gets," she described, "I'm almost free. There were no expectations of me now and I knew I could survive."

Her first step was to get a job, but she had never held a job in her life. She had supported her husband in the restaurant business, but she had never taken the lead in their business and her job had always been at home with her children. She began to take stock of her assets and liabilities. Part of her rehabilitation therapy had included making bead jewelry. While it might not sound like much of a business, making jewelry was at least a start so she began marketing her work. But selling beads wouldn't pay the bills. She realized she had a gift—her chair. Even thought the chair confined her, in another way it freed her and provided an opportunity. She realized that with her rehabilitation experience she could reach others and help them recover. She called the Shepherd Spinal Center, the very place she had been treated in the months following her accident, and inquired about a job. At first she was told there was nothing available, but she wouldn't accept no for an answer. This perseverance characterizes her life in general and it is this character trait that contributed heavily to her recovery. It is interesting how many of the life-tools we need in a crisis are things we have practiced throughout life without even knowing it. Minna had plenty of practice with perseverance. She endured the transition from Korea to the United States and accommodated quickly to life in the United States. She persevered as she learned the language. Many immigrants live in the United States for years and never learn the language. Minna learned English within months. Minna endured the difficulties of college life and she graduated. She persevered through the rough years of her marriage. Again, many marriages end at the first sign of difficulty, but Minna worked through it. These practice runs prepared her for the long-distance race she had to run as a she persevered through the pain of the loss of her husband and as she learned her new "normal" as a paraplegic.

After six weeks of telephone calls, a part-time job as Peer Support Co-ordinator at Shepherd came available. The position was perfect. She could work 20 hours each week, earning enough money to feed her family. It was in a facility she knew, doing what came naturally to her, and it was already accessible to her wheelchair needs. She could work flexible hours, allowing her to be home when her children came home from school and maintain her job as a mother. But the best part about this job was that it confirmed in Minna that she had a place in life. Her life didn't end on that highway median in South Carolina. She now had a new purpose—a purpose she attacks with passion. Her redefinition was underway.

"What I realized is that I had to scale down my life. I couldn't have the house I had before, or the things that used to be important to me, but that's OK."

TURNING POINT

Her house is smaller and her life is simpler, but she has learned to adjust. I saw sincerity in her eyes as she explained to me more about her transition in thinking. "This wasn't the picture I always had for myself. I had to totally readjust my thinking."

This process is called "reframing" and is an essential part of recovery. We all have a mental picture of what we are and what we think we should be. When life's circumstances make it impossible for us to be what we thought we could be, we either quit or reframe our lives and adjust. Reframing allows one to see the glass as half full rather than half empty. Every experience is open to interpretation. Even the most tragic circumstances could have positive outcomes. Over the years I've had many patients who initially saw a tragedy in life from only one perspective—a devastating "bad" experience. However, they often later say, "It was the hardest, but the best thing that ever happened to me." For example, one patient of mine explained that her husband left unannounced and she and her children had no notice, no money, and no resources. I saw her for the first time at the beginning of the crisis. She was alone, broke; she had three children to feed; and she had no marketable job skills. She was on the verge of suicide and it was only her love and concern for her children that kept her from taking her own life. Five years later I saw her in a grocery store. She had gone to college, become a teacher, and remarried. She told me her life had never been better. She was happier with herself than she had ever been; the man she married treated her better than her first husband ever had; and he loved her children and supported her career. "If my first husband hadn't left me, I would still be unhappy, my girls would have a crummy father, and I would still feel like dirt. I'm glad it happened." Their separation and divorce hadn't changed. It was the same event. What changed was her perspective on the event. She reframed it. Unfortunately for the therapist, it is very hard to help people see their experiences in a new frame while they are in the midst of their crises. Some people do this more easily than others, but for all of us, the initial emotional response to a tragedy makes it difficult to see beyond the moment even when our brains know that something better might lie in the future. Our feelings overpower what our minds try to tell us. *Affect always trumps logic.*

Reframing has helped Minna see that even though she is in a chair, she still is a "whole person" and her life can be just as full and exciting as it ever was. As Minna says, "One is not the sum of defective parts. Ninety-five percent of what I do is the same as everyone else." She shops, cleans, takes care of her children, and she continues to love cooking. Several months into her new life at home, Minna reached a turning point in her recovery when she realized she could still "flip food"—a skill she demonstrated for me. Flipping involves turning food in a skillet without a spatula. Knowing she could still maneuver in a kitchen helped her to realize that she would be OK—that she could have a new normal.

Spinal injury involves loss—loss of mobility, loss of dreams, and loss of identity. In order to cope with loss, patients have to address two major questions—"Who is in control?" and "Who is responsible for fixing it?" Each of these questions can be addressed from an internal or external direction. These two questions and the two ways in which they can be answered can be demonstrated in a two-by-two matrix (see table 3.1).[1]

The four quadrants identify the four ways in which one perceives locus of control and locus of responsibility for a given situation. When the person sees the responsible party as "someone out there," his locus of responsibility is external. When the person sees himself as responsible, his locus of responsibility is internalized. When one believes someone or something "out there" is in control of what happens in the person's life, his locus of control is externalized. On the other hand, when one supposes he or she is in control of what happens to him/her, locus of control is internalized. In recovery, locus of responsibility is important because when the patient sees herself as responsible for fixing her problems, she is more likely to take initiative to work toward solutions as opposed to the patient who sees recovery as someone else's responsibility. Locus of control and locus of responsibility are sometimes described as "explanatory style." Explanatory style has a significant impact on how one copes with difficulties. For the spinal-injury patient, believing one is in control of the situation and also

Table 3.1 Locus of Control / Locus of Responsibility

I am in control of myself and I am responsible to fix it. (IC/IR)	Someone/something else is in control and I am responsible to fix it. (EC/IR)
I am in control of myself and someone else is responsible to fix it. (IC/ER)	Someone/something else is in control and someone else is responsible to fix it. (EC/ER)

responsible for fixing it (IC/IR) leads to motivation to move forward. An explanatory style that supposes others are responsible (blaming), and that others are in control and responsible to fix it (EC/ER) leads one to wait on others to fix something that can only be fixed through one's own efforts. Therefore, healing is much more difficult for some with the EC/ER explanatory style.

One of Minna's many strengths is her IC/IR explanatory style. She knows that it was she, in fact, who was at the wheel of the vehicle. God is not to blame. The truck driver is not to blame. Life deals difficult circumstances and Minna accepts it at that. One turning point for her came when she realized no one could help her recover if she didn't take control herself. The obvious therapeutic question is, can one change his or her explanatory style? The short answer is emphatically yes. While evidence suggests that a negative explanatory style tends to persist throughout life, change is possible. In his book *Learned Optimism: How to Change Your Mind and Your Life,* Martin Seligman outlines the powerful effects of learning an optimistic attitude. Learning to change one's approach to life from negativity and externalization to positivity and internalization reduces symptoms of depression and enhances performance, careers, interpersonal relationships, and even, according to Seligman, a person's health.

Another part of recovery is processing the many emotions and thoughts that come along with a spinal injury. Some researchers advocate stage theories of recovery. Theorist Elisabeth Kübler-Ross proposed that the process of resolving grief is predictable. According to Kübler-Ross, people suffering from grief experience five stages as they cope with loss. These stages are denial, anger, bargaining, depression, and acceptance. Grieving individuals don't always go through these stages in this order, but these five stages are not uncommon. Spinal-injury victims experience denial. A common response to spinal injury early in recovery is the patient's belief that she will "walk again no matter what the doctors say." It is important not to discourage individuals from trying because it is internal locus of responsibility to get better that helps one endure the hours of painful and difficult therapy. However, continually reaching for a dream that cannot be inevitably sets the patient up for discouragement. When the patient realizes that she can no longer deny the obvious, she then becomes angry. "Why me?" is the most common response. Angry patients may not only fail to participate in their own recovery, but they may actually rebel against their physicians and therapists. Eventually, anger gives way to bargaining.

The patient may bargain with "God." "If you let me walk again, God, I promise to . . ." While miracles may be possible, this bargaining process usually doesn't result in healing and one is left without options. This leads to hopelessness, which then creates depression. With depression comes anxiety, fatigue, withdrawal, and listlessness.

While depression is very common, research appears to indicate that not all SCI patients experience depression. There are two conditions where patients do not experience depression—either denial [an unhealthy coping mechanism] or true acceptance of one's situation [more common in internal locus of control individuals than those with external locus of control]. Minna was not one of the lucky ones who experienced no depression. While Minna was able to conceal her feelings from her family and friends, she was drowning in despair. Her culture dictated that she put the best public face on any event no matter how she felt inside. Yet each day as her children left the house for school she found herself lying in her bed, staring at the ceiling, and crying much of the day away. While depression isn't ubiquitous, it is very common. However, it isn't endless. Most studies of spinal-injury patients indicate that when depression exists, it tends to abate by around 30 days. But this may be an oversimplified view of depression. Just as Kübler-Ross theorized in the grieving process, it is likely that spinal-injury victims cycle in and out of the various stages of adjustment that accompany trauma. Minna's depression was long-lasting—nearly a year. The turning point for Minna came one day as she lay staring up at the never-changing ceiling paint. She decided her life had to be more than that. As she transitioned from a stage of despair and inaction to one of action, Minna was ready to take control of her life and make the best of what she had left of it. Her determination, along with a strong sense of purpose, motivated her to get out of bed and begin her new life.

Finally, when depression has run its course, one begins to accept the limitations as well as opportunities that the loss has provided. By this stage, patients see their limitations in a realistic light, but still see the value of hard work, coping with their pain, and enduring therapy. Not only do they begin to cope better with their circumstances, but they are able to help family and friends cope as well. Kübler-Ross developed her five-stage theory to address grieving during the dying process, but the theory is applicable to almost any kind of significant loss. Not every patient goes through these stages in exactly this order and it is possible that after achieving a level of acceptance, one may cycle back through previous stages, but as a general theory, these stages provide a predictable and useful guide for understanding an individual who has suffered a significant loss.[2]

Other theorists have developed similar adjustment theories specifically for spinal-injury victims. These theories all include similar stages to Kübler-Ross's theory. For example, Katz describes the stages of recovering from trauma as recognition, acceptance, need for understanding, and action. Yet other researchers reject the notion of adjustment-stage theories as myth. They suggest that each patient is different and every situation is so different that it is impractical to attempt to apply an overly simplistic theory to adjustment. Even so, these theorists acknowledge that patients progress at different rates through the process of learning to care for themselves, manage their pain, and cope with their limitations. Perhaps most encompassing is the idea that there is rehabilitation variation depending on personality type, coping style, and even the type of treatment environment one encounters. I agree that we should never force a theory to fit the circumstances, but I find Kübler-Ross's theory very helpful. This theory is not a road map that identifies every turn to the smallest detail, but it can operate more like a compass that can point me in the right direction when I am trying to understand a patient's symptoms and behavior. It can also be helpful in predicting what I might expect in a patient during the recovery process.

It is not uncommon to think that we might rather die than go through life as a paraplegic. We seldom appreciate how easy our life is and how quickly we can do things because of our ability to move until that mobility is limited. Spinal-injury victims often, at least initially, focus on limitations—about what they *cannot* do. This only leads to frustrations. Somewhere during their recovery they must shift their thinking to what they *can* do rather than what they *cannot* do. A major transition in Minna's recovery began when she came to this realization. Her body had healed a great deal, but her thinking remained broken until she realized all that was possible even from her chair. In the years since her accident she has learned how to function quite well. She can care for herself and her children. She can drive, cook, and she is even fortunate enough to be able to have sexual relations with her new husband. In order to achieve this healing, Minna had to redefine who she was. No longer was she defined by her race, gender, marital status, motherhood, or even as a paraplegic. Until the day she decided to get out of bed and move on with life, her life was defined by someone else—her husband, parents, children, and culture.

As a part of her adjustment, Minna had to determine for herself what she was and what she wanted to be. She decided she would always be a mother and her limited mobility wouldn't change that. She accepted her life as a paraplegic, but she began to understand she was still Minna. The characteristics and personality that made her Minna, mother, and daughter were still there even though she looked different. Most importantly, she decided that she, and only she, was in control of what she became. Husband, parent, culture, or children would no longer be in control of who she was and how she saw herself. She seized the power to control her own life that was always there, but for some reason she had never been able to see it. Getting out of bed and looking for a job was the first step in taking control of her life.

There are several other factors that aided Minna's recovery. Abreaction, as discussed in chapter 2, is common with many forms of trauma and it is an attempt to gain control over the trauma. Minna may have been demonstrating abreaction by applying to work at Shepherd Spinal Center. By moving from patient to teacher/counselor, Minna was forced to relive her trauma each day. She had to see patients in various stages of recovery, undoubtedly remembering her own recovery as she watched each patient. Working at Shepherd also helped her gain control over the disability that otherwise controlled her. Working at Shepherd was invaluable in her recovery.

A social support system is vital to trauma recovery. A social support system provides impetus to make progress. While Minna doesn't consider herself close to her father, she has always had a close relationship with her mother. Her children were also a vital part of her social network as she learned to cope with her new life. Social support can also provide the encouragement and focus that help one move through the stages of recovery. A counselor was a major component of Minna's social network and recovery who provided these assets. During her rehabilitation at Shepherd, Minna had an individual counselor who was experienced with working with SCI patients. The counselor helped her to set short-term and long-term goals, but for Minna, it was the short-term goals that were most helpful. She wanted to walk again, a common dream of paraplegics, but that was a dream that would not be realized. Her counselor helped her establish realistic, attainable goals.

"I had goals for the week and after two years, I realized I had made great progress, but they were small attainable goals," she said.

Minna's counselor knew what she was doing. Reaching goals is impera-tive to avoid learned helplessness. If Minna's only goal was to walk again, she would have continually been disappointed. The research is clear that when one is continually frustrated by failing to reach a goal, she eventually decides that nothing she does will make any difference. She learns that she is helpless so she quits trying. In a classic experiment, Seligman and Maier subjected dogs to mild shocks in three different conditions. In two condi-tions, the dogs had some control over the shock. They could make it stop by pushing a lever. The dogs in the third group, however, were harnessed to the dogs in the second group and were totally at the mercy of the dogs to which they were harnessed. In other words, the dogs in the first two groups had control over their environments and their efforts to stop the shock re-sulted in relief from their discomfort. However, the dogs in the third group learned that there was nothing that they could do to stop their pain so they eventually quit trying. When all of these dogs were put into different con-ditions where they each had total control, the dogs who had learned to be helpless wouldn't even try to find a way to escape their pain even though, in this condition, their efforts would have helped. They learned to be help-less. Minna's counselor helped her avoid learned helplessness by providing small, short-term goals in which she could succeed. Through these small successes, Minna saw purpose in her endurance and efforts.

Virtue also played a significant role in Minna's healing. I saw clearer virtuous characteristics in Minna than in any other survivor I interviewed for this book. Other than the fact that she still finds it difficult to forgive herself for the accident, Minna is very forgiving of others. She quickly looks beyond thoughtless comments, stares, and awkwardness that are daily routines for paraplegics. Her forgiving attitude has allowed her to overcome the strained relationship with the Korean community and her parents. She is exceptionally grateful for what she has and she is quick to remind others to be thankful for the many gifts they have in life. She knows how easily we can take things for granted and how quickly they can be taken away.

"On my good days I say God's been good to me in the sense that he's given me two lives so I can experience life more fully—one as a walking person and one in a chair. And both can be beautiful and both are worthy of living and both to be honored."

Her optimism and future orientation is inspiring. Since the day she de-cided to get out of bed and get a job, Minna has moved beyond feeling sorry for herself and she has taken control of her life. Instead of despair over what she has lost, her life is full of hope. "I see hope in me!" she excitedly told me the first time I met her. Virtue is not always synonymous with religion, but it often goes together. Minna describes herself as spiritual, although not necessarily religious. She attends an Episcopalian church and her Christian faith helps her through her darker hours.

CONTINUED EFFECTS

The most obvious continued effects of Minna's accident are her physical limitations and the absence of her husband. Without question, Minna struggles most with guilt, anger, and frustration—guilt for being the driver that ended her husband's life and took her children's father—anger and frustration at how the accident has made her life harder. She deeply regrets that her children have grown up without a father.

"The guilt is still raw," she said in our last interview.

"We weren't finished," she says of her husband.

Things were improving in their marriage and she rues the loss of the future they could have had together. Minna is a very forgiving person but understandably has a difficult time forgiving herself. In my final interview with her, tears quickly pooled in the corners of her eyes when I asked how she was doing with this part of her recovery. She is an amazingly strong woman, yet in some ways exceedingly vulnerable.

Minna has found new love, a counselor at the Shepherd Center named Wayne. She dated Wayne for six years before marrying him in June 2007. Her new husband is nothing like her traditional Korean family might have expected. He is Caucasian, a Texan, and very patient with her. Her relationship with Wayne is good and she is as "happy as ever." He knows her intimately, "warts and all." With this new marriage, she says that she is completely an open book—something that she was just learning with Tony before his death. She remarked that the difference with this marriage and her former marriage is that this time it was something she chose for herself rather than something she believes she needed to complete her existence. She has found peace with herself. When asked who has her back now, she answers, "Me. And it's not as scary as I live it, but it is scary."

In some ways she still struggles with her former self. Prior to her new relationship with Wayne, the desire to fit the archetypal model of a Korean woman led her on occasion to feel incomplete without a husband, but most of the time she is comfortable in her own skin. When I asked her what was most frustrating for her now, she didn't hesitate for a moment. "Access," she said. Being able to go where everyone else goes without having always to sit in the back of the bus or on the front row of the movie theater. She greatly desires a "universal design of things" that accommodate people with spinal injury. Even going on vacation is a challenge because she has to find out about accessibility before making plans. She named a favorite location, Napa Valley in California, because in "wine country, I don't even have to call ahead. I know they can accommodate me and that is liberating."

There is a fine line between denial and acceptance. At some level, I'm sure Freud would argue that Minna is in denial. "Do you hate your chair?" he might ask. I am confident she would answer in the negative, but deep down I can't believe she doesn't. She admitted to me, "If I could take a pill and it would cause me to forget everything I've learned since my accident, but I could walk again, I'd take it because I wasn't a bad person before." However, the level at which she may be denying her resentment for her condition is minimal enough that it doesn't prevent her from functioning. In fact, it would be unhealthy for her to start each day with the acknowledgment that she "hates her chair." That would lead to resentment and a negative attitude. Instead, she starts each day, not worrying about what she wishes, but rather accepting what she cannot change—what *is*. If you can't change it, make friends with it.

When my clients have some monster in their lives that torments them, it is often easiest for them to pretend it isn't there, to deny its existence. For example, survivors of sexual abuse in childhood have tried to convince me that the abuse doesn't affect them. Of course it does, but to admit that it does means one has to embrace a frightening and unpleasant part of one's past. I suggest to my clients to consider the event like living next to a house with a mean dog. If you pretend the dog isn't there, you may end up getting bitten because you wander too close. By acknowledging the existence of the dog, you can learn to deal with it and maybe even make friends with it. At the very least, you will learn how close you can get to the dog before you are in danger and that knowledge allows you to control the danger that exists. Would these clients prefer that the "mean dog" didn't exist? Of course they would, but the fact is they cannot control the existence of the dog so they must learn to live with it. Wishing gains them nothing. Embracing what we can control and becoming the masters of our lives is the beginning of the road to overcoming the demons that torment us.

CONCLUDING REMARKS

Minna continues to make beaded jewelry, which she sells in 550 boutiques nationwide, in Canada, and in the Virgin Islands. Beading is now more of a pastime for her than therapy, but she still enjoys the relaxing activity that allows her to be productive, earn extra income, and think about life.[3]

Over time Minna gained some motion and sensation in her legs. She has feelings of pressure on the underneath side of her legs and sensation on the tops. She feels pressure in her buttocks, but no sensation. The control she has gained in the muscles of the tops of her legs allow some independent movement of her legs. During my final interview, she was able to lift her legs to a footstool on her own. Even with this progress, though, she will never walk again.

Minna's children are teenagers and are doing well. Her son dotes on her and remains her protector. Minna has adjusted her obsessive attitude about housekeeping. "I used to be fanatical about cleaning the house," she said, "but, nowadays it's like are your socks clean? Are your underwear clean? If so, have a great day and I love you." In her recovery, she allowed herself to let go of the pressure to "measure up" that used to control her.

Minna doesn't wait for people to ask her about her disabilities. She is an open book and she comes right out with what she knows may be an awkward thing on a person's mind. For example, during one of our interviews, she came right out and said, "I know you won't ask about this, so I'll tell you." She proceeded to tell me about sexual intercourse as a paraplegic and the minimal sensation she has in her pelvic region. She discussed embarrassing sexual situations that have arisen because of her paralysis and how she deals with it.

Despite her dependence on others for some tasks, Minna sees herself as independent. We all have limitations, Minna recognizes, and she notes that "just because you have help doesn't mean you aren't independent." Independence is defined by the person. As I thought about this comment, I realized that even though I am not in a wheelchair, I am heavily dependent on others for a variety of things, yet I see myself as independent. This realization may have been one of the most significant issues in her recovery. Even though she needs others, she acknowledges that it is good to be OK on her own. When I interviewed her the first time, Minna was unmarried and she had a scary future ahead. Marriage is important in the Korean community, and she wrestled with her prior notion that "completeness" meant "husband." She has come a long way. The date of our last interview came one week after her daughter, now 18, was crowned homecoming queen. Minna has moved on and healing, although not complete, is certainly well on its way. Minna minces no words. She still has bad days and she still finds some of the everyday chores of life very frustrating. Every day she is faced with the difficulty of getting in and out of a vehicle, the simple task of pushing a grocery cart while also maneuvering her wheelchair, and many other tasks that a walking person does without thinking. Simple tasks that took Minna only seconds to do as a walking person now take minutes. Yet she doesn't see herself as damaged—only different than she was. Researcher Mark Katz notes that healthy recovery is evident when "adult survivors [learn] to see themselves as strong and courageous, and not as damaged." This describes Minna to a tee. Minna is an inspiring woman. When I first met her, I was hoping that I might bring encouragement to her through my interviews and our discussions of surviving trauma. In the end, it was Minna who brought encouragement to me and she became my teacher.

NOTES

1. This model has been used by a number of theorists in a number of applications. For example, see Sue, D. W., and Sue, D. (2008).

2. Elisabeth Kübler-Ross died in August 2004 after a series of health problems including several strokes in the 1990s. It was reported that she recanted her theory at one point, but those reports were false. Kübler-Ross's son told me that she was misquoted frequently and never said anything like that to him. He also stated that "approximately 20–35% of what I have read about her is incorrect, misleading, or complete fiction. For the record, this statement [that she recanted her theory] is ridiculous . . . What she might have said was that people are not robots, and do not go through the stages in order."

3. For information on beaded jewelry designs by Minna, see designsbyminna.com.

REFERENCES

Burns, M. O., & Seligman, M.E.P. (1989). Explanatory style across the life span: Evidence for stability over 52 years. *Journal of Personality and Social Psychology, 56,* 471–477.

Byzek, J. (October 2003). Bring it on. *New Mobility.* Retrieved January 8, 2004, from http://www.newmobility.com/articleView.cfm?id=758&srch=minna%20 hong.

Katz, M. (1997). *On playing a poor hand well.* New York: W. W. Norton & Company.

Seligman, M.E.P. (2006). *Learned optimism: How to change your mind and your life.* New York: Vintage Books.

Seligman, M.E.P., & Maier, S. F. (1967). Failure to escape traumatic shock. *Journal of Experimental Psychology, 74,* 1–9.

Sue, D. W., and Sue, D. (2008). *Counseling the culturally diverse: Theory and practice* (5th ed.). New York: John Wiley and Sons, p. 304.

Trieschmann, R. (1988). *Spinal cord injuries: Psychological, social, and vocational rehabilitation* (2nd ed.). Atlanta, GA: Demos Medical Publishing. Retrieved January 5, 2010, from http://books.google.com/books?id=bIWcEXA0uB8 C&pg=PA99&lpg=PA99&dq=trieschmann+poorly+localized+diffuse+vis ceral+pain&source=bl&ots=DHPOZl847B&sig=iruX-Jc1fNhyZrr94-CSf1 OCXPE&hl=en&ei=G1xGS4z4EZG1tgeLwqX6AQ&sa=X&oi=book_result& ct=result&resnum=1&ved=0CAoQ6AEwAA#v=onepage&q=&f=false.

4

DANGEROUS HOUSES: SURVIVING ABUSE

When I look at the world I'm pessimistic, but when
I look at people I am optimistic.

—Carl Rogers

For me, home was more peaceful when Daddy wasn't home.
I got nervous when suppertime approached because I knew he
would be home soon and I didn't know what I might have done
to displease him. It always gave me an unbelievable sense of
peace when he walked passed me and went to his chair in the den
to watch TV. If I was ignored I knew I was safe—at least
for a while.

—Anonymous

Seven-year-old Adam (not his real name) concentrates on the project in front of him. He is coloring on a piece of paper on the floor in my therapy room and I am sitting close beside him. Crayons litter the floor and he thinks carefully as he selects each color. He leans back against me like a baby bird snuggling beneath its mother's wing. This simple behavior says, "I trust you" and it is a very good sign.

As he colors, his head is bent forward exposing his neck. I can easily see the fading remnants of a bruise in the shape of fingers and similar bruises are visible on the exposed skin of his arms. I know there are more bruises in places I can't see. I also know that he would never lean back against his stepfather like he is doing with me. It wouldn't be safe for him. The touches he receives at home are not gentle ones.

Adam's world is very small. He lives in a small trailer and attends a small elementary school. He doesn't play sports, take piano lessons or engage in any other activities outside his home. He has never had a party or been to a sleepover at a friend's house. Chances are good that he never will. His world is small, but it is very crowded. Brothers, sisters, mother, father, stepmother, stepfather, teachers, social workers, counselors, doctors, lawyers and judges—these are the people that inhabit his world.

He looks forward to coming to see me once each week. When his world and mine overlap, it is just the two of us. We play in the sandbox, draw pictures, or play with puppets. I learn a lot about his world from the way he plays, his choices of toys, and the emotion he puts into the activities of our sessions together. Sometimes he tells me stories of yelling and hitting, and other times he tells stories of policemen and social services workers.

In his case, there is little I can do to make his home-life easier. The law has done little to protect him and as well-intentioned as they have been, social agencies have in many ways made his life harder. He is a powerless child at the mercy of a world of adults who like to think they care, but in reality they care more about their own interests and personal agendas than they do about children like Adam. To most of the people in his life Adam is just the troubled kid that makes teaching harder or the disruptive child that parents don't want their kids playing with. They can't understand him and many of them don't try. Even his caseworker is too busy and too emotionally jaded to connect with Adam. I can only help him cope. It breaks my heart, but I've seen it many times.

It always surprises me how the things of the world that otherwise would be important to me seem to fade in their significance when I am working with a child like Adam. In this quiet hour I don't think about politics, world affairs, politics, my religion, or even my family. I concentrate fully on Adam. I am his for one hour. He knows he is safe with me and I will always honor and respect him, his thoughts, and his dreams. He knows I will not betray his secrets or laugh at his fears.

In some ways he is an enigma to me. He giggles as he tells me about something funny his sister did at home. How does he find happiness in this life he lives? Maybe it is just a way to cope or more likely it is that the chaos is his "normal." He doesn't know any other life.

When our time is up he rises to leave. Adam doesn't look back as he exits my office. He copes by living from moment to moment, investing only in that moment—no future and no past.

People often wonder how I work with children like Adam. "How can you sleep at night?" they ask shaking their heads. I can sleep because I know that even if it is only for one hour, I can make a child's world a little more tolerable. I know I am helping create a better world for children like Adam because for one hour they can know they are safe and secure and that I really do care about them. I have no hidden agenda. I can sleep because even though I know I am helping to make his world better, he also teaches me. Working with children like Adam helps me to put life in perspective. It makes me a better father and a better human being. This is my calling and I wouldn't have it any other way.

For more than 20 years I've dedicated my clinical work to children. Hundreds of children have passed through my office doors and over these many years I've seen almost everything. Some of my children have been in treatment for cancer, AIDS, leukemia, and other terminal illnesses. Many of them have since passed away. Some have survived fires and others have survived tornados and hurricanes. Others have been exposed to unimaginable tragedies—parents killed in front of them, war, or torture. But the saddest cases for me are those that involve intentional abuse—either sexual, physical, or both. I've seen children burned, stabbed, cut, poisoned, and beaten nearly to death. Equally sad are those children who have been psychologically tortured by cruel caregivers. Several of my clients have had their lives repeatedly threatened by mothers and fathers. On two separate occasions I've worked with children who have been forced to dig their own graves and then were buried up to their necks in those shallow graves, left overnight to wonder if they would ever see the morning sun. I've learned a lot about these children from watching them heal and I've gained tremendous respect for their courage. I've also learned a great deal from resilient children I never knew, but whom I got to know through their biographies. I've read many of them—Pat Conroy's *The Great Santini,* Dave Pelzer's *A Child Called It,* Jennings Burch's *They Cage the Animals at Night,* and others.

For example, in his moving biographical saga *They Cage the Animals at Night,* Jennings Michael Burch chronicles his experiences as a child lost in the foster-care system. He was given up by his own mother, literally dropped off at a children's home because she was unable to care for him. He was then mistreated in foster care in group homes as well as in private placements. He spent much of his boyhood waiting on his mother's return, a hope that was never realized, and in her absence he found comfort in a stuffed animal. Theory tells us that a boy like Jennings should have grown up hardened, jaded, and delinquent, but just the opposite happened. Not only did he survive an extremely lonely and painful childhood, but he also became a healthy adult and social advocate for children.

The title of this chapter comes from a line in a book by Pat Conroy entitled *My Losing Season*. Conroy notes that because of his father's volatile temper and explosive outbursts he and his brother played together in the "softened laughter of children who grew up in dangerous houses." This statement demonstrates one of the keys to survival—accurately assessing one's surroundings. Conroy's father, a marine colonel named Don Conroy, was abusive to Conroy, his siblings, and his mother. Pat Conroy was never certain when his father might physically lash out at him so he learned to read the context of his father's presence to lessen the likelihood of being targeted. But Colonel Conroy's most damaging interactions with his son didn't involve physical abuse. Conroy says that his father never had a kind word to say, never hugged him, called him a "loser," and regularly told his son how much better he (the Colonel) was than his son. For example, one Christmas Conroy presented his father with a special gift of a pen set. He was so proud of himself and was certain that his father would like it. Instead, his father simply threw it in the trash. Even his successes were diminished by his father as flukes, luck, or worthless. When Conroy won a sportsmanship award while at the Citadel, his father called it the "pussy award" and when Conroy won most valuable player his senior year at the Citadel, his father said, "they must have been a shitty team" to give Pat the award. Conroy suffered some of the same types of physical and psychological humiliation at the hands of his abusive basketball coach during his college years at the Citadel as he did from his father. He lived a life from one tragedy to another—one abuse to another. Like many children who are abused at home, I suspect that the abusive basketball coach seemed normal to him—business as usual. But the abuse and humiliation that defeats so many children seemed only to make Conroy stronger. His successes in life include numerous best-selling books and several classic movies, including *The Great Santini, Lords of Discipline, The Prince of Tides,* and *Beach Music.* Conroy reminds his readers that as abusive as his father was, he still loved him. This theme, as hard as it is to imagine, shows up often in children who are abused and the story of Dave Pelzer is one of the best examples.

SEVEN STRATEGIES FOR SURVIVAL

By far, the most unbelievable story of child abuse that I've ever studied was the case of Dave Pelzer. Most known for his biography *A Child Called It,* Pelzer was the most seriously abused child in the state of California who didn't die from his abuse. Pelzer's early life was unremarkable until his mother started drinking sometime around his seventh year. His mother had the capacity to be a loving and empathetic woman, but for some inexplicable reason she turned on Dave. "Whenever Mother was patient and kind, she was my 'Mommy.' But whenever Mother became cross and snapped at everything, 'Mommy' transformed into 'The Mother'—a cold, evil person capable of unexpected violent attacks." She began to abuse alcohol and the more she drank, the more abusive she became. She began to talk to him cruelly, beat him, humiliate him, and starve him mercilessly. By his eighth birthday she began to dehumanize him by calling him names. He was no longer "David," but instead referred to as "The Boy," "It," and eventually his real name was never spoken in the house. His brothers, in an apparent attempt to gain favor with their mother, turned on him, too. As time went on, the abuse got worse. She stuffed a baby diaper in his face and made him eat the feces, forced him to drink Clorox and ammonia, and forced him to eat his own vomit. As she starved him she forced him to vomit each day to make sure he hadn't eaten. He was not allowed to sleep in the house. Instead, he had a filthy bed in the garage. The Mother created numerous ways to punish him for the slightest infraction. Once, she forced him to lie in a cold bathtub with only his nose exposed for hours on end. She made chlorine gas and forced him to stay in a small bathroom as the gas overcame him. She regularly made him sit on his hands with his head thrust backwards in the "POW" position for hours. Pelzer chronicles being held over a hot stove as his mother tried to make him lay on the lit burners, being forced to stay outside in the winter with no coat, and being forced to mow grass and work for neighbors while his mother kept the money for herself. After one altercation with him, she stabbed him in the abdomen and then refused to take him to the hospital. Each time he suffered injury from these cruel behaviors, including the time he was stabbed, Dave had to care for his own wounds. His father, a fireman, feebly tried to protect him, but eventually quit trying. After being stabbed, Dave stood before him bleeding from the knife wound, but his father told him to get back to work doing the dishes so he wouldn't upset his mother any more.

As if this weren't enough, he was mentally tortured, made to sit on the basement stairs while the family ate, and after starving him for days his mother would put food in front of him and then snatch it away just before he could eat it. She gave him chores to do with a time limit—threatening no food if he didn't finish on time. He was so hungry he stole food from lunch boxes at school and begged for food from neighbors until his mother caught him. Pelzer says he ate only about once every three days. He never stopped hoping for the "old" loving mother and once thought "Mommy" might have come back. One day his mother apologized to him, hugged him, and let him interact with the family and play with his brothers. He thought the torture was over, but later learned that child protective services was on the way and his mother's apology was just a scam. The beatings resumed immediately after the social worker left their home.

I've read everything available about Dave Pelzer searching for clues to his resiliency. In scouring his history, I found seven strategies that Pelzer used to survive and these strategies are common among the many survivors I've interviewed. As you have seen in previous chapters, forgiveness, gratitude, and hope are important. Pelzer also demonstrated a powerful sense of self-reliance, depersonalization, effective coping strategies, and a stubborn will to survive.

Forgiveness

As I described in detail in chapter 2, forgiveness is an important part of healing.

In a public speech, I once heard Dave Pelzer describe his mother in loving terms and he said he didn't hold the abuse he suffered at her hands against her. I couldn't imagine how he could forgive her, especially given the fact that she remained unrepentant even as she faced death. In one of his last face-to-face encounters with his mother, she continued to blame others and make excuses for her behaviors. She was still as vile and hateful toward Dave, by then a successful adult, as she had been in his childhood. He writes:

Breathing heavily, I continued to rage to myself. "Do you realize what I can do to you now, at this very moment? I could wrap my hands around that swollen neck of yours and squeeze the life out of you . . ." A freezing sensation crept up my spine. Oh my God! I warned myself . . . Suddenly the light dawned on me: it was the chain, the chain linking me to my mother . . . I could become the person I most despised. Closing my eyes, I erased the thought of revenge and flushed away any feelings of hatred that I held against Mother. I could not believe the intensity of my rage. Taking a slow, deep breath, I cleared my head before raising my face and staring into my Mother's eyes. For my own peace of mind I told myself, "I'm never gonna be like you!"

Dave's transition to forgiveness came when he realized he could not continue to wallow in his grief and regret. He notes that the more he interacted with other survivors of traumatic childhoods, the more he realized he could not carry his resentment any longer. "I forgave her. I forgave 'The Mother,'" he said. Dave decided to let it go.

Research has also shown that forgiveness provides healing because it creates room for growth in several areas. One theorist explains that it isn't just forgiving that heals, but that forgiveness provides "prosocial changes in one's basic interpersonal motivations following a serious interpersonal offense" and it "promotes relationship harmony." He goes on to say that "forgiving one's transgressor leads to the re-establishment and preservation of supportive, caring relationships between victim and offender." Re-establishment of a relationship with Dave's mother never happened, but his willingness to forgive freed him to have loving relationships with others, especially his own son.

Gratitude

Emmons and Crumpler describe gratitude as feeling "indebted for a debt that can never be repaid." In spite of the seemingly hopeless circumstances in which people find themselves, survivors have an amazing ability to see the silver lining in the dark cloud. It is hard to imagine seeing Pelzer's childhood as a "debt that can never be repaid," but Dave describes himself as "lucky." He notes: "I'm so lucky. My dark past is behind me now. As bad as it was, I knew even back then, in the final analysis, my way of life would be up to me. I made a promise to myself that if I came out of my situation alive, I had to make something of myself." He continues: "I'm so blessed. The challenges of my past have made me immensely strong inside. I adapted quickly, learning how to survive from a bad situation. I learned the secret of internal motivation."

Hope

Goal-directed expectations involve two parts—determination and a belief that "successful plans can be generated to reach goals." This research distinguishes between "little optimism" and "big optimism." Little optimism is the hope for small steps, such as Pelzer's belief he could get through the night, while "big optimism" involves long-range beliefs, such as Pelzer's belief that he would overcome his mother's behavior no matter what she threw at him. Loss of hope is the beginning of the end. For many, their hope comes from a higher power. For others, such as Minna Hong about whom you read in chapter 3, it is their children or family members. For Dave it was his younger brother, Kevin. He loved his brother deeply and the life he saw in that baby, even though his mother was behaving cruelly to Dave at the same time she was showering Kevin with affection. Dave loved Kevin and that love kept him going. Dave also harbored a life-long memory of a trip his family had taken to a quiet waterside retreat—a time before "The Mother" had appeared. This memory gave him a sense of safety when he was forced to retreat inside his head. Well into adulthood he dreamed about owning a log home along that river, warmed by a fireplace and "the smell of redwood trees." "Of all the things she did to me, Mother could never get me when I thought about the river. As a kid, that dream gave me something to live for." When one runs out of dreams, one quickly runs out of energy to survive.

Self-Reliance

In his first book, Pelzer acknowledges that at some point he realized there was no one who could save him. He was on his own. His mother was his perpetrator, his father's feeble efforts to help him were ineffective, his brothers turned on him, and even a visiting social worker had been conned by his mother. "I came to believe if I were to survive, I would have to rely on myself." He lived up to his commitment. For example, nearly starving to death, Pelzer was forever seeking food. On one occasion after finding food in the school cafeteria and eating frozen hot dogs and tater tots he realized he could indeed take care of himself. "After filling my stomach I returned to the classroom, feeling so proud that I had fed myself." "I was on my own and every night I prayed to God that I could be strong." Like Pat Conroy, who learned to maneuver amid the secret hushes of dangerous houses, Pelzer learned to analyze his mother's moods, motives, and predict her behaviors. He writes: "I knew I had to be prepared to deal with anything that Mother might throw at me . . . I knew why Mother had followed every step I took. She wanted to maintain a constant pressure on me, by leaving me unsure of when or where she would strike." This is common among abused children who are survivors. They develop an uncanny ability to read social situations, moods, and to predict outcomes of various behaviors. From that information they time their movements and carefully select their words. "As a shivering child in the garage . . . [I was always] thinking of what I could learn from the situation, and do whatever it took to somehow make things better. I had always formulated the ultimate plans and broken them down to the tiniest detail. This strategy helped me prevail over Mother."

A Stubborn Will to Survive

In each abusive situation, Dave created ways to save himself. He had a powerful will and he was a quick thinker. He writes that he decided to find ways to defeat his mother any way he could. "I knew if I wanted to live, I would have to think ahead. I could no longer cry like a helpless baby. In order to survive I could never give in to her. That day I vowed to myself that I would never, ever again give that bitch the satisfaction of hearing me beg her to stop beating me." He had many opportunities to match wits with her. Once as she tried to break him, teasing him with food then taking it away before he could take a bite, he forced himself to stand firm and he refused to give her the satisfaction of his tears. Even after the incident when she stabbed him and his logic told him that he needed help, he refused to seek help from her. Lying in his bed in the garage, after awaking covered in his own blood and realizing his wound was infected, he said, "I wanted to go upstairs and ask Mother to clean me up. When I was half-standing, I stopped. 'No!' I told myself. 'I don't need that bitch's help.' I knew enough about basic first-aid training to clean a wound, so I felt confident that I could do it alone. I wanted to be in charge of myself. I didn't want to rely on Mother to give her any more control over me than she already had." This is consistent with research. Individuals who overcome their abusive childhood experiences often have a "strong sense of control over future events and the impact they would have on their lives. They felt a sense of control over their destiny. Non-survivors felt just the opposite, as though nothing they did really mattered, so why even try."

Depersonalization

"The Mother" depersonalized Dave by calling him "The Boy" or "It." This is a common behavior in perpetrators. It is easier to be cruel to a thing than a human being, a son, or someone with a name. Dave used the same strategy to cope with his mother's cruelty. He called his mother "The Bitch" and "The Mother." By creating "The Mother" she wasn't "mommy" anymore and he could still love mommy. He even referred to his home as "The House." While depersonalizing is not a healthy coping strategy if it is ubiquitous or haphazard, it can be especially functional when deliberately applied. For example, doctors, nurses, EMT workers, and other emergency personnel utilize this strategy every day to cope with the tragedies they face, but they can return to a more normal mode of functioning when they leave work.

Effective Coping Strategies

Abused children often retreat inside themselves and Pelzer was no exception. A social worker had visited the Pelzer home and his mother, after a few days of preparation, was able to effectively convince the woman that Dave was fine. When the social worker left and the beatings resumed, Dave said, "I settled back into my routine and relied on my solitude to keep me going." Comfort in solitude worked for him. Pelzer also describes himself as having two identities—one that was "It" and the other was what he called his "Clark Kent" personality. "I knew I had an inner strength, a secret identity that no one else realized. I came to believe if Mother shot me, the bullets would bounce off my chest." Pelzer didn't let his loneliness control him and he didn't immerse himself in his alter ego without forethought. Just as he did with depersonalization, he was able to use these skills when they were needed, but also he was able to reemerge when he wanted to. He was able to control his rage, manage his hurt, and "push his feelings down" when he needed to. As a side note, it is interesting that his pet was a box turtle named Chuck—a creature that could easily hide inside a hard outer shell, but one that could come out and move around effectively when it chose.

SECRETS OF RESILIENCY

So what can we conclude about boys like Dave Pelzer, Pat Conroy, and Jennings Michael Burch? Resiliency is a paradox. "In an encounter with hardship, people can develop strengths or resiliencies. However, no one is a super kid—able to escape unscathed. At the same time, few people are completely vulnerable. Most have the capacity to act on their own behalf—to learn and to grow in the fight to prevail." If they were each simply genetically gifted with resilient, survivor spirits, there is little to learn and even less we can do short of genetic engineering. Fortunately, this is not the case. Researchers have noted a number of common characteristics in resilient people and these characteristics can be cultivated. They include strong esteem, independence of thought and action, give-and-take in personal interactions, open-mindedness, flexibility, insight, empathy, communication skills, tolerance for stress, finding meaning in life, and faith in a higher power to which a person can turn. But does this teach us anything? For example, "tolerance for stress" seems self-evident and we know that early experiences predispose children to behave in ways that are not always socially acceptable or functional. In his amazing research, Bruce Perry has found that early exposure to trauma deeply impacts future behavior. These early experiences predispose children to respond to life in more negative ways later in life. "This might also be called the 'snowball effect': when things go right early on, they will tend to continue to go right and even self-correct if there are minor problems. But when they go wrong first, they will continue to go wrong. This effect is literally built into the architecture of our brains and bodies." These traumatized children are more likely to make future choices that almost ensure future trauma rather than choices that would avoid it. As Perry says, "They prefer the certainty of misery to the misery of uncertainty." From this evidence, it would be easy to be discouraged and assume these children are doomed from the start.

Fortunately, however, research demonstrates that resiliency is far more than genetics or the luck of the draw. For example, Katz has been found that "among those who overcame abusive childhood experiences, there was often a strong sense of control over future events and the impact they would have on their lives. They felt a sense of control over their destiny. One's perspective on control over life can be learned and unlearned. The environment in which one recovers following trauma has also been shown to aid in recovery. In his research with the children who survived the Branch Davidian cult, Perry found that "the children who did best after the Davidian apocalypse were not those who experienced the least stress or those who participated most enthusiastically in talking with us at the cottage. They were the ones who were released afterwards into the healthiest and most loving worlds, whether it was with family who still lived in the

Davidian ways or with loved ones who rejected Koresh entirely." There are many other skills that can be learned. As Howard and Johnson note in their 2000 study, "Perhaps the most powerful [reason for research into resiliency] is that it purports to: . . . promote hope rather than despair, empowerment rather than alienation, survival rather than victimization and pro-action rather than reaction." Even though boys like Dave Pelzer appeared to learn them on their own, they can be fostered in therapy, nurturing environments, and through mentoring.

But resiliency isn't as simple as learning a few skills. I spent more time researching for this book than any other book I've written—almost 10 years from my first interview until I submitted the final draft to my publisher. During the interim, numerous friends and colleagues have asked me about the book. When I explain that this book is about resiliency, they inevitably ask the same question. "So, what did you find?" I wish it were easy to answer that question. For one thing, it would make me less boring at a cocktail party when I'm asked the question, but also because it would make intervention simpler. But in order to adequately answer the question I have to explain how I came about my answer. First I searched the research available on resiliency and I looked for common themes among dozens of studies. From this process I was then able to develop a list of characteristics that I should expect to see in people who appeared to be resilient. Next, I took that list of characteristics and applied them to the survivors I studied to see if they were present in these individuals. From this three-step process I have found that resiliency, rather than a single list of factors, is instead a combination of factors that can be divided into three groups—risk factors, resiliency factors, and protective factors. *Risk factors* are those issues outside the person's control that put him or her at risk for trauma. There are a number of these factors including repeated exposure to trauma, severity of trauma, and parental criminality. A child repeatedly exposed to mild trauma is at risk in some ways equally to a child exposed to a single severe trauma. Not only is parental criminality and parenting style important, but the mental health of parents, especially mothers, is crucial. Schroeder and Gordon have discovered that children of depressed mothers adjust more poorly; depressed mothers perceive their children more negatively; and they [depressed mothers] may be "less organized and provide less stimulation" to their children.

Another risk factor is prolonged exposure to television. Television is not completely without value and it has become an easy target for special

Table 4.1 Risk Factors

1. weak, neglectful or abusive parenting
2. low family income
3. large family size
4. parental criminality
5. low IQ
6. poor child-rearing techniques/parenting style
7. long hours in front of a television
8. repeated exposure to trauma
9. severity of trauma
10. mental health of the mother

interest groups since its inception, but it may be that television itself is not the problem. Instead, the amount of time in front of the television is really the issue. Long hours in front of the television may interrupt social interaction, thus weakening social skills and stunting emotional regulation by reducing the time one has to practice emotional regulation. In one study, for example, it was found that "seriousness of crimes for which men and women were convicted (age 30) was highly correlated with time spent watching television at age 8." Children who spend hours in front of the television are less imaginative and, consequently, likely less competent at problem solving. It should be noted that *what* children watch on television is just as important as *how much time* they spend watching television. In summary, the research is fairly clear that children who spend less time in front of a television and more time reading, playing, and interacting with others generally adjust better to life.

Almost anything could be a risk factor and as I addressed in chapter 1, trauma is sometimes defined by the individual experiencing it. One writer notes that "given sufficient exposure to miserable social, familial, and educational environments, all children and youth fail to do well—each child has a tipping point." But the major risk factors present in the research can be seen in table 4.1.

Resiliency factors, also called "personal traits," are those strengths, skills, and characteristics that increase the likelihood that an individual will overcome a trauma. Resiliency factors are personal characteristics that the individual brings to the table that reduce the likelihood of negative responses to trauma. Some of these traits are predispositions—they may be genetic—but others are traits that can be fostered in the right environment. Therapists, for example, can assist individuals dealing with trauma by strengthening resiliency traits. Teaching a child social skills, coping skills, and problem-solving strategies, and helping him look to the future can help build internal resiliency (see table 4.2).

Ideally, children are most stress resistant when they have "compensatory doses of psychological nurturance and sustenance." Such children are more likely to have a "consolidation of confidence, optimism, and ability to seek/respond to help when needed." Research regularly shows the importance of "good intellectual functioning and a close relationship with a caring parental figure" in creating such an environment. Children who are intellectually competent and who have close, caring relationships with mentors are more likely to have a strong sense of self. Likewise, individuals

Table 4.2 Resiliency Factors

1. effective problem-solving skills
2. effective coping skills
3. strong self-image
4. sense of control over life
5. effective social skills
6. internal locus of control
7. feeling that the world is orderly, meaningful, and that one has a place in it
8. confidence
9. abstract thinking
10. intellectual competence
11. personal competence
12. courage—seeing self as courageous rather than damaged
13. virtues—hope, forgiveness, gratitude, humility, perseverance
14. autonomy
15. optimism
16. empathy
17. open-mindedness
18. flexibility
19. impulse control
20. sense of humor
21. ability to delay gratification
22. alert/attentive
23. easy temperament
24. ability to appraise situations
25. altruism—responsibility to help others

with a strong sense of self are less affected by the perspective of others. They can assess situations more accurately and make objective decisions more reasonably. Objectivity, in turn, produces a higher sense of subjective well-being, something that is a critical part of adjustment to life's traumas. Researchers have found that people generally adjust to life changes fairly quickly—often in just a few months—to major life events (i.e., spinal injury, loss of a loved one). "People do not so much totally habituate to their conditions as they adjust expectations to the amount of pleasure they desire and the relative amount of happiness they report." The quicker one adjusts to life changes, the faster a sense of subjective life satisfaction will return.

Another resiliency factor is abstract thinking. This allows one to find solutions for the dilemmas that confront them—a problem-solving strategy. Likewise, the stronger one's coping strategies, the less likely the person is to fall victim to traumatic experiences to begin with. People with poor coping strategies and poor problem-solving strategies often make poor decisions that place them in a position where trauma is more likely. For example, I have had several adult female clients over the years who were rape victims. Several of these women made poor choices that put them in the position to be raped. While they were in no way responsible for their rapes, if they had better problem-solving strategies, it would have been unlikely that they ever would have been in the place where they were raped or with the people who raped them.

Several personal factors have to do with one's personal perceptions about life. For example, a personal sense of control over one's own fate, a personal feeling that one counts in life, a sense of purpose in life, and a sense of personal competence are all important personal factors. Meaning and purpose are important components for all of us, but especially for adolescents. A 2009 study, for example, showed that believing that one "mattered" in life was negatively correlated with depression and anxiety. These factors all pertain to *efficacy*—the belief that one's behaviors will lead to effective solutions. When one believes his or her behaviors will lead to a desired effect, he or she is more likely to continue to endure, search for solutions to problems, and implement those solutions.

People who are independent and autonomous have an internal locus of control and are more likely to see themselves as responsible for taking care of their own problems than one who has an external locus of control. Strong verbal/communication skills are important for several reasons. These skills allow one to communicate effectively when help is needed, to learn from others who have stronger skills, and to develop stronger social relationships. Strong social skills are important for human interaction and foster caring relationships in life, another resiliency factor. Other resiliency factors, seen in table 4.2, are open-mindedness, flexibility, a sense of humor, impulse control, courage, and empathy. In other words, resilient people tend to be fun people to be around and they make friends easily.

Finally, *protective factors* are those factors that can intervene and mitigate the effects of trauma as well as weaknesses in resilience. Schroeder and Gordon note that risk factors result in heightened probability of psychopathology while protective factors are those attributes that temper predictions of psychopathology. For example, those who adapt well have a sense of control, at least one supportive adult involved in their lives, and they take responsibility for helping someone else. Helping, an altruistic behavior, is not an uncommon treatment for depression and trauma. When people reach out to others, several things happen. They have less time to focus on their own problems; they see that the world is continuing to function despite their personal life disruptions; and they are able to put their difficulties in perspective in a way that is difficult when one spends too much time in isolation (see table 4.3).

Caring relationships could include parents, siblings, religious leaders, teachers, or others who are involved in a person's life. These relationships both model and teach good social skills as well as other resiliency factors such as problem solving and coping. High expectations from others help the individual aim high, develop strategies for reaching goals, and also provide the impetus for people to overcome. These people want to please the people who are important to them. As is true with risk factors, one of the most important protective factors is good parenting, but there are gender differences. For boys, a self-confident and educated mother is an important correlated resiliency factor while an educated and self-confident father is a resiliency factor for girls.

Anyone who has gone through a 12-step program of some kind will recognize that belief in a higher power is important. All 12-step programs, including AA, have as one of their tenets the belief that one cannot succeed alone and that the person must look toward a higher power for help and meaning. Belief in a higher power is very important because it gives people the motivation to hang on—even in the face of dismal circumstances.

A child who is predisposed, because of internal strengths, to handle trauma will overcome in spite of the presence or absence of protective

Table 4.3 Protective Factors

1. strong social support system
2. caring relationships
3. high expectations from others
4. faith in higher power
5. altruism—helping others
6. parental involvement
7. education
8. educated, self-confident mother (for boys)
9. educated, self-confident father (for girls)
10. learning to talk about painful experiences
11. learning about others who overcame similar experiences
12. social organizations including schools and neighborhood groups
13. finding success—we learn to be successful by succeeding

factors in the environment. This is the type of child who never had an adequate adult role model but survived anyway, and this may explain why boys like Dave Pelzer survived while others in less severe situations did not. On the other hand, a child who is weak in resiliency factors but is immersed in many protective factors will be more likely to overcome trauma despite deficits in his internal resiliency. The greatest advantages are for individuals who have few risk factors and who also have both resiliency strengths as well as protective factors present in their environment.

So the answer to the question "What did you find?" comes down to these three areas. I need to know what risk factors are present in a person, what resiliency factors he or she brings to the situation, and what protective factors are present. As a therapist, my goal is first and foremost to prevent trauma to begin with. If I can reduce risk factors by parenting-skills training or by creating safer environments for children at school, day care, church, scouting, or other places they frequent, I can reduce the possibility of trauma from the start. For this reason, the majority of the public presentations I do worldwide involve children in one way or another. I speak to schools, parenting groups, church groups, physicians, and pastors. When these caregivers are better informed, educated, and prepared to work with children, the likelihood of a child being victimized by a perpetrator is reduced and the likelihood of a child being a victim of an accident is also reduced because with proper training caregivers are more sensitive to risks in the environment. In assessing children who have been traumatized,

I seek to discover the traits they have as assets, and I try to teach them skills that shore up their resiliency to the trauma they have endured. When possible, I also work to strengthen the protective factors in their environments by providing skills training to parents and social organizations, and I do my best to help the child succeed using the skills he or she has available.

CONCLUDING COMMENTS

Children survive abuse for a variety of reasons. For some, like Dave, they refuse to be beaten. Many children in much less severe situations are defeated, in part, because they quit. They are mentally beaten in a way that Dave could not be beaten. The mind is a powerful tool. As William P. Young says in his novel *The Shack,* "Such a powerful ability, the imagination . . . but without wisdom, imagination is a cruel taskmaster." For those who lack this internal strength, the need for healthy models, mentors, and an involved community is imperative. Bruce Perry neatly summarizes the need for community. "For years mental health professionals taught people that they could be psychologically healthy without social support and that 'unless you love yourself, no one else will love you.'. . . The truth is, you cannot love yourself unless you have been loved and are loved. The capacity to love cannot be built in isolation."

As for Dave Pelzer, his father began spending more and more time away from home and he eventually divorced "The Mother." By age 12, five years after "The Mother" appeared, a schoolteacher noticed that Dave was being abused and contacted authorities. Child protective services finally intervened effectively and "The Mother" was unable to con her way through the interview. Dave was removed from the home and he spent the remaining years of his childhood in foster care. At age 18, he joined the Air Force and spent some of his military years aboard a B-1 bomber. As with Murray Lynn, I'm quite certain that Sigmund Freud would read a lot into Dave's choice of career—fighting the enemy while flying safely above it all in a protective vessel. Interestingly, Dave's brothers all chose military careers living a life of uniforms, structure, and black-and-white orders with no room for interpretation. As for the dream about living in a log home along the river, Dave eventually realized this dream, living for a time in a quiet house on the riverside. But his nightmarish past haunted him well into adulthood and he could find no peace within himself, even at his dream home. "For nearly a week I shut myself completely off from the outside world. My days consisted of waking up at four or five in the morning so I could scour every inch of every object within my surroundings. Every day, after more than nine hours of cleaning the house, I'd remove, wash, and restack the virtually empty refrigerator shelves; then on my hands and knees I'd scrub the baseboards until the paint nearly rubbed off. I thought if everything around me was perfectly immaculate, somehow my life, too, would be in order." This "redoing" as it is called in therapy, was an attempt to please his mother, even though she wasn't there. This behavior is reflective of a common process. Even in adulthood, abused children continue to engage in behaviors to satisfy the abuser. They subconsciously believe that if they are good enough, clean enough, successful enough, or smart enough, the pain will stop. "My guilt consumed me to the point that several times when I dared myself to see a movie, I'd instead return home, as if I could not allow myself to escape my reality for just a few hours. Somehow I thought the pleasure of seeing a movie took something away from Stephen [his son]." By reliving his confinement and abuse, Dave put his world in order—he was most comfortable with what he knew even though it was dysfunctional. Almost all abused children, even the ones who survive with minimal effects, engage in this behavior. We gravitate toward what we know because there is comfort in the familiar, even when the familiar does not serve us well. But no matter how hard he worked he eventually realized he would never be good enough: ". . . no matter how hard I worked, no matter how much effort I applied, I would never be good enough. I couldn't make my marriage work. I threw away a career with the air force so I could chase my tail trying to prove myself as a speaker, just to end up being labeled as a victim of abuse rather than a person with an inspirational message." In these words I hear his mother's voice telling him he is "chasing his tail." The fact is Pelzer is a very successful man in many ways, but he'll never hear that from "The Mother" in his head. Hopefully, he will come to believe what his audience and readers know—that his story is powerful and his books and speeches have been incredible catalysts for healing. He admits that he still uses depersonalization to cope with his stress. "At times I'd still stutter, but somehow I'd find a calmness, tap into the audience, and let things happen. When the subject matter became too serious, I'd fire off comical impersonations, one after another, while maintaining my focus of driving my message home." When he finally realized he could never please his mother, he found a sense of peace.

Is Pelzer really happy with life? Who knows? It is possible he is just deluding himself. Sophocles argued that optimism "prolongs human suffering." Likewise, Myers comments that "seemingly happy people" may "merely be in denial of their actual misery." Happiness is subjective and maybe Sophocles is right, but perhaps Dave really is happy. He functions, finds pleasure in life, and does the business of life as is required of him. Maybe that is enough. Katz notes that "successful individuals who overcame earlier adversities were often able to define themselves more around their multiple talents than around their areas of vulnerability." Dave has definitely found his strengths in his public appearances and his writings.

Following the publication of his first book, *A Boy Called It,* Pelzer launched a very successful career as a writer, comedian, and motivational speaker. As I've described, Dave's childhood still affects him. As a child he had an alter ego—his Clark Kent personality. As an adult, Pelzer relies heavily on changing voices in his comedy routines. Could you guess his best and most frequent impersonation? It is Arnold Schwarzenegger as the Terminator. Maybe this isn't the same as Superman, but in some ways it might be better—Arnold is a real person. So is Dave.

As for Adam, the boy I mentioned in the opening story of this chapter, he is doing fine. He survived his dozens of trips to court, foster homes, and social workers. Middle school was hard for him, as it is for most kids, but he made good grades in middle school and in high school, ran track, and learned to play the trumpet. He never had a party, as I guessed he wouldn't, but that doesn't seem to have mattered. He entered college at a prestigious southern university in the fall of 2008, and his grandfather recently told me he is enjoying college "too much." Good for him. After surviving a childhood like his he deserves some playtime. Maybe that will in some way make up a little of what he missed in childhood while he sat in courtrooms and therapists' offices.

REFERENCES

Conroy. P. (2002). *My losing season.* New York: Doubleday.

Diener, E. (2000). Subjective well-being: The science of happiness and a proposal for a national index. *American Psychologist, 55,* 34–43.

Dixon, A. L., Scheidegger, C., & McWhirter, J. J. (2009). The adolescent mattering experience: Gender variations in perceived mattering, anxiety, and depression. *Journal of Counseling & Development, 87,* 302–310.

Emmons, R. A., & Crumpler, C. A. (2000). Gratitude as a human strength: Appraising the evidence. *Journal of Social & Clinical Psychology, 19,* 55–69.

Gil, E. (1991). *The healing power of play: Working with abused children.* New York: The Guilford Press.

Hosen, R., Solovey-Hosen, D., & Stern, L. (2002). The acquisition of beliefs that promote subjective well-being. *Journal of Instructional Psychology, 29,* 231–244.

Howard, S., & Johnson, B. (2000). What makes the difference? Children and teachers talk about resilient outcomes for children "at risk." *Educational Studies, 26,* 321–337. ERIC Document: ED419214, p. 334 in Dryden, J., Johnson, B., Howard, S., & McGuire, A. (1998). Resiliency: A comparison of construct definitions arising from conversations with 9–12 year old children and their teachers. Proceedings of the American Educational Research Association Meeting, San Diego, April 13–17.

Katz, M. (1997). *On playing a poor hand well.* New York: W.W. Norton & Company.

McCullough, M. E. (2000). Forgiveness as a human strength: Theory, measurement, and links to well-being. *Journal of Social & Clinical Psychology, 19,* 43–55.

McWhirter, J. J., McWhirter, B. T., McWhirter, A. M., & McWhirter, E. H. (1998). *At-risk youth: A comprehensive response.* New York: Brooks/Cole Publishing Company, p. 81.

Moffatt, G. (February 2005). One quiet hour. This article first appeared in my newspaper column in *The Citizen,* Fayette County, GA.

Myers, D. G. (2000). The funds, friends, and faith of happy people. *American Psychologist, 55,* 56–67. p. 57.

Pelzer, D. (1995). *A child called It.* New York: HCI.

Pelzer, D. (2000). *A man named Dave.* New York: Plume.

Perry, B. D., & Szalavitz, M. (2006). *The boy who was raised by a dog.* New York: Basic Books.

Peterson, C. (2000). The future of optimism. *American Psychologist, 55,* 44–55.

Project Resilience. (1999). Resilience as paradox. Retrieved November 24, 2003, from http://www.projectresilience.com/resilience.htm.

Schroeder, C. S., & Gordon, B. N. (2002). *Assessment and treatment of childhood problems: A clinician's guide* (2nd ed.). New York: The Guilford Press.

Suh, E. M. (2002). Culture, identity consistency, and subjective well-being. *Journal of Personality & Social Psychology, 83,* 1378–1391, p. 1378.

Thompson, C. L., & Rudolph, L. B. (1996). *Counseling children* (4th ed.). New York: Brooks/Cole Publishing Company, p. 4.

Young, W. P. (2008). *The shack.* Los Angeles: Windblown Media, p. 141.

5

━━━◆◆◆◆━━━

EIGHT DAYS IN MARCH:
SURVIVING VIOLENT CRIME

A hero is an ordinary individual who finds strength to
persevere and endure in spite of overwhelming obstacles.

—Christopher Reeve

It was Saturday, March 28, 1987. The Crowe family was doing what most families do on weekends. They worked around the house, ran errands, and tried to squeeze in a few hours of recreation at the end of a busy week. Tammy Jeanette Crowe, a 20-year-old scholarship student at Clayton State College, was preparing for registration for the spring quarter that was set to begin in just a few days and she was hoping to enjoy the last few days of her quarter break with her friends. None of them could ever have known the horrifying turn of events that lay ahead of them that day and how their lives would change forever.

In the comfort of her parents' home, Tammy chatted on the phone with her good friend Beth. Beth and her husband had just moved into a new apartment and they had invited Tammy and her boyfriend, Wayne Legg,

---

The information from this chapter, especially the details of Tammy's ordeal, were gleaned from dozens of police reports; transcribed interviews with Tammy by investigators; interviews with David Eatherly; victim impact statements by Tammy, her parents, and Wayne Legg; and my own interviews with Tammy and her husband. Material in quotations is either directly quoted or paraphrased from one or more of these sources.

over for the evening. Wayne and Tammy would be the first guests in Beth's new apartment near Piedmont Park in Atlanta. Tammy's parents, Merle and Larry Crowe, kissed her good-bye as they slipped out of the house to run errands. It was 3 PM. Tammy arranged with Beth that she would stop at Kroger and pick up some strawberries on her way to meet Wayne at his parents' house. The two of them would ride together to Beth's apartment from there. When Tammy finished her conversation, it was 3:25 PM, and she pulled the front door closed behind her, got into her 1974 Ford Mustang, and headed north toward Atlanta.

It had rained the night before, but it was a beautiful sunny day as she stopped at the Kroger parking lot in Riverdale as she had planned and pulled into a parking space. As she turned off the boom box sitting in the floor between the seats (her car radio was broken) she was approached by a Caucasian man wearing blue jeans, a striped shirt, and purple sunglasses with pinkish-purple lenses. David Eatherly, age 27, had a mustache and a pack of Kool cigarettes in his shirt pocket as he leaned in the window of Tammy's Mustang and told her his battery was dead and he needed a

Tammy and her husband Wayne in Fayetteville, Georgia in 2009.

jump. He asked if she would help and she agreed. He then pointed to a red Ford short-bed pickup truck parked about 10 spaces away and two rows over. She pulled her car around in front of his truck, unlatched the hood of her car, and walked to the front of the vehicle. "The latch sticks sometimes," she told him, but he already was lifting the hood of her car. At first he had told her that he had jumper cables, but then said, "Did you say you have cables? I'd rather use yours because mine are broken." So she went to the trunk of her car to retrieve her jumper cables and handed them over to the man. He told her to start her car as he appeared to connect the cables to her battery. She sat in the driver's seat of her car, the door open and one leg out on the pavement, and prepared to start the car for him. In an instant the passenger door opened, and the man slid across the seat and put a knife to Tammy's throat. Immediately she began to pray in her mind that God would protect her.

"If you do anything stupid, I'll slash you open right here!" he ordered. "I need to borrow your car. Some men are after me because I owe them a lot of money and they are trying to kill me."

He forced Tammy into the floorboard on the passenger's side, but the boom box was in the way. He moved it to the seat and Tammy sat compressed into the small space with her head back against the seat. He warned her not to scream and closed the door. She heard the hood of her car close and the man got into the driver's seat, again holding the knife to her throat. It was about 4 PM as he drove out of the Kroger parking lot.

"I'm just going to drive down the road about a mile," Eatherly said as Tammy shuddered with fear. She couldn't see out the windows from her position on the floor, but she felt the vehicle enter the busy highway.

"Are you going to hurt me?" she cried.

"I'm not going to hurt you. Do you have any money?"

"Just 12 or 13 dollars is all I have," she answered.

They drove quietly for the next 10 minutes with only the sounds of Tammy crying and noise from the road until Tammy felt the vehicle leave the roadway. She was shaking uncontrollably when they pulled into the deserted parking lot of the W. E. Pruitt Company, a concrete manufacturing company. Eatherly was a truck driver and worked for Pruitt so he knew the terrain. He pulled to the back of the property near two dump trucks and stopped. He grabbed Tammy's purse, opened it, and held it out in front of her, instructing her to slowly remove her wallet. Tammy complied and handed the wallet over to Eatherly. He took all of her cash—a grand total of $12—and searched every pocket and compartment of the wallet for more.

"If I find any more money and you lied to me, you've had it," he threatened. "Do you have any bank cards?"

She didn't—no bank cards, no credit cards, and no other cash.

"You had better not be lying if you know what is good for you!"

After searching the wallet, he threw the wallet and purse in the backseat and got out of the car, putting her car keys in his pocket. Rounding the back of the car he opened the passenger door and demanded that Tammy get out. He constantly was looking around as if to make sure no one could see them. He had a mesh-like belt wrapped around his hand, the end dangling. At the time, she thought he might be intending to use it to drag her. From her sitting position and with the boom box in the seat, she had trouble getting out of the car. He became impatient and dragged her out by her arm. She looked around and realized her predicament. The business was deserted because it was Saturday and she was at his mercy. He pulled her toward a wooded area abutting the parking lot, dragged her by the arm through the tree line, and they stumbled down a steep embankment. About 30 yards into the woods they came to a stream.

"This'll do," he said and then demanded that she remove her clothing. She refused, begging him not to "do this." She felt exposed already. She was wearing only small running shorts, a white tank top, and tennis shoes. He grabbed at her shirt and threatened her yet again with the knife saying if she didn't obey he would cut her clothes off, so she pulled her blouse over her head. Again, she begged him not to rape her, but instead he pulled at her bra and tried to force it off, but it wouldn't unclasped. Tammy unhooked the bra and tried to cover herself with her hands. Eatherly, cursing at her, pulled her shorts down to her ankles and demanded she remove her shoes. As she did, she saw him unbuckling his belt and unzipping his pants. She was crying uncontrollably and shaking so badly she nearly lost her balance. He forced her to sit on a fallen tree trunk and stood in front of her, his genitals exposed, and demanded she commit fellatio on him. "Suck it," he ordered. Once again she begged him not to do this, but he forced himself in her mouth. Pulling her by the hair, he forced her until she gagged, yet she feared if she threw up he would hurt her so she tried to comply with his demands. He slapped her on the head and complained that she wasn't doing it right.

"Do it right or I'll cut you up," he heartlessly said, but having no sexual experience, Tammy was in a catch-22. She didn't know what to do, but if she didn't perform to his satisfaction, she feared he would kill her. He gave her instructions and she did her best to follow his directions. After about five minutes, he ordered her to bend over the log and he fondled her breasts as he sodomized her until he lost his erection. Fear and disgust were so powerful that Tammy nearly lost consciousness as he penetrated her. Then he forced her to again perform fellatio to erection. Forcing her on her back he raped her vaginally. For the next 30 minutes he repeatedly forced her from one sexual act to another until she lost count. If he heard her quiet cries, he heartlessly slapped her and told her to "stop sniveling."

Apparently tired of standing, he sat back on a fallen log and told Tammy to kneel in front of him and again forced himself into her mouth. As she did, she realized he had stuck the knife in a tree next to him about six feet off the ground. From his sitting position, she realized he couldn't reach it. Another advantage was that his pants were around his ankles. She hoped that this gave her the opportunity she needed to escape. With all the power she could muster, she shoved him and turned to run. Unfortunately, he never completely lost his balance and didn't fall completely off the log. Another misfortune was the boggy stream. It had been raining and the water was cold and deep and the sand was soft. As she tried to run, the soft sand gave way; her leg sank up to her calf; and she fell face first into the sandy soil. Eatherly was on top of her in an instant. Rolling her over, he beat her in the face with his fists calling her "whore" and "slut" and grinding her face in the sand. He was furious. He rolled her back over onto her stomach and grabbed her hair by the handful.

"Crawl like a lizard back to where we were," he screamed as he half-dragged her through the sand back to the fallen tree. Again he forced himself into her mouth, but she protested saying she had sand in her mouth and in her eyes. It made no difference. He forced her anyway. When he had exhausted himself, he stood up and looked at his wet and sandy clothes. He cursed her saying, "I can't believe what you did to my pants! You got my pants all dirty. Now I've gotta run around with dirt all in my pants. You're gonna pay for that!" Again he grabbed her by the hair and pulled her across the creek. "I need to find someplace to hide you," he said aloud to himself as he surveyed the woody area around them. He seemed to take sadistic pleasure in forcing her to walk through briars and thorns.

She did her best to keep up, but he seemed to deliberately pull her through every sticker bush and even forced her so hard through tree branches that they broke. If she stumbled, he called her "clumsy" and demanded that she hurry up. Her face was bleeding from the beating, her legs were numb from abuse and covered with dirt and blood. Finding a clearing on the other side of the creek, he forced her one last time to perform fellatio. When he was done he said, "Turn around on all fours."

She was expecting him to enter her again, but he had other plans. She was horrified when she felt him reach around her from behind and the cold blade of the knife made contact with her neck. In one quick swipe, he pulled the knife across her throat. Fortunately, the blade was dull and did not sever any major vessels, but he pulled the blade across her throat a second time. This attempt on her life was enough to release every ounce of panic within her. She screamed and kicked hysterically and fought him with every ounce of strength she had. She grabbed for the knife and actually managed to gain control of it. For an instant, she saw panic in his eyes as it appeared to her that he thought she might hurt him or get away. Cursing at her and scrambling for the knife, he dove on top of her and bit her hard on her shoulder drawing blood, but she held fast to the knife, unable to swing it in any way that was defensive. He grabbed her hand and bit down hard on her knuckles until she lost her grip. Once again in control of the knife, he went into a frenzy and began stabbing Tammy in the chest as she fought against him with all her might. Seven or eight times, she felt the knife plunge deep into her body glancing off of her ribs. As her mind raced for a solution she realized that if she kept fighting he would keep stabbing so she relaxed. Immediately, he stopped. As he stood beside her bleeding body she whimpered, "Why are you doing this? I've never done anything to you and I have a life to live. I have a boyfriend and I've never had any kids. I go to church, I go to college, and I'm a good student and I have a future. Why!?" With a sinister grin spreading across his face he replied, "Because I'm sick, lady." She stared at him in disbelief. As she lay there dying, she could see blood squirting from the puncture wounds in her chest as she tried to talk and reason with him, promising that if he let her go she wouldn't tell anyone.

"No way! They'll put me in prison," he argued and then attacked her once again with the knife. She felt the piercing pain of the blade and heard the sickening sound of her lungs collapsing and filling with fluid. Then one last time he stabbed her, low in the abdomen near her hip, and he gave the blade a final twist, as if to say good-bye. He withdrew the knife, stood up, and paused. Her energy to fight was gone and he was out of breath. He looked at what he had done. Tammy was a bloody mass mixed with dirt and sand. Eatherly stumbled a few feet away and threw up.

Tammy lay as still as she could. She could hear Eatherly walking around and through her blurred vision she caught a glimpse of him picking up her clothing. Then it was quiet. Fearing he would return, Tammy pretended to be dead, but when she didn't hear anything for several minutes she sat up. Her head was swimming and she was close to unconsciousness. As she tried to stand and walk, she lost her balance and fell. To her horror, she heard him returning. Lying face down, she tried to breathe as shallow as she could, but the knife had punctured her chest and lungs and each breath produced a gurgle and rasping noise. She felt his presence as he walked up behind her and she heard him unzip his pants. She braced for more abuse, but it didn't come. Instead, she realized he was masturbating. He moaned and she heard something hit the ground beside her. He had satisfied himself as he watched her—a common behavior among rapists and serial killers. (Eatherly never ejaculated during the rape except perhaps autoerotically. That evidence was not recovered. Ironically, a rapist can sexually engage with a victim for nearly an hour, as Eatherly did with Tammy, but still never reach climax. The only way to reach climax for him was to look at her torn and bleeding body—a certain symptom that his assault on Tammy was more than just a one-time impulsive act.) She heard him zip up his pants and then in a smooth motion, she felt the mesh belt, the one he had around his hand much of the time he was raping her, slip around her neck and tighten. As she fought for breath, her legs spasmed, and the world began to spin. She felt like she was drowning, struggling to get to the surface for air, but there was no surface. Her vision went black and she lost consciousness.

David James Eatherly had a checkered past. Despite several military decorations, including one decoration for saving a man's life, his life was troubled. His father, a retired Army Sergeant Major, described a tense relationship between David and his brother in which they didn't get along at all, a relationship that was sometimes physical. According to his father, David's brother despised him. Eatherly had been addicted to drugs since age 12 and drug troubles were the common theme in his adult life. Eatherly had several run-ins with the law, his first arrest on drug charges in Texas as early as 1977. Drugs had destroyed his marriage to Angela Anderson, whom he married in 1979 and with whom he had a daughter in 1981. He earned a GED with marginal scores before entering the Army in 1979, but his marriage was rocky and drugs were ever-present. He was refused reenlistment in December 1984 because of a positive drug test for marijuana. His discharge was listed as "under dishonorable conditions—misconduct." His parents were devastated at how drugs were eating away at him.

After his marriage with Anderson ended, David began seeing a woman named Mona Ragland and the two moved in together in 1985. He worked as a truck driver in Kentucky, but drugs continued to control his life. Violence was a part of his history. His arrest record in Kentucky shows that he was arrested for (but acquitted of) assault in North Carolina in 1984 and that he had at least one arrest for assault in Kentucky in 1986. His military record includes a history of being "unable to control his temper and impulses" as well as a history of domestic violence. Following an altercation while still married to Anderson in 1984, Eatherly attempted suicide by cutting his wrist.

Ragland and Eatherly moved to Georgia, in part in an attempt to escape the drug usage that was consuming more and more of David's life. Eatherly held several jobs as a truck driver and he had worked as a driver for W. E. Pruitt, the owner of the property where he assaulted Tammy Crowe, for a year prior to the attack. In January 1987, just a few months before the attack, Eatherly was arrested in Georgia on drug charges. Drugs destroyed his relationship with Ragland just as it had with Anderson. On March 28, she had had enough. They argued that morning over his drug use. "Do you want me to leave?" he asked her. She didn't answer, but her silence gave him an answer. He left the house, found a drug dealer, and purchased some cocaine. After injecting it, an atypical but potent way to use cocaine, he drove around searching for more drugs. He purchased several more hits of cocaine and drove to the Kroger parking lot in Riverdale to use the drugs. As he consumed them, he realized he was broke so he decided to rob someone. Sitting in his 1985 silver Pontiac Fiero, he waited until he saw a Mustang pull into a parking space "kind of away from the store and away from the other cars" in the parking lot. He had a victim in his sights.

When Tammy regained consciousness, she found herself lying in a sticky pool of blood and dirt. Flies were swarming her wounds and she felt like a dead opossum on the side of the road, but she also realized she was still alive. She lay there quietly for what seemed like 30 minutes to her, afraid he would return and brutalize her further, but with each breath, she heard the sucking sound from her chest wounds and saw blood spurting from her torso. She knew she had to take her chances. She sat up and was stunned at the amount of blood that was gushing from her body. She recalled the little first aid training she had recently had in a health class and she assessed her injuries. Knowing her chest wounds were severe, she did the only thing she could think of to stem the bleeding. She packed them with sand hoping it might slow the bleeding enough to coagulate the blood. She stood, barely conscious, and realized she didn't know where she was. She wanted to walk away from the parking area, away from where the man might be waiting, but she knew she had to get help soon and returning the way she came was her best bet. Naked and shivering, she was having trouble even standing upright. Racked with pain and struggling to breathe, she was almost certain she wouldn't live. At that point she decided a goal might simply be to make sure her body was somewhere where it would be found quickly so her parents would know what had happened to her. She hoped that she might even be able to tell someone what happened before she died, giving a description of the perpetrator so that he might be caught. She waded through the cold water in the sandy stream, once again sinking knee-deep into the sand and falling into the frigid water. She sat there for a moment watching her lifeblood pour out of her, amazed she hadn't yet bled to death.

As she finally reached the other side of the creek, she approached the almost 45-degree incline to the parking lot and it seemed an impossible barrier, but she refused to quit. She sat on a log at the base of the hill and wondered aloud, "How long does it take to die?" Pushing with her feet and pulling herself with branches up the hill, she finally reached the pavement and paused to rest. She saw that her car was gone and instinctively looked toward the road about 100 yards away and began stumbling in that direction. As she moved toward the road she saw a boy on a bicycle and tried to yell at him, but her voice was hoarse from screaming. As she tried to yell, an 18-wheeler drove by on the road and drowned her out. The biker never saw her. Undeterred, she continued toward the road and then she saw two men on motorcycles about to ride down the hill off of the road and into the pit. She began waving her arms. Robert Day, a foreman at the W. E. Pruitt Company and Timothy Irish, ironically a high school friend of Tammy's who had dated her sister, were out enjoying the day when they saw a nude and bloody woman weakly waving at them. The pair raced to her rescue. Helping her to the ground, Day covered her body with his sweatshirt while

Irish drove off to get help. Within minutes EMTs, police, and rescue personnel were on the scene. Tammy's condition was critical so a Life Flight helicopter was ordered. Her bleeding had slowed. Tammy told them she had tried to slow the bleeding with dirt and sand, but it wasn't helping. An EMT pulled the cellophane from a cigarette wrapper and placed it over the most serious area of bleeding in her chest until more permanent treatment could be rendered. Doctors later told her that the sand she packed in her wounds probably saved her life, but she was still losing blood. It was about 5 PM.

Around that same time, Merle and Larry Crowe were finishing their errands with a stop at Kroger in Riverdale. They looked across the parking lot and noticed a number of police cars had converged in one area of the lot and they wondered to each other what was going on. Driving home, they prepared supper. Around 6 PM the phone rang. It was Wayne Legg looking for Tammy. She was supposed to meet him by 4:30 and hadn't shown up. Merle told him she didn't know where Tammy was and that she would let Tammy know he had called if she called the house. Fifteen minutes later the phone rang again. Expecting to hear Wayne's voice again saying that Tammy had arrived, she was stunned to hear a woman on the other end of the line asking to speak to a relative of Tammy Crowe. "I'm her mother," Merle said.

"This is Anita Ray calling from Georgia Baptist Hospital. Your daughter has been brought here by Life Flight helicopter. She has been raped and stabbed. Will you come?"

Merle screamed and dropped the phone, yelling at Larry that they had to go. Confused, Larry picked up the phone and heard the same message. They raced toward the hospital in downtown Atlanta. Fighting downtown traffic, they finally arrived at the hospital 40 minutes later, wondering the entire trip if Tammy would be alive or dead when they arrived. Parking their car illegally at the curb, they raced inside to the emergency room and asked about their daughter. Moments later Ms. Ray, the woman who had called them, came out to meet them and took them into a room adjacent to the ER. Fully expecting to hear that Tammy had died, they were relieved when they learned she was conscious and talking. In fact, it was Tammy who had given ER personnel her home phone number. They were angry that Ms. Ray hadn't told them on the phone that Tammy was at least conscious, but they were grateful she was still alive. Ms. Ray left and they called Wayne's parents and left a message for him about what had happened. About 20 minutes after their arrival, a physician met them and explained Tammy's injuries. She had been stabbed 10 times; the knife had slashed her arms and chest in five places; she had suffered multiple abrasions and cuts; she had been beaten; her lungs were punctured; and she had lost over half the blood in her body—almost four quarts. It was likely she would need surgery. Also, her eyes were damaged because of the beating and because sand had gotten into her eyes and ground into the sclera. She wore contact lenses and those lenses cut her eyes as her attacker beat her. The sand and dirt made things worse as it acted like sandpaper between the cornea and the lens. Despite these many injuries, they were hopeful that she might survive. The doctor told them that they could see Tammy after they had a chance to clean her up. Again they waited. Eventually, a nurse came to get them and led them through the trauma area to Tammy's bedside. What they saw was beyond imagination. Tammy was almost unrecognizable. An oxygen mask covered her nose and mouth and tubes were running in and out of her body several places. Dried blood covered her body and was matted in her hair. It was even stuck beneath her fingernails. Round teeth marks were visible on her shoulder and her hand. Her face was swollen and the whites of her eyes had hemorrhaged so much that all they could see was blood and blue irises. Pure blood was running through the drainage tubes in her side to a receptacle on the floor. Tammy looked up at her parents and through her voice weakened from screaming she was barely able to be heard. "Mamma, did they tell you what that man did to me? I was just trying to help him. He said he broke down. Now nobody will love me because I'm dirty." Her parents were devastated. When Wayne arrived she asked him if he still loved her. He too was heartbroken that she would even ask.

Other family and friends began to arrive as the evening wore on. By 8 PM, Detective T. W. Justice of the Clayton County Police had interviewed Tammy and she was able to give him a great deal of detail about her assault. She had described the events, described her attacker, and identified the weapon as a wooden-handled butcher knife. By 9 PM they were informed that Tammy's abdominal bleeding hadn't subsided so they would need to operate. While Tammy was in surgery, two detectives met with the Crowes and explained what they knew so far. They had recovered Tammy's car and were searching the site of the assault for clues. By 5:30 PM police had already found the site of the attack, followed the trail of blood as well as Tammy's barefoot prints in the dirt, and even made plaster casts of a man's shoe prints, but there was no sign of Tammy's clothing or personal effects. The perpetrator had her name, address, pictures of her family, and her keys. Police were concerned for Tammy's safety so they posted a guard outside her door. (The guard remained throughout her hospital stay, even walking the halls with her.) She was listed in hospital computers under a false name. They were taking no chances. After three more hours of waiting the doctor told them things looked much better and they expected her to recover. The worst was over, but she would spend three days in ICU and five more days recovering in the hospital before she could go home.

After strangling Tammy, Eatherly had gathered up the knife, his belt, and Tammy's clothes and returned to her car. He then drove back to Kroger and parked at the far end of the parking lot. As he walked from Tammy's car to his own, a number of people noticed the dirty and blood-covered man carrying women's clothes crossing the parking lot, but no one called the police. He drove his own car back to Ragland's house, showered, washed the bloody knife and returned it to the kitchen drawer, and put his dirty clothes in the laundry. Apparently, Ms. Ragland unknowingly washed away the evidence on his clothes later on. He put Tammy's clothes in a paper grocery bag and left them in his car. He was out of money, out of drugs, and he knew he was in trouble. He found some drugs in the house to help him sleep, took them, and went to bed. He stayed there for most of the next several days.

Tammy slept very little her first few days in the hospital. Even though she was heavily sedated with morphine for pain and Valium to sleep, she awoke nearly every hour in pain and crying. Tammy's injuries were severe. With her lungs punctured and filling with fluid after the attack, emergency workers had to insert a drainage tube into her side between her ribs. This painful experience often results in breaking of the ribs—ribs that were already damaged from the beating and scored by the penetrating blade of the knife. She was in excruciating pain and her bandages had to be changed twice each day—a procedure that was so painful her mother could not stay in the room during the procedure. After three days in intensive care she was moved into a regular room and her mother was able to clean her up. She still had sand in her hair and blood under her fingernails. Her mother said it took two days of cleaning to get the blood completely out of her hair and from beneath her nails. Tammy lost 10 pounds while she was in the hospital. She was exhausted with the slightest exertion and her hospital stay stretched into a total of eight days. Wayne never left her bedside as she recovered. By 5:30 PM on Monday, Detective Jewett paid a second visit to Tammy in the hospital. Her first words to them were, "Y'all haven't caught him yet, I gather?" The answer was no. Tammy didn't realize it, but only a small percentage of stranger rapes are ever solved. The vast majority of rapes are committed by people who know the victim—boyfriends, coworkers, and dates. Only about 28 percent of all rapes are committed by complete strangers and these rapes are very hard to solve. Even having a suspect in the first two or three days is improbable, but Detective Jewett was working fast and he had a number of very good leads. Almost half of all rapes are never even reported, let alone solved. The United States Department of Justice reports that in 2006 almost 45 percent of the 158,020 subjects they surveyed either chose to report to an agency other than police (9%), didn't see the need to report because the sexual assault or rape was thwarted during the assault and it was not seen as important enough to report (10%), or it was seen as too personal to make public through reporting to police (25%). In this one survey, that means that almost 70,000 rapes or sexual assaults were not reported to police. Of those that are reported, the Bureau of Justice Statistics reported in 1998 that only about 20 percent of rapes brought to trial end in conviction. Rape is a very hard crime to report, investigate, and prosecute. The believability of the victim is crucial. In cases where the victim voluntarily engaged with the victim, but later claimed rape, the victim is seen as somehow responsible by investigators as well as juries. Tammy noted in one of our interviews that she was lucky she had been physically attacked and not just raped because she knew she was more believable and they took her more seriously. She was exactly right.

Detective Jewett presented Tammy with a picture of the pickup truck she had described to them from the Kroger parking lot. The truck turned out to belong to a Kroger employee. Eatherly had simply used that vehicle as part of his ruse. He also showed Tammy a pocketknife they had found at the crime scene, but she told them that this wasn't the knife he had used on her. Jewett said that a police sketch artist would be coming by later that night to create a composite sketch. The artist came by as promised. By Friday, April 3, a composite sketch of the suspect was released to the media. The sketch portrayed a Caucasian male in his thirties, 5 feet 10 inches tall, weighing approximately 150–165 pounds, with dark brown hair, a thick mustache, and aviator sunglasses. Even though Tammy's idea about her attacker's age was off, her description was strikingly similar to Eatherly. He was indeed 5 feet 10 inches; he weighed 145 pounds; and he looked very much like the composite. A reward fund was established by a local

Kiwanis Club and donations totaled $2,000 for information on Tammy's attacker.

Later that week, Eatherly was feeling the pressure from public attention to the case. He took the grocery bag containing Tammy's clothes that had been in his car for a week and threw the bag into a wooded area in Peachtree City, Georgia, near a plant where he had worked. He shaved his facial hair and drove to Pruitt where he talked with several employees. Everyone was aware of the assault because it had taken place on their property. Several of his coworkers had also seen the composite sketch on the news and noted the likeness to Eatherly. "If it isn't you, then you have a twin," they teased. Eatherly panicked. He knew it was only a matter of time before the police caught up with him. He quit his job and shaved his mustache. On Monday, April 13, he told Ragland that he was going to Bowling Green, Kentucky, to his parents' house. He told her that if anyone from Pruitt called, she should tell them he had gotten another job and he wouldn't be returning to work. By Thursday, April 16, two-and-a-half weeks after the attack, the personnel director at Pruitt called the Clayton County Police saying Eatherly resembled the composite, that he had altered his appearance, and that he had not been coming to work. The next day, Detective Justice learned that Eatherly had an outstanding warrant from Fulton County, and because of his police record, Eatherly's fingerprints were on file. By 9 PM on Saturday, three weeks after the attack, they were able to match his prints with a latent handprint that they lifted from the hood of Tammy's car. Eatherly was clearly their suspect. Thirty minutes later Tammy was in the police station looking at a photo lineup of six men. Instantly she identified number two as her assailant—a positive ID on Eatherly.

On Sunday, April 19, Bowling Green police were alerted that Eatherly might be in the area and that he was wanted in Clayton County. By 2:30 PM that same day Officers David Brewer and Randy Schocke stopped Eatherly in his vehicle—a woman named Evelyn Rechelle Britt was in the passenger's seat. Eatherly was arrested without incident. The next morning, Detective Jewett and Lieutenant Reynolds from Clayton County interviewed Mona Ragland and executed a search warrant on her property where they retrieved six Chicago steak knives along with other items. By the end of the day, they had driven to Bowling Green where Eatherly had already signed an extradition waiver and by 10 PM that night Jewett and Reynolds began their first interview with Eatherly. He admitted that he had attacked Tammy and that he was under the influence of drugs at the time.

He confessed that one of the Chicago steak knives that had been confiscated during the search of Ragland's home was, indeed, the knife he used in his assault on Tammy. His description of the attack, while accurate, was laden with excuses and conditions. For example, he argued that he only intended to rob Tammy and that he was under the influence of cocaine when he started raping her, a statement that was probably true. He said that when he started to come out of his drug-induced state, he realized he was in trouble. This was a convenient excuse. Lots of people do drugs but never rape or assault anyone. Not only that, he raped her viciously and repeatedly. His history is aggressive and I have no doubt his choice of victim had a sexual component. He could have robbed anyone, but he picked an attractive young woman. Second, he told Jewett that he tried to kill Tammy to hide the evidence, but when he realized she wasn't dead, he tried to "put her out of her misery" because he thought she was "suffering" and he figured she was going to die anyway. Again, that might sound logical to him, but it is a ridiculous excuse. He is the one who caused Tammy's misery and suffering over the course of an extended, brutal attack. To suppose that he suddenly got a conscience and felt compassion is absurd and it certainly doesn't explain his apparent autoerotic sexual behavior just before he strangled her. Third, he later told his attorney that he didn't stab Tammy until she began to fight. Again, this statement was true, but it doesn't include the fact that she didn't begin to fight him until he tried to slit her throat—a conveniently omitted detail. Fourth, even though he claimed to be remorseful, in his interview with police he said that Tammy "wasn't real bright" because she didn't scream or try to run while they were still at Kroger. In his interview with police he failed to mention that he threatened to "cut her up" if she did either thing. Beyond that, to blame the victim for her terror is cruel. In reality, Eatherly was a sexual predator and that is the way he behaved.

Eatherly was extradited back to Georgia on Tuesday, April 21. Investigators drove him to Dividend Drive in Peachtree City where he had indicated he discarded Tammy's purse and clothing. Just as he had described, about 25 feet off the roadway, investigators located a brown Cub Foods grocery bag. Inside were Tammy's purse, clothing, and an insulin syringe that Eatherly had used to shoot cocaine. While investigators looked through the bag, Eatherly said he felt sick and vomited in the woods.

On Wednesday, Tammy positively identified her personal effects and also listened to some of the tape-recorded interview with Eatherly. She was certain that the voice—a voice she will never forget—was that of her attacker. On Saturday police visited Eatherly in the Clayton County Detention Center and he voluntarily supplied head hair and pubic hair samples. The case against him was strong. He was charged with five counts—count one, armed robbery; count two, kidnapping; count three, rape; count four, aggravated sodomy; and count five, aggravated battery. Initially he pled not guilty, but after his psychiatric evaluation showed him competent to stand trial, he changed his plea to guilty. The district attorney, Robert E. Keller, had asked for life on counts one through four and for 20 years on count five. He said that Eatherly's actions were "despicable, heinous, repulsive, and abhorrent," and that "not even the lowest animal on the face of the earth should be treated" like he treated Tammy Crowe. He later noted in a letter to the department of pardons and paroles that "but for her strong will to live, the case would have been a death penalty murder." At sentencing in September of that year, Eatherly was guarded personally by the sheriff of Clayton Country. Eatherly's attorney, K. Van Banke, said a life sentence was overkill and instead petitioned for a lesser sentence along with "banishment from the county and state upon parole." He argued that Eatherly was completely remorseful for his actions and a reason for his guilty plea was that he "didn't want to put the young lady through any more." He said Eatherly wasn't the beast he had been described to be and that he went to Kentucky, not to flee the law, but to spend his last days of freedom with his family. Banke asked the court to consider a sentence of 10–12 years. When Banke said his client didn't intend to kill Tammy, Larry Crowe sprang to his feet and screamed, "Bull—, the son-of-a-bitch tried to kill her. He tried to kill her twice!" Deputies surrounded Mr. Crowe and there were no other incidents. Like Mr. Crowe, I find it odd that if he really was remorseful and if he really wanted to spend his last days with his family, why was he driving around Bowling Green with Britt, the woman in the car when he was arrested?

Only about one in five rapes are ever reported to police. Of those that are reported, few perpetrators are arrested. Less than half of those arrested are convicted and when they are convicted, few serve time in prison. Of those who are arrested, convicted and sentenced to jail, the average sentence is 11 months. But Eatherly was sentenced much longer. Judge Stephen Boswell didn't accept Banke's argument and he sentenced Eatherly to two concurrent life terms on counts one, three, and four, 20 years on counts two and five, and 20 years of probation following release. He was also ordered to pay $19,363.09 in restitution. Detective Jewett was awarded the medal of merit by the Clayton County Police for his work on closing this case and he was also recognized by the Metro Atlanta Chamber of Commerce South Council for his work leading to the conviction of David Eatherly. Jewett, however, humbly credited Tammy's strength and determination for his success.

While it is possible that Eatherly could eventually be granted parole, it is unlikely he will be paroled anytime soon. The psychologist who did his competency evaluation noted that Eatherly had a diagnosis of "mixed substance abuse" and "antisocial personality disorder" and that "treatment, per se, is not essential for his adjustment in a free or incarcerated society and his prognosis at best is poor." He has come up for parole hearings several times, but he has been denied. Under Georgia law, Eatherly is eligible for a parole hearing every seven years. He was denied parole in 1994 and 2001, and he was most recently denied parole in 2008. His case will come up for review again in 2015. The Board of Pardons and Paroles in Georgia is reluctant to release violent offenders, but when he was first sentenced, the district attorney told Tammy that Eatherly would most likely serve 20–30 years. As of this writing, Eatherly has been in prison in Georgia for 22 years. In 2015, he will have served 29 years so parole is a distinct possibility.

SURVIVING

One of the biggest factors in Tammy's recovery was her determination to live. The same internal strength that drove her to walk up that hill has assisted her recovery. She wrote in her victim impact statement: "I will *not* allow that . . . *thing* to ruin my life. I fought too damn hard to live just to let the aftereffects kill me." But the road to emotional recovery was a difficult one. In the early days after her release from the hospital, Tammy struggled to make sense of the randomness of the crime that nearly took her life. She cried, was afraid, and couldn't see how God could allow this to happen. She told me that at times she would literally stand in her backyard and scream at the sky during the night. She perceived a black hole deep within her and she wondered if she would ever feel whole again. She wondered if she would ever be sexually desirable to a husband and she especially needed to know that Wayne found her attractive. She was angry with God and had a very hard time the first Easter after the attack. She sat in the church "in a rage" and she just wanted to stand up and scream. It was "like having a gun, but nobody to point it at," she said. It took six months to let go of that level of rage and a year until she didn't think of it every day, but after nearly two years of counseling, recovering from her physical wounds, and working through her thoughts, she reached a point of transition. She came to the realization that bad things happen. She came to grips with the randomness of the event and that "God didn't do it" to her. When I asked her about "forgiveness," she said that she came to realize it wasn't "God" or anything else that caused her experience. "Bad things happen sometimes for no reason at all." She forgave God by letting go of the anger she felt, though she does not forgive Eatherly and she still gets angry at the mere mention of his name. That resolution was the beginning of her psychological healing. She realized that recovery was her responsibility. In fact, Tammy has a tremendous sense of personal responsibility that drives her in all she does.

Patient support from others during her recovery were important to her. Having someone who would listen to her was also important. In all recovery, victims of trauma need a sponsor. A sponsor is someone who provides financial and emotional assistance during recovery. Without both, victims might not ever recover. Along with her parents, Wayne was also Tammy's sponsor. She said the key turning point for her was Wayne's reaction to her in the hospital. He didn't blame her at what she said may have been "my most vulnerable point." If he had reacted differently—if he had seemed distant, blamed her, or appeared repulsed by her—she would never have had a good relationship again with any man, and people would have said it was the rape when, in fact, according to Tammy, it would have been Wayne's response.

She still had a lot of healing to do. I first interviewed Tammy in 2000. My last interview was almost 10 years later. I saw a much more confident and healed individual as those years passed. She notes that the incident made her "meaner" and less empathetic of whining. She earned a brown belt in karate and feels more confident that she would never be that vulnerable again. But even though the event had negative effects, it also made her more determined. "I refuse to let it stop me from doing what I need to do" and "it has made me stronger." In some ways, it made her a better wife and mother. She recognizes that her stable home and supportive parents helped in her recovery and made her more confident. She is making every effort to provide the same thing for her own children. She has applied the confidence she learned from her parents. "I used to be afraid of failure, but this [incident] was the worst it could get so I'm not afraid to fail."

I asked Tammy if she could change her life and erase this event, if she would. As hard as it is to imagine, she said no. As is so often true, she recognized that despite the many negative outcomes of her trauma, she also gained something. "If it hadn't happened, my life would be so different. I might not have married Wayne. We were trying to decide what to do and this event solidified our relationship in his mind. I would definitely go through it all again if undoing it would mean losing my children."

I've investigated dozens of murders and many of those victims had lesser wounds than Tammy. I don't blame them for dying, of course, but I can't help but ask the question why she survived and they didn't. By all accounts, her story is one of amazing resilience. She lost enough blood that she should have died before she ever walked out of that ravine. Her blood pressure should have been low enough that merely standing up would have caused her to be dizzy and nauseated. Even if she had maintained consciousness, she shouldn't have had the strength to stand, walk, or climb, and psychologically she should have been defeated. Being brutalized as she was would be enough to defeat most of us. Having the perpetrator return twice to finish her off should have been enough to mentally defeat her, but again, it didn't. Some of Tammy's physical strength came from the fact that she was physically fit. Her regular exercise, according to her doctors, probably saved her life. But this doesn't help us understand how she could overcome the loss of blood as well as the mental torture of her attack. She was mentally and physically strong. I wanted to know why.

All the factors that I see in resilient patients exist in Tammy. She is internal in her locus of control. She has a stubborn streak that gives her enough energy to face down danger and threat. She had meaning in life. She cared deeply for her parents and even if she didn't survive, she wanted to be certain her body was found quickly so her parents could get on with life. As I found with all the subjects I interviewed for this book, Tammy embodied virtues that helped her survive. She finds happiness in life and what it brings, even when life brings difficulties and pain. Her circumstances do not determine her attitudes or moods. She is humble and grateful for the blessings she has in life—her parents, family, husband, and children.

On March 1, 2009, almost 22 years after her assault, I visited the crime scene. I told Tammy I was going and without a hesitation she said, "I'd like to go with you." I wasn't sure what to expect from her, but I was honored that she wanted me to be the one to walk those steps with her. It was the first time since a Life Flight helicopter lifted her from the scene that she would have seen it. Ironically, it had rained all weekend and the sun came out just as had happened all those years ago. As it turned out, though, she chose not to go. She may have been too busy with work and family or maybe she was wasn't ready yet. Either way, it was her choice and I respect that. At the scene, I parked and walked in silence. I studied the path she took and little had changed. The trees were taller, but everything else was just as it was. In many ways she has left her trauma among those trees. Life goes on and Tammy is strong. Like each of the victims I've described in this book, she inspired me with her strength.

CONCLUDING COMMENTS

It is nearly impossible to imagine the effects of violent crime on victims. For someone like Tammy, just the pragmatic, short-term effects of the event are extensive. For example, because her purse was stolen, she had to get a new driver's license, new insurance cards, and a new school ID. Personal photos and special notes are gone forever. Her glasses were in her purse so she needed to get her glasses replaced, and her contacts were lost in the assault so they, too, needed to be replaced. Her vision was very poor so she needed to get her lenses replaced quickly and that added expense to the process. Her keys were stolen, but she couldn't simply get new copies. Because the perpetrator knew her vehicle, it had to be re-keyed, and he had her address from the information in her wallet so her home needed new locks as well. Rekeying all of these locks can be very expensive. Expenses are associated with everything as well as time to get it done. Hospital bills need to be paid. Dental bills may have been incurred if teeth are chipped or lost during an assault. Again, more bills. Tammy was in the hospital for eight days. If she were employed, she would have lost wages for those days plus whatever time she needed to recover at home. As it was, she lost an entire quarter of her college career. She was forced to find a job that she could do given the limits of what she was able to do because of her injuries.

The emotional effects of violent crime are devastating. Each time the victim looks in the mirror, she sees the results of the event and scars are ever-present reminders of life's most humiliating experience, and with each day's mail come bills that also serve as reminders. The victim fears that the perpetrator might show up at work or home because he has addresses, identification, and phone numbers. Rape victims live with the feeling of "dirtiness," being unlovable, and their husbands and boyfriends have to live with the fact that victims may associate them with their perpetrators simply because they are male. They have to be careful about hugging their loved ones or coming up behind them. What would be a nice surprise for the normal couple could easily be a conditioned reminder of rape. Wayne noted in his victim impact statement that, "I can't hold her tight or squeeze her. It hurts her to be held tight. I can't hold her arms or hands because of the scars there. You would have to see her stare at her hands and arms or see her stare at her reflection in the mirror. Now if we married I don't know how she will react to making love with me. Sometimes she will flinch if I come up from behind her and grab her tight." Other conditioned responses are common—sensitivity to sounds, certain kinds of movements, geography, certain kinds of automobiles, or even weather. Anything that could be associated with the attack could become a conditioned reminder. Tammy remembers that Eatherly smelled like stale cigarettes and to this day that smell causes her stomach to lurch as her body remembers the vicious attack. Loved ones of the victim are subject to conditioned responses, as well. Mrs. Crowe noticed that for many months, every time the phone rang when Tammy was gone her heart "jumped into her mouth" as she recalled the frightening call from the trauma center.

Rape victims may fear pregnancy depending on the time of their monthly cycle the assault took place. Imagine the overwhelming news that one may be carrying a rapist's baby. Fear of venereal disease is another realistic issue. Tammy was given large doses of antibiotics in the hospital in the hopes that any exposure to disease would be stemmed. Tammy began to experience jaundice in June of 1987, two months after the attack. It was then that she discovered that she had contracted hepatitis from a blood transfusion she received while in the hospital. This was the beginning of the nationwide awareness of a frightening disease called AIDS and the International Red Cross was just beginning to screen its supplies for HIV. Tammy was afraid she might have contracted AIDS as well. Her father helplessly noted, "He couldn't kill you then, but he is going to kill you one way or another." Fortunately, she has not tested positive for HIV or AIDS.

Victims are forced to relive the event every time an investigator or lawyer appears for questions. Tammy was interviewed three times during her hospital stay. She had to tell her story to family members, rape-crisis counselors, her boyfriend, police, and attorneys. When the case eventually went to court she had to tell her story to the court in her victim-impact statement. Each time Eatherly comes up for parole, she has to once again make the case for how his behavior has impacted her life and why he should stay in prison. The victim has to personally follow the perpetrator in prison. Through the Internet the victim can usually find out when a parole hearing is imminent. Each time it comes up, the whole thing starts again—phone calls, letters, and hearings. The need to stay on top of this process is driven by the victim's fear that the perpetrator might one day get out and finish what he started. No matter how many years of good behavior in prison or apologies extended by the perpetrator, the victim will never feel safe if he is released. (The state of Georgia passed a Victim's Bill of Rights in 1995, giving the victim the right to be notified about arrest, trial, parole hearings, appeals, and other important steps in the process. However, the victim is required to make initial contact and provide contact information to various agencies. Even then, the victim is not always notified.)

Humiliation and feelings of responsibility are common. Victims feel responsible for being victimized and they question their decisions. "What ifs" plague them. "What if I didn't stop at Kroger?" "What if I didn't stop at *that* Kroger?" "What if I had parked in another spot?" "What if I had screamed or tried to run?" These questions can be overshadowed by the biggest question, "Why me?" Tammy noted, "I was lied to and tricked into dropping my guard"; therefore, "I found myself pinned under a sweaty, heavy, complete stranger who stank, no reeked, of cigarette smoke." She recognized that she was tricked, but she felt guilty just the same. Coping with a sexual assault is challenging because even though the victim is never to blame, she often can see things she did that might have made it easier for the perpetrator to either target her or to take advantage of her. Tammy told me that she has never helped any stranded motorist since that day because she believes if she had not stopped to help, she wouldn't have become a victim. Another mistake Tammy made was letting Eatherly drive her away from the public parking lot. You should never, ever, let a perpetrator take you away from a public place. The best bet is to play it out there, even if the perpetrator threatens your children. Even if he harms you or your children, at least you will be in a public area; you will have access to help. If he takes you away to some secluded place, he has complete control and can not only harm you anyway but can also extend the length of time it takes to do so. Would Eatherly have killed Tammy if she had screamed and fought at Kroger? Probably not. Even when he tried, he failed. It is likely if she had fought with him in her car there in the parking lot, she would have escaped with her virginity intact and with minimal injury. We'll never know, but when a victim is faced with these thoughts, it is easy to feel stupid, responsible, and embarrassed. Yet it is unfair to suppose that a young, idealistic woman would have any reason to know such things or reason to distrust someone in the middle of a busy parking lot on a sunny Saturday afternoon. Likewise, when confronted with the horror of being overpowered by someone with a weapon, no one can know how he or she would respond. I have reviewed cases of police officers who were so frightened when confronted with an armed perpetrator that they literally allowed the perpetrator to walk up, take the officer's gun, and shoot him with it. That is why Eatherly's statement that Tammy "wasn't very bright" because she didn't scream or run was so thoughtless (not to mention evidence of Eatherly's egocentric, self-centered thinking).

Tammy learned a valuable lesson from her experience. Today, Tammy says that when any male approaches her in a parking lot, she makes eye contact. That one behavior is enough to deter some perpetrators. In my work I've been told by dozens of prisoners that if their intended victim makes eye contact they will pick another victim. Eye contact not only lets the potential perpetrator know that you see him and may be able to identify him, but it takes away his element of surprise.

Even though she would do things differently if confronted with a similar situation today, Tammy did several things right. Once she was under his control, she tried to follow his orders. When it became clear he was going to continue to hurt her, she took advantage of an opportunity to run. Unfortunately, the elements worked against her, but it was a good idea. When he tried to cut her throat, she fought back. Perpetrators count on the passive compliance of their victims. Even if she had died, she would not have made it easy for him. Eatherly claimed that he didn't try to kill her until she fought with him. This is ridiculous. He intended to kill her all along. He was in a hole and he had decided to end her life and eliminate the evidence before she ever tried to run. She did the right thing. Once she found herself alone and bleeding, Tammy had the clarity of mind to assess her resources. She made a decision about which direction to walk, and even though she thought she would die, she was able to think about where she might be most easily found. She had the mental acuity to remember her health-class first aid training and she improvised a solution to slow her bleeding by packing her wounds with sand. Finally, she maintained enough mental focus to provide investigators with an impressively accurate description of her perpetrator that quickly led to his arrest.

Wayne asked Tammy to marry him even while she was still in the hospital, but she said no. She didn't want a "pity marriage." Over time, though, she agreed and on December 16, 1989, two-and-a-half years after her attack, they married. They now have two boys, ages 9 and 15, and both Tammy and Wayne are high school teachers. Tammy teaches social sciences, psychology, history, government, and sociology and she is the yearbook faculty sponsor. She approaches her classes and the yearbook with the same tenacity that helped her survive her assault. When she told me she had become the yearbook sponsor, I said, "And I bet it is the best yearbook they have ever had." "Yeah," she said matter-of-factly. "It has won a bunch of national awards." I wasn't surprised. In terms of her recovery, she says, "This is a war I will win. He will not imprison me."

Tammy's theme song is "Get Over It" by the Eagles. The lyrics include the lines "spend all their time feelin' sorry for themselves, victim of this, victim of that . . . get over it . . . But the big, bad world doesn't owe you a thing . . . get over it . . . You drag it around like a ball and chain, you wallow in the guilt; you wallow in the pain. You wave it like a flag, you wear it like a crown, got your mind in the gutter, bringin' everybody down. Complain about the present and blame it on the past. I'd like to find your inner child and kick its little ass . . . get over it." Trauma is no excuse to quit, Tammy told me. She lives in the same way she expects others to live and, as she demonstrated in 1987, she refuses to sit down and die.

Tammy is not fully recovered and probably never will be. She still gets angry at the mere mention of her perpetrator's name. In her victim-impact statement to the court, she noted that:

Never, never will I feel completely clean and whole again . . . I'll always have mental scars to go with my physical ones (of which there are many!). They are a mocking reminder of what someone can do to you and quite possibly get away with. I cannot forget being completely vulnerable and powerless; degraded and abused . . . dragged around and treated like something lower and more unimportant than anything you care to name. I'll see his face the rest of my life . . . feel that knife over and over in my dreams . . . see him grinning like he could do whatever the hell he wanted to me, and no one could stop him . . . see him thrusting his dirty, smelly repulsive penis into my face . . . how many others has he done this to that we know nothing about? How many will he do this to in the future? I have flashbacks and nightmares; I go on crying jags. I see the whole thing over and over and over until I feel like I want to die just to escape.

She would love to see him in prison for the rest of his life, even though parole is likely. But her anger doesn't possess her. Her life continues and she will continue to grow, teach, mother, and live. Eatherly couldn't stop her in 1987 and he won't stop her today.

REFERENCES

Bureau of Justice Statistics, U.S. Department of Justice. (1998). Crime and justice in the United States and in England and Wales, 1981–96. Retrieved December 3, 2009, from http://www.ojp.usdoj.gov/bjs/pub/html/cjusew96/cpo.htm.

McLain. S. (1987, September 9). Riverdale rapist sentenced: Two life terms, 20 years. *Clayton Daily News*, p. C1.

McLain. S. (1988, March 11). CCPD detective awarded medal of merit. *Clayton Daily News*, p. 1A.

Rockmagic.com. (2009). Get over it guitar chords. Retrieved April 28, 2009, from http://www.rockmagic.net/guitar-tabs/eagles/get_over_it.crd.

Sexual Assault Statistics. (2008). Men against sexual assault at the University of Rochester. Retrieved April 28, 2009, from http://www.sa.rochester.edu/masa/stats.php.

U.S. Department of Justice. (2008, August). Criminal victimization in the United States, national crime victim survey, table 27. Retrieved December 4, 2009, from http://www.ojp.gov/bjs/pub/pdf/cvus06.pdf.

U.S. Department of Justice. (2008, August). Criminal victimization in the United States, national crime victim survey, table 102. Retrieved December 3, 2009, from http://www.ojp.gov/bjs/pub/pdf/cvus06.pdf.

6

———◦•◦•◦———

UBUZIMA BUFITE IMPAMVU:
GENOCIDE IN RWANDA

Great minds have purposes, little minds have wishes.

—Washington Irving

In more than two decades of work in the field of psychology, trauma, and aggression, I've spoken to millions of people through TV, radio, my books, newspaper columns, articles, and in public appearances in multiple countries on five continents. But nothing was as heavy a burden for me as the assignment to address a mere 50 people that I accepted in the fall of 2008. My commission was to bring a message of forgiveness and healing to the victims of the 1994 Rwandan genocide. Representatives from various areas of the country would attend this three-day conference and then the attendees would take my lessons back to their provinces. The hope was that they could then bring healing to thousands of Tutsi across the country— widows, children, and other survivors of the holocaust that befell Rwanda in 1994. It might seem an odd time to begin healing, over 14 years after the fact, but a new twist in their existence was underway. Many of the Hutu

---

Unless a source is noted specifically, the information included in the chapter was acquired through personal interviews with Rwandan political officials, Rwandan residents (both Hutu and Tutsi), and also from information provided by the genocide museum in Kigali known as the Kigali Memorial Center.

perpetrators of the genocide who were prosecuted and imprisoned had served their sentences and were being released. These men and women were returning to their homes—literally moving in across the road and next door to the very families that they terrorized 14 years earlier. They were moving right back into the very neighborhoods where they mutilated, raped, and killed nearly one million Tutsi beginning in April 1994. It was hard for me to imagine what this wrinkle in daily life might mean to a wounded country.

I leapt at the chance to address the group, but I wondered what on earth I could say to people who had endured such a devastating tragedy—a holocaust that was more vicious in some ways than what the Germans did in World War II. I realized it was very possibly the most important assignment I had ever accepted. If I did my job right, even though my audience would only be 50 people, the cumulative effect of my work could easily reach thousands and I might help bring healing to this beautiful country. This trip came on the heels of many years of interviews and research I had conducted on healing and forgiveness and the timing couldn't have been

Pius Nyakayiro in Kigali, Rwanda in 2008.

better. I had the chance to put the ideas I present in this book into practice on a grand scale. I couldn't imagine a more difficult place than Rwanda to test my idea that virtues—purpose, hope, gratitude, and forgiveness—were the keys to healing.

It was October 2008, late winter in the southern hemisphere. As my plane soared at 35,000 feet over the deserts of Libya and Sudan on the way to Rwanda, I realized what a huge continent Africa is. For more than two hours we flew over endless desert and it became apparent to me that Rwanda is an isolated country. Landlocked and one of the smallest nations in Africa, Rwanda is hidden away in the south-central part of the continent, nestled between Tanzania, Burundi, Democratic Republic of the Congo, and Uganda. It measures just 26,338 square kilometers (10,169 square miles)—smaller by 700 square miles than Hawaii. The population of this tiny country is just over nine million people. More than 24 hours after I left home, after brief stopovers in Belgium and Uganda, I touched down in Kigali, Rwanda.

Prior to its colonization by the Germans in 1895, Ruanda-Urundi was an "uncivilized" nation by western standards, its various tribes living in huts, farming, hunting, and existing as they had for centuries with traditional language, religion, diet, and customs.[1] The Tutsi arrived in Rwanda sometime in the 16th century and for most of their prewestern history, even though they were outnumbered by Hutu peasant farmers, Tutsi chieftains ruled over the Hutu, sometimes cruelly, through a feudal system called *ubahake,* a system where power was based on the number of cattle one owned. The Tutsi formed a dominant class akin to European nobility. They were upper class and they took advantage of it. While it was possible for the Hutu to rise in power, the "feudal system placed the Hutu in a position of almost permanent inferiority." Western expansion became an important part of Rwanda's history as European ideas, language, and culture merged with the traditional cultures during 60 years of occupation. The Germans occupied Rwanda until 1916, a mere 20 years, when Ruanda-Urundi was invaded by Belgium. The Belgians already occupied the neighboring Belgian Congo (later known as Zaire and today known as the Democratic Republic of the Congo) and the 1916 invasion of Ruanda-Urundi expanded their land holdings to the east. Belgium officially occupied Rwanda from 1923–1962. These 50 or so years of occupation greatly affected the Rwandan people. Rwandans were largely Christianized, and French became the national language and still is today, although

Kinyarwanda is the native language that was, and continues to be, spoken on the street.[2]

During the Belgian occupation, Belgian leadership favored the Tutsi tribal leaders. Nearly all tribal chiefs were Tutsi, despite the fact that the Hutu tribe outnumbered them almost eight to one. Tutsi leaders enjoyed the favoritism they received from the Belgians and this favoritism undoubtedly fueled racial tensions under Belgian rule.

In 1962, when Rwanda gained independence from Belgium, the Hutu tribe was tired of being treated as second-class citizens. A year earlier in 1961 they took advantage of their numeric superiority in a general election. This election put the Hutu in the position of leadership, a position they enjoyed through the 1980s while the favoritism shown to the Tutsi was still fresh in their minds. The Hutu leadership began a process of ethnic cleansing that continued for more than three decades. But the first attempt to rid Rwanda of Tutsi happened even before the Belgians left. In 1959 as a transition in power from Belgium to Rwanda was in process, nearly 150,000 Tutsi were exiled to bordering countries. Despite the ominous signs of a potential genocide, the Belgian government left the ethnic battles to Rwandans to work out for themselves.

The Tutsi endured two decades of humiliation and oppression. Just as it happened in Germany prior to World War II, the Hutu government became more and more oppressive, and more and more aggressive. Sporadic murders, arrests, and deportations were not uncommon. Throughout the 1960s, many Tutsi were resettled in an area known as Bugesera in northeastern Rwanda, and as many as 700,000 Tutsi were exiled. By 1973, things got worse. Juvénal Habyarimana, a military officer who was the former minister of defense, seized power from the sitting President Grégoire Kayibanda just three months after Habyarimana was promoted to major general. Habyarimana was staunchly anti-Tutsi and two years after overthrowing the government, he established his own military called the National Revolutionary Movement for Development (MRMD). From the onset of his reign until 1992, Habyarimana ruled as de facto dictator. In 1990, the growing overt hatred of the Tutsi became apparent to anyone paying attention with the publication of the "Ten Commandments of the Hutu." Published in the Hutu paper *Kangura,* these rules told Hutu how to view the Tutsi. Here is a synopsis:

1. A Hutu is a traitor if he marries a Tutsi woman, hires a Tusti, keeps a Tutsi as a mistress, or even befriends a Tutsi.

2. Hutu women are more beautiful, conscientious, and better mothers than Tutsi.

3. Hutu women should ensure their husbands and brothers do not engage with Tutsi women.

4. All Tutsi are dishonest, Hutu are ethnically superior, and anyone engaging with Tutsi in any way are traitors of the race.

5. All power positions (political, military, etc.) should be held by Hutu.

6. Education must be conducted and enjoyed by majority Hutu.

7. The army should be exclusively Hutu.

8. No mercy should be shown to Tutsi.

9. The Tutsi are the Hutu common enemy both inside and outside Rwanda.

10. Hutu ideology must be taught ubiquitously.

If this message of hate was too cryptic, it was clarified by Leon Mugesera, a senior member of Habyarimana's party, in 1992 when he said, "The fatal mistake we made in 1959 was to let [the Tutsi] get out . . . They belong in Ethiopia and we are going to find them a shortcut to get there by throwing them into the Nyabarongo River. I must insist on this point. We have to act. Wipe them all out!"[3]

The Tutsi began to organize themselves in exile. In the mid-80s, a military movement known as the Rwandan Patriotic Front (RPF) began in Uganda. Some of these RPF troops had been refugees since the 1959 deportation. By 1990, the RPF resistance movement invaded the northern portion of Rwanda. This was the first military opposition Habyarimana had from the Tutsi, but inroads were being made in politics, as well. In 1992, the first multiparty elections were held and a Tutsi woman named Agathe Uwilingiyimana was elected as prime minister. In August 1993, the RPF and Rwandan government signed a peace agreement and the United Nations sent a team to Rwanda under the command of Major General Roméo Dallaire, a French Canadian, to enforce peace.[4] The team was labeled UNAMIR—United Nations Assistance Mission to Rwanda. This was a label full of irony since history has shown the United Nations rendered very little assistance during the genocide (except for the valorous efforts of General Dallaire and his men) and, in fact, inhibited assistance that was requested.

Even as political freedom was expanding with the addition of Tutsi representation in government, Habyarimana was operating in a Nazi-like fashion. He was sole commander of the military in a single-party system. He organized a youth military-training program that involved heavy indoctrination in anti-Tutsi thinking, much like the Hitler Youth program during World War II, and Tutsi continued to be jailed, exiled, and murdered. The final step toward genocide was the registration of all Rwandans. Just as Hitler forced the registration of all Jews for the purpose of identifying and locating "undesirables," the primary purpose of the registration was to make it easier for the government to locate and identify Tutsi. The registration of Tutsi was critical. While some Hutu are taller than the Tutsi, it is impossible to definitively identify a Hutu or Tutsi by appearance alone. The only way Hutu leaders could know who was Tutsi and who was not was by checking documentation. Clearly stamped on one's documentation was tribal identity.

In January 1994, Dallaire notified his superiors that a "third force" was operating in the country. An informant had disclosed to Dallaire that the president's party was going to derail the peace process; mass killings were being planned, including killing some of Dallaire's Belgian soldiers; and that the UN was being targeted to force the UN to leave. That third force likely referred to the Interahamwe. The Interahamwe were a paramilitary organization sponsored by Habyarimana's government, but these militia operated without the constraints of law and gave Habyarimana deniability. Even when the genocide began, Habyarimana claimed to be against the militants behind the attacks, but his government did almost nothing to stop the killings. The word "Interahamwe" means "those who fight together."

In August 1993, 2,500 UNAMIR troops arrived in Kigali with the intentions of supporting the cease-fire. Despite ominous warnings from Dallaire, the United Nations was still telling expatriates in Rwanda that it was safe, even though political assassinations were occurring on almost a daily basis. Regardless of the cease-fire between the RPF and Habyarimana's government, small massacres of Tutsi occurred several times between October 1990 and February 1994. The killings became more brazen and more frequent as April approached and the Hutu militants were convinced the UN would do nothing to stop them. Unfortunately, they were right.

In April 1994, Habyarimana had visited Cyprien Ntaryamira, the Hutu President of Burundi. The two men were negotiating peace possibilities between Tutsi and Hutu. In the late evening of April 6, the plane carrying the two presidents approached the Kigali airport in Rwanda, and was shot down. The plane fell to earth and pieces actually fell into Habyarimana's own presidential compound near the Kigali airport.[5] Within hours, the military under the command of Colonel Théoneste Bagosora, head of military operations in Rwanda, had taken control of the country; road-blocks were established; and home searches were being conducted. One of history's most gruesome genocides was underway. Almost immediately, Dallaire realized the prime minister should be in charge and he recognized the potential for a political coup. Dallaire met with Colonel Bagosora and insisted that he step aside, but Bagosora refused.

The genocide was carefully planned. Dallaire notified his superiors as early as 1992 that Hutu militia were stockpiling munitions as well as over a half million machetes, that they were creating death lists, and that the Hutu were planning a massacre, but he was forbidden by his superiors from tak-ing action. Committed to peace, the UN severely limited Dallaire's budget, denied his requests for a minimum of 5,000 troops, and when he planned a raid on one home known to contain as many as 135 weapons, he was told to stand down. He warned, "If you don't stop these weapons, some day those weapons will be used against us." This was just a few weeks before the genocide began and Dallaire couldn't have known how right he was.

In January 1994, an informant from Habyarimana's own security guard informed Dallaire that registration of Tutsi was underway specifically in preparation for extermination of Tutsi civilians and that there was also a plan to kill Belgian peacekeepers with the UN in order to force a UN withdrawal. Both plans were put into effect almost immediately following Habyarimana's death under the direction of Colonel Bagosora.[6]

Upon the death of President Habyarimana, mass executions began. Just as Dallaire had been warned, a hit list of Tutsi leaders was immediately put into use giving the international community the illusion that the killings were exclusively political in their motivation—a sad, but common behavior in many nations experiencing political turmoil. At the top of the list was Tutsi prime minister Agathe Uwilingiyimana. With Habyarimana's death, Prime Minister Uwilingiyimana was legally in charge of the nation, but she realized that as a Tutsi, her life was in jeopardy. Ten Belgian and five Ghanaian peacekeeping members of UNAMIR attempted to protect her and even tried to help her escape the renegade militia by climbing the wall of her compound, but shots were fired over their heads forcing them back into the compound. Even under fire, the peacekeepers had orders from the UN not to return fire. They were soon surrounded and Uwilingiyimana surrendered. A half an hour later, she was shot to death.[7] The Hutu militia released the four Ghanaian peacekeepers, but took the 10 Belgian soldiers back to the Belgian army base. Meanwhile, Dallaire was driving all over Kigali in a desperate attempt to use diplomacy to stop the pending genocide. As he drove by the Belgian army barracks, he saw the 10 soldiers laid out on the ground. He knew he could do nothing to save them so he proceeded on to meet with Bagosora. He told them he knew of their plan to force the UN out and he argued that the United Nations would stay no matter what, but his pleas were ignored. While he was meeting with Colonel Bagosora, the 10 Belgians were beaten, shot to death in cold blood, and their bodies were mutilated with machetes. The wall at the Belgian army barracks against where they were killed remains in Kigali, bullet holes splayed across its face.[8] By 9 PM on April 7, less than 24 hours after the plane crash, more than 1,000 bodies filled the morgue at Kigali hospital. A horrifying prophecy, this fulfilled the words of the informant who had told Dallaire about the hit lists and pending genocide. He told Dallaire in his message that "in 20 minutes his personnel could kill up to 1,000 Tutsis."

On April 8, President Clinton ordered all 267 United States citizens to evacuate Rwanda and he ordered the embassy closed, just as all the other foreign embassies were closing. The next day, military troops from various countries, including 1,000 Belgian paratroopers, landed at the Kigali airport to organize the evacuation of their expatriates. Foreign troops sped in trucks and cars all over the country picking up their citizens, but no Rwandans were allowed to be evacuated. If one's skin was white, he could be saved, but if one's skin was black, he stayed. By April 10, only one American was left in Rwanda, the director of the Adventist Development and Relief Agency (ADRA), a man named Carl Wilkens.[9]

Just days into the massacre, the United States sent a reconnaissance team of marines into Rwanda on a one-day fact-finding mission. They reported that there were "so many bodies on the streets that you could walk from one body to another without ever touching the ground." Even with this knowledge, Dallaire was ordered by the UN to avoid armed conflict.

Just as the Hutu had hoped, the death of the Belgian peacekeepers created a cry from home for the return of all Belgian troops and on April 19, they withdrew. In the United States, Secretary of State Madeleine Albright had been ordered to petition the UN for a withdrawal of all UNAMIR forces. Dallaire was more hamstrung than ever, but the worst was yet to come. By April 25, the United Nations inexplicably cut his troops to just over 500. Originally, Dallaire was ordered to withdraw from Rwanda completely, but he defied that order and this fraction was allowed to remain. With only 500 peacekeepers for the entire country and no authority to take offensive action, Dallaire was forced to witness the horrors happening around him as a bystander. He wrote later, "My force was standing knee-deep in mutilated bodies, surrounded by the guttural moans of dying people." Westerners left Rwanda and the Interahamwe were free to kill at will.

The killing started in Kigali, but soldiers branched out through the countryside, recruiting hundreds of Hutu civilians to assist in the genocide. Tutsi were shot, speared, knifed, hacked to death with machetes, clubbed, raped, burned, blown up with grenades, chased with dogs, and drowned. Relative killed relative and neighbor killed neighbor. Men, women, and children—no one was spared. During the first few days of the genocide, in an attempt to save themselves, Tutsi civilians clustered in areas where foreigners were housed—hospitals, churches, and offices. But their efforts were futile. As troops arrived to escort expatriates to safety, they were specifically ordered not to include Rwandans. In one case, as reporters and troops liberated a few Westerners from a mental hospital, they passed Hutu gangs with machetes and guns around the building. Rwandans seeking refuge pled to be taken with them, but their pleas fell on deaf ears. As the caravan pulled away, screams and gunshots could be heard as all of the refugees were bludgeoned and shot to death. On April 15, two weeks into the genocide, in the eastern town of Nyarubuye, 5,000 Tutsi sought shelter in a church only to be shot and hacked to death. Their bodies remained where they lay for months. Even some religious leaders were complicit with the perpetrators. For example, Father Athanase Seromba, a Hutu priest at Nyange, a town on the northern border with Uganda, did nothing to save the people seeking refuge in his church. Tutsi refugees had gathered inside the church in Nyange where they were under constant attack and were deprived of food, water, and sanitation. As they assembled, Seromba was accused of asking them the whereabouts of Tutsi who were in hiding. He then turned that list over to the Hutu militia. Then, with 2,000 of his own Tutsi congregants inside his own church, Seromba gave Hutu perpetrators information as to where the "weakest parts of his church" were so they could lob hand grenades into the packed building. He then personally gave the order to bulldoze the church, killing the ones who had survived the bombing.[10]

In May, frustrated that his efforts to get help from the UN were refused and that his talks with the Hutu government got him nowhere, Dallaire arranged a meeting with the leaders of the death squads. They met in a hotel in Kigali and Dallaire said that they arrived with "blood spots on their hands." He realized at that moment he was talking to "evil." His negotiations that day did nothing to stop the killings.

Meanwhile in May, the United States communicated with the commander of the RPF and encouraged them to halt their march toward the capital. The U.S. position was that if the RPF negotiated with the Hutu government, the killing would stop, at least temporarily, and buy the country time to reach an agreement that would save the lives of thousands of Tutsi. This position was naïve. The Hutu had preplanned their attack down to the smallest detail. They were intent on ethnic cleansing and if the RPF had slowed their advance, it would only have given the Interahamwe more latitude for killing in the countryside. While negotiation might work in many cases, when a military power is intent on a plan, negotiation will not work. This had already been demonstrated in Rwanda. Kofi Annan, for example, held the position prior to April, that letting the Hutu government know that the world community was aware of its plans for ethnic cleansing would keep the Hutu in line. He believed that fear of UN and world sanctions would stop them. This, too, was naïve. It was the Hutu plan all along to force the UN out by killing the Belgian soldiers. They had no fear of sanctions.[11]

Making the most of the resources he had to work with, Dallaire attempted to create safe havens around Rwanda, many of them in soccer complexes because they were easiest to defend. Sadly, in some cases it simply provided the Interahamwe easy access to large groups of victims who were ruthlessly murdered. But in many cases it worked. Despite few or no weapons, inadequate equipment and desperately few troops, in several cases UNAMIR troops were able to repel attackers simply by their presence. Even when unarmed, UN guards, sometimes only one or two, were able to keep militias from killing by simply saying, "Stop, this site is protected by the UN." One of those safe havens was the Hôtel des Mille Collines, also known as Hotel Rwanda and made famous by the movie

Hotel Rwanda starring actor Don Cheadle, who portrayed hotel manager Paul Rusesabagina. Rusesabagina allegedly provided shelter for Tutsi as they sought refuge in the hotel, narrowly escaping death many times from Hutu militia. However, Rwandans told me that they do not believe his story and, in fact, believe he was a co-conspirator. They believe his story was fabricated to further his own political aspirations. In order to validate the incredulity of Rusesabagina's story, one Rwandan told me, "Hundreds of people have been honored in Rwanda for helping during the genocide, but not one person has come forward to validate Rusesabagina's story." The most likely story is that the people seeking refuge in Hôtel des Mille Collines were saved because of the regular presence of UN members and an eventual evacuation by the UN. One of these UNAMIR members was Captain Mbaye Diagne from Senegal. Captain Mbaye, as he was known, saved hundreds of lives by smuggling people from one safe haven to another and he was a regular visitor at Hôtel des Mille Collines specifically to demonstrate to the militias that he was watching over those refugees.[12]

However, no place in Rwanda was completely safe from the marauding killers. Not even the Red Cross was spared. On one occasion Hutu militants stopped a convoy of Red Cross trucks clearly marked with their Red Cross insignia. Inside some of the vehicles were wounded Tutsi. Six patients were pulled from the vehicles and slaughtered. To quote one survivor, the Hutu didn't refer to individuals who survived their vicious attacks as "wounded," but rather as "those not finished off."

It is embarrassing and infuriating that the United Nations and the U.S. government wrangled over terminology while it was perfectly clear that genocide was occurring. As late as June 10, spokesmen from the U.S. State Department were still stumbling over their words and trying to avoid the use of the term "genocide." For example, after well over half a million Tutsi had been slaughtered, when asked how she would describe what was occurring in Rwanda, a U.S. State Department spokesperson told a Reuters correspondent:

> Well, I think . . . as you know, there's a legal definition of this . . . clearly not all of the killings that have taken place in Rwanda are killings to which you might apply that label. . . . But as to the distinctions between the words, we're trying to call what we have seen so far as best as we can; and based, again, on the evidence, we have every reason to believe that acts of genocide have occurred.

One would be hard pressed to find a better example of political double-speak. It was argued that the airport was under Hutu control and that the UN (and the United States) couldn't get troops into the country even if they wanted to, but this was a false claim. The director of the Red Cross in Rwanda stated that whenever he asked for extra nurses, doctors, or other medical help, his reinforcements arrived within days. If the United States had the motivation to help, they could have taken control of the country in a matter of days. The most honest statement that was made by any U.S. official during the entire genocide was when one Clinton administration official said, "We don't have friends, we have interests and there are no US interests in Rwanda." The UN approved 5,000 troops on May 15, but little action came from it because, according to Kofi Annan, contacts with more than 80 countries brought no commitment for troops. Help was finally in the offing when the U.S. government in late May gave approval to send 50 armored personnel carriers (APCs), but it took three months before they arrived because of bickering in Washington about who would pay for it. By then the killing was over and the APCs were no longer needed. Bill Clinton acknowledged in 2002 that Rwanda was a big regret to him and that the United States could have saved "at least half of them."

In fairness to the UN, it should be noted that the RPF was opposed to the presence of UN troops. The resistance movement feared that a strong UN presence in Rwanda would strengthen the Hutu government, making it less likely that the RPF would achieve its political goals. Even so, an agreement to help didn't come from the United States until late in May when most of the Tutsi victims had already been killed and, just like help from the UN, by the time a decision to help was approved, it was too late. The RPF took control of the country on July 19. Ironically, by the time the Clinton administration took action to help, most of the aid that eventually reached Rwanda went to refugee camps on the border of Rwanda. These camps housed mostly Hutu refugees who were dying of hunger, cholera, and thirst. Little U.S. aid actually helped the Tutsi whom it was intended for. The United States could have helped stop much of the killing if the Clinton Administration had acted quickly and decisively, but both Democrats and Republicans in the United States were complacent about the situation in Rwanda. It pains me to believe that both parties sacrificed thousands of Rwandans for political expediency. For those who cared or realized the scope of the genocide, fear of another Somalia debacle loomed large. For much of the time the genocide was underway, the Clinton administration was actively counting the cost of intervention. For example, Dallaire was asked on July 29 by a U.S. army officer "precisely how many Rwandans had died" and when he asked why, he was told that "one American casualty was worth about 85,000 Rwandan dead." It is hard to think that race didn't matter. It is nearly impossible to imagine a situation where a half million Frenchmen, Italians, or Englishmen were being slaughtered and the world not jumping in immediately with all its resources to help. The simple truth was that the world didn't want to be bothered with Rwanda and the United States led the way to apathy. The world had forgotten the people of Rwanda and the fact that I had to tell their story to introduce Pius Nyakayiro, discussed below, is demonstrative of that fact. Sadly, the words of Martin Luther King, Jr., ring true—"In the end, we will not remember the words of our enemies, but the silence of our friends."

PIUS NYAKAYIRO

On my first visit to Rwanda in 2008, I met Pius Nyakayiro. His reputation literally preceded him. A group of Americans I met in Rwanda had already met him and told me a little of his story. Equally interesting to me as a mental-health worker was the way they described his demeanor. He sounded mentally healthy and easygoing. I was doing research for this book and I thought Pius might be too good to be true as a research subject. Part of the purpose of my trip was to interview not only survivors of the genocide, but survivors who were highly functioning and when I heard the brief account of his story, it became obvious to me Pius was the one I wanted to write about. I met him for the first time outside the largest prison in Kigali. I knew him before he ever spoke a word. Standing only five feet tall he was hard to miss and his infectious smile was possessing.

Pius was born and raised in a Catholic family located in an eastern province of Rwanda. Like most Rwandans, his family was of modest means. The seventh of nine children, he was nearly last in line for an education, but he was able to eventually finish his primary grades. Pius was active in his Christian faith throughout his youth and it was this foundational belief system that became the primary hinge on which his later healing would turn. In 1990, still a part of the Catholic Church, Pius had become influenced by the teachings of Protestant Christianity, teaching that contradicted Catholic doctrine. Consequently, he was forced to leave the Catholic Church in 1992. As a result, he and several others who had been forced out of the church started their own house church. His former friends from the Catholic Church were unhappy with his heresy so they made trouble for him that eventually led to his arrest. Catholic theology was wedded within the government and during his week in prison he was told not to continue his Christian teachings. But he continued anyway and eventually joined the Apostolic Church for Revival in Rwanda, where he continues to practice his faith today. This stubbornness and courage would also be his assets for recovery from the trauma that awaited him in 1994.

Pius was only 24 years old in 1994—a young man in Rwandan culture. Because of the political unrest, the rumors of civil war, and the growing violence, many Rwandans had sought refuge in neighboring countries of Uganda, Burundi, and Tanzania, and they followed the peace talks from there. The northern part of the country was partially controlled by the RPF, but even there, villages were skeptical of strangers, even Tutsi, and they were resistant to others moving into their villages. Pius's father realized that in the face of looming trouble in Rwanda, Pius would be safer in Nairobi, Kenya, so he gave Pius some money and sent him to Kenya in hopes that he would be safe from whatever fate lay ahead for his people at home. Along with four other Tutsi, he boarded a bus for Kigali where he would catch a plane to Nairobi. When they reached the town of Rwamagara, half way to Kigali, the driver told them he could not go any further that day. They planned to spend the night in Rwamagara and get up early in the morning and continue to Kigali on another bus, but when they awoke the next morning, they heard an announcement on Rwandan National Radio telling them that "the President of Rwanda together with other high rank authorities have been killed" and that "everyone is requested to stay at home for security purposes." It later became clear that this order was issued to make it easier for the killers to find Tutsi. Pius and his group sought refuge in a nearby house because it became apparent that killings were taking place everywhere in the country. They spent two weeks in their hiding place starving, fearful, and waiting for death—all the while they could hear gunfire everywhere around them, knowing that people were being dragged from their various hiding places. Pius knew it was only a matter of time until they were discovered.

One day, the sound of people being killed was closer to their hiding place than ever before and all day long Pius could hear people being dragged from various hiding places and murdered. That evening, the Interahamwe found them. "What are you doing here? Why are you here?" they asked, but neither Pius nor his friends had any answer for them. The militants told them they "had to be killed." A woman who was with Pius tried to encourage the group and said, "If it is God's will we will die, but if it's not we won't die." The soldiers laid everyone down side-by-side and they felt death upon them. Reaching for the few dollars he had in his pocket for his trip, Pius offered the money to the men and said, "Don't defile yourselves by our blood and if you accept, God will likewise have mercy on you." The men took the money and left, but before leaving they told the group, "You deserve to die because you are no better than the others, but we won't kill you because we made an agreement." Pius and his friends breathed a sigh of relief as the men departed, but minutes later their hearts sank when they saw the men returning. Pius thought he was going to die, but luck was on his side.

To their surprise, the men approached and asked if the group knew of a better hiding place where they would be safe from other soldiers seeking to kill them. Stunned at the purpose of their return, Pius and the group were unfamiliar with the area and, therefore, had no other ideas. The men took Pius and his friends to the home of a local pastor. They told the pastor they wanted the group protected and they charged the pastor with ensuring that nobody find out that they were hiding there. The soldiers said they would be coming back to make sure the group was still alive. The pastor did as he was told, but the soldiers never returned. He hid them in a dark room where they stayed for two weeks without a shower and with food only every three days. But their main problem was not food or water. The ever-looming specter of death shrouded them like a veil each day as they heard death all around them. During these two weeks, over 100,000 Tutsi were murdered. After their two weeks in hiding, they heard the sounds of a military convoy heading their way. To their relief, it was the advancing RPF. An RPF officer explained that the area was still unstable and that they wanted to move the group to a safer location. Pius was relocated to a refugee camp where he heard hundreds of stories of the killings that had taken place all over Rwanda, but he received no information about his family or his church brothers and sisters. He remained in the refugee camp for two more months as the genocide raged around him, but his desire to know the fate of his family overcame his natural need to remain safely inside the refugee camp. The RPF was gaining control of the country, so in late June, he left for home to see if anyone was still alive. When he arrived in his home village no one was there—no people were on the street and many buildings in his hometown were destroyed. Dead bodies were everywhere.

He went to a refugee camp, which was nearby, and found two people who were members of his church who gave him news about his family. Some were killed, he was told, and others had fled the country, but there were no other specifics. He learned more information about his church family. His church was thriving when the genocide began in 1994, but by the end of the genocide, most of Pius's church friends had been killed or had escaped to Tanzania. Only three church members remained in Rwanda. That was all he knew.

The country was slowly coming under the control of the RPF, but it was still a dangerous place. Scattered bands of militants were still terrorizing various areas of the country and Pius learned this firsthand. One evening on his way back home from a refugee camp where he had been searching for survivors he knew, he ran into a lone Hutu man on the road. The man attacked Pius and dragged him into the forest where he beat him mercilessly and threatened to kill him. Once again, Pius believed he was going to die and he prayed that God might receive his soul. But for some unknown reason, the man suddenly stopped beating Pius and ran away. To this day, Pius is still unsure what frightened the man off, but whatever the reason, it saved his life. Pius crawled to safety in a nearby banana plantation where he spent the night hiding, bleeding, and near death. The next morning he summoned the strength to walk to an RPF military camp where he explained what had happened and he was taken to the hospital. Pius spent a week in the hospital recovering. While in the hospital he learned the fate of his family. Twelve members of his immediate family had been brutally killed—an uncle, his father, three sisters, two of his brothers, three nieces, and two cousins—along with many of the members of his church. After leaving the hospital, Pius returned to the camp where he was staying and spent another month there.

When he left the hospital, the genocide was ending, but he found his country devastated. Everywhere he looked he saw crying widows, orphans, homes destroyed, and there was no food for anyone. He was angry with God, bitter, full of hate, broken, and he had no hope. He describes that point in time as a time when he hated everybody, including himself; life was meaningless; and he could see no reason to keep on living. In the meantime, the man responsible for beating Pius had been captured and imprisoned. One day soldiers brought the man to Pius and asked him, "What do you think we can do with this man? We want to show you that we are not supportive of the bad things he did to you." Full of bitterness,

Pius didn't know what to say so the commander ordered his men to beat the man severely with sticks.

In August 1994, Pius moved on to Kigali to try to start life over. Even though his theology had taught him for years that he should forgive those who wronged him, now he was faced with the reality of having to live what he taught and he found it nearly impossible to do. The magnitude of his pain and devastation was beyond comprehension. He prayed that he would feel some forgiveness for those who had destroyed his world, but he did not know how he ever would. Then, after believing that God had called him to continue his church work, he was able to release his hatred and hopelessness and embrace the faith that had always sustained him. He believed that he could not continue his work with hatred in his heart. Not only did Pius let go of his anger and hurt, but as those accused of perpetrating the genocide were tried and imprisoned, he saw the opportunity to practice what he preached. Along with his spiritual and emotional healing, he began to feel a great burden for the people in prisons, widows, orphans, and the reconciliation of Rwandan society that had been torn by the genocide. Through the Internet, he found the Web site of *Good News Jail and Prison Ministry*. From that very moment he realized prison ministry was his calling. He began working in prisons, ministering to the men and women there. By 2006, he officially became a prison chaplain, ministering to thousands of the perpetrators of the very genocide that destroyed his family and country. Today Pius is married, has a four-year-old child, and is the country director of all the prison chaplains in Rwanda. This is a mammoth job. The prison in Kigali where I first met Pius was originally built to house 2,500 inmates. At its peak after the genocide, it housed over 7,000 inmates. When I visited, there were almost 4,000 inmates housed there, including many women with young children. A prison in the southern city of Butare was built for 3,000 inmates and when I visited that prison in 2008, the population of the prison was over 5,000. Many of these inmates have no bed, no blanket, and no shoes. They sleep on the floor or outside on the ground. Women with children are allowed to keep their children with them until the children reach their third birthday. There were about 60 toddlers and infants in both prisons I visited. The conditions were stark and Pius works daily to help meet the basic needs of these forgotten people.

There was one final act of forgiveness that Pius felt he had to express. Many years after the genocide had ended, he was on the street in Kigali and he saw the man who had tried to kill him. Pius tried to catch up with him, but the man saw Pius coming and ran away. He couldn't have known that all Pius wanted to do was to greet him, shake hands, show him love, and most importantly let him to know that Pius had forgiven him. He never was able to fulfill this wish, but in a way with each prisoner he visits he demonstrates his commitment to forgive.

TURNING POINT

Ubuzima bufite impamvu. These Kinyarwandan words are written across the outside wall of a modest wooden building in Kigali where I visited a number of survivors of the genocide. Both Hutu and Tutsi meet here regularly. The translation of these words in English is "Life with purpose." These are words that describe Pius. He recovered from the unthinkable because he saw purpose in his life. As much as I try to keep religion out of my writings, this is one place where it is nearly impossible. As you will read in chapter 8, there are a number of things that help individuals recover from traumatic events. Many of these things have nothing to do with religion. Murray Lynn, for example, whom you read about in chapter 2, has abandoned the teachings of his Jewish traditions. While he is active in his synagogue, he told me he sees religion as a collection of "myths and stories." But I've interviewed dozens of survivors and as much as it might be distasteful to those in the secular world, for most victims of trauma whom I've studied, religion was indispensable. Forgiveness, as it is taught in Christian faith, is exceedingly helpful. I suppose it is possible to find forgiveness outside of religion, but religion makes it easier because one is answerable to a higher power rather than exclusively to oneself. This higher calling provides a powerful motivator to do something that ironically is in the individual's best interest anyway. Without this motivator within the bounds of religion, people often find it difficult to forgive. It is possible to let go of one's rage, or at least set it aside, without formal religion, but it is rare. For example, after finding out who was responsible for killing her family during the genocide, one woman I interviewed in Rwanda had hired an assassin to kill the perpetrator, but she later called it off for fear of "cursing her bloodline." She didn't forgive, but her worldview that taught her that her behavior had an effect on her descendants, something bigger than herself, motivated her to withhold her anger. The turning point for Pius was not just his desire to forgive. His religion taught him that he should be forgiving and he deeply wanted to forgive from the very beginning. What made the difference was the decision to do it. By forgiving, Pius was willing to release the chains of memory that bound him to the past and the pain that resided there. I once heard a famous pop psychologist say that forgiving people who haven't asked for it cheapens forgiveness. This is a very narrow view of forgiveness. Forgiveness isn't just about giving grace to a wrongdoer, although it can include that. Rather, forgiveness is freeing oneself. It is the decision to move forward, to release one's hatred, vengeful thinking, and loss, and move on toward the many possibilities remaining in one's future. As psychiatrist Gordon Livingston writes, "Widely confused with forgetting or reconciliation, forgiveness is neither. It is not something we do for others; it is a gift to ourselves." When one forgives, grace is not only possible, but likely because one has released the things that make grace difficult.

A powerful lesson in forgiveness comes from the story of Immaculée Ilibagiza. In her book *Left to Tell,* she describes her harrowing escape from the Interahamwe by hiding in a tiny bathroom in the home of a Hutu priest with seven other women for 91 days during the Rwandan genocide. Immaculée lost almost half her body weight during her three months in hiding and when she emerged, she found herself face to face with a Hutu man with a machete. He intended to kill her, but through her internal strength and powerful gaze, she "stared him down" and survived. Afterward, she found that nearly her entire family had been brutally slaughtered. Hate and rage consumed her for her loss, but through constant prayer and her religious teachings, she found the forgiveness not only to move forward, but to confront the man who killed her "favorite brother." The man had been known to her family and she says that she was able to face him with no hate in her heart. Her story was immortalized in the film *The Diary of Immaculée.*

I was once talking with a fellow therapist who was very unhappy in her job and how her employer often put her in questionable ethical situations. "Why not just quit?" I asked her.

"Because I'm afraid of being unemployed."

We talked for a while about the irony of her comment. "What would you say to a client who was in your situation?" I asked her. She admitted that she could see that leaving her job would help her, but she was bound by her own fear of the unknown. She understood the truth of how finding a new job would be in her own best interest, what I was saying, but she couldn't let go of her fear of not having a job—her fear of the unknown.

Forgiveness is like that. It is in our own best interest, but our fear of the unknown—fear of letting the perpetrator get away with it, fear of justice going unserved, fear of dishonoring oneself by letting go of our vengeful thoughts—causes us to hold on to the very thing that holds us captive in the pain of the past.

CONCLUDING COMMENTS

The genocide came to an end in July 1994 as the RPF won the war. By that time, over 800,000 Tutsi had been killed. The end of the war is the only thing that brought an end to the genocide. It is interesting to note that if the RPF had taken the U.S. position to cease their push toward the capital and negotiate with the Hutu government, almost certainly more people would have died.[13]

Even though the genocide ended in 1994, the killing in Rwanda didn't end. In 1997, 317 Tutsi refugees were massacred in the Mudende refugee camp in northwestern Rwanda and again in 1998, returning refugees were slaughtered by Hutu in Rwanda. Even today, 15 years later, murders continue. Many of these murders are committed by Hutu attempting to silence witnesses of the genocide. In addition to the 800,000 men, women, and children who were murdered during the genocide, thousands were maimed, 300,000 children were orphaned, and 85,000 children were left as head of the household because their parents were killed. The killing goes on in one final cruel way—through the AIDS virus. Over 500,000 Tutsi women were raped during the genocide. Some of them survived only to live with (or die from) the complications of AIDS. These women also transmitted AIDS to their children, thus perpetuating the effects of the genocide to an entirely new generation. I said earlier that in some ways the genocide in Rwanda was worse than Hitler's genocide in Germany. If the killing in Rwanda had continued at the same rate for the same length of time Hitler's regime was exterminating Jews, approximately 22,400,000 people would have died—more than three times Rwanda's population at the time.

The United States government doesn't bear the blame for U.S. apathy alone. Even though I was not in Rwanda during the genocide, I have felt personally touched by the tragedy. I followed it on the news in 1994 and was frustrated when I tried to explain to my students what was happening and they just didn't seem to grasp the gravity of the situation. The citizens of the United States are fickle as the wind in their opinions about foreign policy and they have little stomach for long-term and expensive (both in dollars and in lives) conflicts, even when it means saving thousands of lives. Describing the apathy of the United States in regard to the genocide in Cambodia in the 1970s, former president Jimmy Carter called Cambodia a "remote part of Asia." That comment is indicative of an ethnocentric worldview. Cambodia isn't remote if you are in Cambodia.

Approximately 100,000 perpetrators were indicted on crimes committed during the genocide. I saw many of them still in prison while I was in Rwanda in 2008, and many more could be seen along various roadsides doing work projects—literally digging and breaking rocks, preparing the ground for gardening, monuments, or beautification. Their uniforms identified the prisoners on the roadside as genocide perpetrators and I am embarrassed to acknowledge that I felt a personal sense of justice as I witnessed these chain gangs, knowing the humiliation they were experiencing.[14] As I traveled the country, I saw many people missing arms and legs, and I couldn't help but wonder if they were survivors. Children were especially hard hit. After the genocide in 1994, many international agencies and in-country groups rallied to meet the needs of the orphans and child victims of the genocide. However, the concentration of their efforts was on physical needs—housing, medical needs, and food—but little energy was invested in trauma exposure and effects. These children are now in their late teens or early adulthood and yet they have never processed what they experienced with anyone. I talked with numerous victims in 2008 who were telling their personal stories for the very first time. Interestingly, while I was researching in 2008, I met a number of Hutu school children who were learning of the genocide perpetrated by their ancestors for the first time. This knowledge created feelings of guilt among even these young children over the behavior of their ancestors even though they were not even born when it occurred. My seminar in 2008 was a starting place for the healing I hope for in Rwanda.

The country itself is healing. The roads of Kigali are decorated with beautiful roundabouts, landscaping, and manicured medians. There is a massive urban renewal going on. Many of the buildings that existed in 1994 are gone and lovely construction has replaced many of the slums and ghettos. I saw entire neighborhoods that were slated to be leveled even today. But while the physical appearance of the country has improved, erasing many of the scars of the genocide, in some ways the country is in denial. There are genocide memorials all over the country and every year in April, the country commemorates the genocide with a week of mourning. However, the reconstruction, as well as the remaining 51 weeks of the year, are symptomatic of the denial I describe. Even the Genocide Museum itself tells a message of no hope. The displays trace the path of the genocide and end with mountains of bones—the arms, legs, and skulls of victims, some obviously infants, crushed and maimed from machetes and clubs. But that is where the story ends in the museum. In order to heal, the country must find a way to embrace its past, but also look forward to a hopeful future.

Many Tutsi acknowledged to me that any time they meet a Hutu, they privately wonder "what they might have done" during the genocide and some victims still suffer severe PTSD symptoms. One woman I met suffers panic attacks that overwhelm her. When they strike, she finds herself screaming, "They are coming again! They are coming again!" Another man described his depression by saying he believed that "God was tired when he made him" and another man said of himself that he had "the blood of a beast." There is no way to know how many victims of trauma exist and how that trauma is affecting them. For example, one woman I interviewed described her mother's depression. After 1994, the woman had two babies die during childbirth. It is tradition in Rwanda to name a baby something that is reflective of one's history. After two deaths, she didn't want to waste time naming the baby because she feared it too would die, so she named it "just wasting time." This is the kind of hopelessness that is still in need of healing.

The airport in Kigali sits high on a hill. At night it is very dark, hardly recognizable as an airport from the ground. As I waited to leave Rwanda, I couldn't help but think what it was like in 1994 when the Hutu military took control of the airport, screaming voices surrounding them as the massacre began in the nearby neighborhoods, valleys, and hillsides. From my first day in Rwanda, I watched the street from the window of my apartment, a 10-foot wall surrounding the apartment complex. I realized the terror one must have felt knowing that the wall wouldn't be enough to stop them—that I couldn't have saved myself and even more frightening, that I couldn't have saved my children. There was no place to hide. That is trauma I can hardly imagine.

In 2008 in the neighboring country of Congo, Congolese rebels battled ferociously for control of the country. A renegade Congolese general named Laurent Nkunda led the rebel forces, claiming to be on a mission to protect Tutsi people in the Democratic Republic of the Congo. Refugees attempted to flee the country for neighboring nations as the Congolese government backed Hutu militia groups, some of whom were perpetrators of the genocide in Rwanda. Once again, the United Nations aid workers, 17,000 strong at the time, were unable to do anything to protect the towns and villages that were threatened by this military advance. The Congolese people threw stones at the UN compound in Goma saying, "The peace-keepers and aid workers have failed to protect them." Maybe the people have learned something from Rwanda in 1994. As many as five million people have been killed in fighting in Congo since 1996. After the Holocaust in World War II, the world said, "Never again." After the genocide in Rwanda, it was said again, and this slogan is found everywhere in Rwanda. Yet the world doesn't learn. Since Rwanda, genocides have occurred in Darfur, Sudan, and Bosnia. The slogan "Never Again" is one that appears hollow in Congo, but if people like Pius Nyakayiro proliferate, they will survive.

NOTES

1. At the time, Rwanda was known as Ruanda-Urundi because present-day Rwanda and Burundi were one country. Both countries gained independence on the same day, July 1, 1962, and have since been independent countries known as Rwanda and Burundi.

2. French is still the national language, but as of this writing, Rwandans are unhappy with the French and avoid speaking it when possible. English is becoming the national education language. As a protest against the French, the president of Rwanda addresses French reporters in English.

3. Mugesera's prediction was right, but the river and country were wrong. By May 1, 1994, the Kagera River in eastern Rwanda that borders Tanzania was practically clogged with the bodies of dead Tutsis.

4. Rebounding from the disaster in Somalia that same month, the United States had refused to participate in this UN mission.

5. No public statement was ever made regarding who was responsible for shooting down this aircraft. However, in December 2008, Rose Kabuye, Rwandan president Paul Kagame's chief of protocol and former RPF officer, was arrested in Germany for conspiracy in connection with the downing of the plane. The French warrant for her arrest had been issued in 2006, one of nine. She was extradited to France where she remains in custody as of this writing. Other arrests and trials are underway. As late as October 2009, a former Rwandan military official named

Idelphonse Nizeyimana was arrested in Uganda and charged with killing Queen Rosalie Gicanda during the genocide.

6. Following the genocide, Bagosora fled to Zaire but was arrested in 1996. He pled innocent. The trial began in 2002 and deliberations began in June 2007. The verdict was finally rendered on December 18, 2008. At that time, the 67-year-old former military leader was found guilty for his role in planning and executing the genocide along with other military officers and sentenced to life in prison.

7. Her children were saved by a UN soldier named Captain Mbaye Diagne, who hid them in a closet.

8. The Belgian army base has been remodeled and is now a college—the Kigali Institute of Technology. Only the entrance to the barracks and the building where the killing of the 10 Belgian soldiers occurred remain as they were as a memorial to their deaths.

9. Carl Wilkens, the lone U.S. citizen in Rwanda, has been credited for "saving more people in Rwanda than the entire US government." When he discovered the Interahamwe had surrounded the Gisimba Memorial Centre orphanage, he petitioned the prime minister, who then saw to their safety. He also negotiated permission with the *préfet* of Kigali to deliver humanitarian assistance aid during the crisis. He was honored in 2006 by *African Rights* for bravery.

10. After the genocide, Seromba fled Rwanda, changed his name to Anastasio Sumba Bura, and moved to Italy where he worked as a priest. He surrendered to a postwar tribunal in 2002, pled innocent, but was found guilty and sentenced to 15 years in prison.

11. It is interesting that this is the very argument that President George W. Bush gave to justify the invasion of Iraq in 2003. Saddam Hussein had made it clear he was not afraid of sanctions and he would do whatever he wanted. It is likely that if he had not been forced from power, Hussein would have eventually continued exterminating the Kurds in northern Iraq.

12. Mbaye was killed in late May 1994 by a mortar fragment that exploded near his vehicle as he drove through a checkpoint.

13. Major General Paul Kagame, the commander of the RPF during the genocide, was elected president of Rwanda in 2000.

14. I also noticed that after such intense exposure to the genocide, I began to see PTSD symptoms in myself. For example, I remember hearing helicopters and seeing soldiers in trucks and on the streets and I felt panic reaction. This phenomenon is called secondary PTSD.

REFERENCES

Amanpour, C. (2008, December 4). Scream bloody murder. *CNN* broadcast.
Barker, G. (Writer, Producer, and Director). (2004). *Ghosts of Rwanda. Frontline*, coproduction with BBC.

Gettleman, J. (2008, October 30). Many flee as Congo rebels approach eastern city. *New York Times.* Retrieved October 30, 2008, from http://www. nytimes.com/2008/10/30/world/africa/30congo.html.

Gettleman, J. (2008, November 3). In Congo, a little fighting brings a lot of fear. *New York Times.* Retrieved November 3, 2008, from http://www.nytimes. com/2008/11/03/world/africa/03congo.html.

Ghosts of Rwanda. Frontline (2004). Co-production with BBC. Writer, producer, and director: Greg Barker.

Ilibagiza, I. Immaculée. Retrieved December 3, 2009, from http://www.immaculee. com/immaculees-story.

Kalafer, S. (Producer), & LeDonne, P. (Director). (2006). *The diary of Immaculée* [Motion Picture]. United States: New Jersey Studios, Hay House.

King, D. C. (2006). *Cultures of the world: Rwanda.* New York: Marshall Cavendish Benchmark.

King, M.L.K., Jr. QuoteDB. Retrieved January 6, 2009, from http://www.quotedb. com/quotes/46.

Lacey, M. (2006, December 14). Rwandan priest sentenced to 15 years for allowing deaths of Tutsi in church. *New York Times.* Retrieved December 3, 2009 from http://www.nytimes.com/2006/12/14/world/africa/14rwanda.htm.

Livingston, G. (2004). *Too soon old, too late smart.* New York: Marlowe and Company, p. 163.

Power, S. (2002). *A problem from hell: America and the age of genocide.* New York: HarperCollins.

Reuters Foundation. (April 6, 2004). Eyewitness: Word games in Washington as blood flowed in Rwanda. Retrieved December 3, 2009, from http://www. alertnet.org/thefacts/reliefresources/108124945499.htm.

7

—•◦◉◦•—

THE BREAKING POINT: PROTECTIVE FACTORS AND SEVEN LIES THAT PREVENT RECOVERY

Almost all our faults are more pardonable than the methods we resort to to hide them.

—François VI, duc de La Rochefoucauld (1613–1680)

In 1985, Simon Yates, age 21, and Joe Simpson, age 25, set out to do what had never been done. They were determined to summit the 21,000-foot Siula Grande in the Peruvian Andes. Several climbers had scaled its peak, but never before, despite many attempts, had any climber ever ascended by its harrowing west face. They were experienced climbers and had scaled peaks in the Alps together. Tethered together, they left their base camp and began their climb with crampons, ice axes, ice screws, pitons, and 150 feet of rope. Three days later around 2 PM they reached the summit and began their descent on the north face, a route for descent that was so treacherous most climbers avoided it as a descent route. As they began their descent, the weather turned for the worst and they found themselves in a blinding whiteout where snow blows so hard climbers cannot even see the ground beneath their feet. Realizing the danger of descending in a whiteout, they built a snow cave and prepared to spend the night.

The next day the weather had cleared enough for them to continue their journey and they descended without incident until late in the day. Joe lost his footing and began sliding. Still tethered to Simon, Joe plummeted down the face and over the edge of a precipice into a bottomless crevasse. As Joe's foot hit a ledge, the pressure shoved his leg upward. This compressed his leg, shoving his lower leg bone through his knee and shattering his femur, the bone between the knee and the pelvis. Above, Simon did his best to stop his runaway partner. Finally his crampons bit into the ice and he had control, but he could see nothing beyond where the rope dropped over the edge of the cliff. He had no way to secure the rope so all he could do was hold on, Joe's full weight on the other end of the rope as he dangled in the air. As Simon held on for life above and Joe hung in the air below, it began to storm again and the temperature was dropping.

Joe assessed his injuries and his situation. Climbing up was impossible and he feared he would die in the crevasse. For nearly two hours he hung by the rope while above, unable to hear him, Simon continued to hold on, nearing the end of his endurance. Suddenly, Joe felt himself falling again. At the top, Simon could no longer hang on and he had cut the rope before he found himself dragged over the ledge, as well. It was an agonizing decision, but neither man could hear the other and Simon was unsure that Joe was even alive. Joe landed on a ledge 150 feet below the surface and pain exploded through his body as the bones in his leg ground together. Even though he knew his chances were slim, he began to formulate a survival plan. He used an ice screw to secure himself to the wall of the crevasse. The rope was still hanging above him and he tugged on it only to see the end fall around his feet. At that moment, he realized the rope had been cut and he assumed Simon believed he was dead. Joe was on his own.

For the next several days, Joe Simpson accomplished the most unbelievable escape from death ever seen in mountaineering history. He spent that first night on the ledge. Surprised the next morning to find himself still alive, Joe waited and hoped Simon would appear over the upper edge of the cliff, but even though Simon had called to him, neither man could hear or see the other. Joe tried to climb up the face, but it was impossible. He could not see the bottom of the crevasse and he only had 150 feet of rope. He realized his only hope was to rappel down into the crevasse in the hopes of finding a way through the ice out of the crevasse and toward the bottom of the mountain. But with only limited length of rope, he realized he might easily run out of rope before finding the bottom. He decided to proceed anyway. He would find a way out or he would die either dangling from the rope or from falling from the end of the rope.

In an amazing stroke of luck, as Joe descended about 50 feet below the ledge where he spent the night, he saw light emitting from an area across a sloping ice surface. In excruciating pain, he inched his way across the slope toward the light, a challenging technical climb even for a climber with two good legs. Reaching the source of light, Joe broke through to daylight. Lying in the snow, he saw the glacier below and realized in his condition, in pain and bleeding, his chances were slim. Even a healthy climber with full equipment and supplies would find the descent from that point exhausting. Joe was bleeding; his leg was broken; and he had no water or food. But he did have assets. He had his climbing gear, his crampons, and warm clothing. Even though exposure and dehydration were serious threats, he pushed himself onward.

In the meantime, after cutting Joe loose and spending the night in a snow cave, Simon hiked down to the edge of the crevasse. He searched as best he could inside the crevasse and called to Joe repeatedly, but when he heard no answer and saw no sign of Joe, Simon had hiked down to base camp. When Joe emerged from the hole in the crevasse, he was able to see Simon's tracks in the snow. He began to work his way down the mountain toward base camp himself following Simon's footprints, but unfortunately, snow was continuing to fall and the tracks became harder to see until it was too dark to follow them. The next day it was sunny and clear, but the tracks were gone. Pushing his pain aside, Joe continued to move down the mountain, sliding along the glacier inches at a time. As he reached the bottom of the glacier, another obstacle loomed in front of him. The ice and snow disappeared and before him were rocks and boulders that stretched as far as he could see. He could no longer slide downhill dragging his leg behind him. He realized he would have to walk through the boulder field. He pulled himself upright and attempted to hop. Almost every time he hopped he fell, but each time he fell he got up again. Joe continued that way throughout the day until darkness fell. The next day, seven days after he and Simon left base camp for the summit, and four days since he fell, he thought he was going to die. He was desperately thirsty, dehydrated, in unyielding pain, and exposed to the cold. But luck was with him as he came upon a pool of water. Long cool drinks from the pool refreshed him and gave him strength to continue on.

As the day wore on he could see a lake he recognized as one near base camp. At that point he realized that Simon and another climber, Richard Hawkings, who helped them carry their gear to base camp, might be gone.

It had been four days and he realized they almost certainly had broken camp and left. In fact, Simon and Richard had discussed leaving the day before, but Simon wanted to stay even though he was quite certain Joe was dead. It was after dark when Joe finally reached the opposite side of the lake where their base camp had been. He called for Simon, but got no answer. He was near delirium, almost unconscious from dehydration, cold, exhaustion, and pain, but suddenly a pungent odor roused his mind. He realized he was crawling through the latrine area of base camp. He was there. Again he called out. This time Simon heard him and came to his aid. Richard and Simon carried Joe further down the mountain where he was airlifted to a hospital. Through the ordeal, Joe lost nearly one third of his body weight and over the course of two years, he had six operations. Today he is climbing again. Simon received harsh words from the climbing community, but Joe holds no grudge against him. His first words to Simon when he saw him back at base camp were that he would have done the same thing. Joe and Simon were reunited in 2003 for the filming of a documentary about their experience entitled *Touching the Void*.

As I began writing this chapter, I was sitting on the front porch of my in-laws' summer home in Florida. The sunset was stunning. Back home in Atlanta, winter was in full force, as much as we get winter, but here the evening air was warm, the breeze was soft, and the colors of the sunset were spectacular. I understand the meteorology of the sunset. The colors are reflections and penetrations of the various colors of the spectrum off of molecules in upper atmosphere (called "Rayleigh scattering") and the relatively longer distance these light waves have to travel at sunset compared to the middle of the day gives us the color we see at sunset. However, even though I understand the science of it, the sunset is so magnificent that I can't think of it in any way other than miraculous. As psychiatrist and pilot Gordon Livingston says about flying: "I've heard the physics explained to me a hundred times . . . but it still seems like a miracle." Even though we know the science of the sunset, we couldn't even begin to reproduce it. It is simply too big. I have felt the same way when I've read stories like Joe Simpson's. His courage, fortitude, and endurance are nothing short of miraculous. His survival seems to defy all logic and even though I understand it, I wonder if I could ever learn to produce that same resiliency in others.

How someone could have the courage, endure the pain, and face the mental hopelessness of a situation like Joe Simpson's is an enigma. So many people have been defeated by so much less. In this chapter I'll unwrap the enigma and examine its parts. We'll look at the reasons why Joe continued to get up, continued to press forward even when all logic and his own pain told him his situation was grim. I've combed the literature for everything I could find on resiliency, talked to as many experts on resiliency that I could find, and I have interviewed dozens of survivors. We know how people are destroyed by trauma, but I want to know how people endure their traumatic experiences, how I might foster that resiliency in my own clients, and how their experiences cause them to grow—something called "posttraumatic growth." An amazing longitudinal study on one of the Hawaiian Islands gave me some answers.

THE KAUAI STUDY

Two researchers named Emmy Werner and Ruth Smith tracked a group of 505 high-risk individuals born in 1955 on the Hawaiian island of Kauai. These children were interviewed, examined, and questioned at various increments over a 30-year period. The study is known as the Kauai Study. Even though the island of Kauai is a tropical paradise, the indigenous children of the island were considered high risk for several reasons. Perinatal complications were common in this population, the community was exceedingly poor, their parents were uneducated, and a host of other ills were common on the island such as "disorganized care-giving," parental desertion, divorce, marital discord, alcoholism, mental illness, and learning disabilities. The community made a perfect case study. Without money for travel, Kauaians lived almost totally isolated not only from the rest of the world in general, but even from the other islands in the Hawaiian chain. Tourists tend to prefer Maui, Oahu, and the Big Island so even tourist influence was minimal. This community provided an ideally controlled setting for Werner and Smith to follow these children from childhood through adulthood to see who coped well despite their risk factors and who did not. Their findings were fascinating. By the time their subjects were 10 years old, one in five had behavior difficulties or learning problems that required more than six months of intervention and by the time they were 18, 15 percent had delinquency records and 10 percent had mental-health problems that required hospitalization or outpatient treatment. In the general population, youth under the age of 19 with delinquency troubles constitute only about .4 percent of the general population, and only about 1 percent of the general population in this age group have diagnosed mental-health disorders. These Kauai data represent a staggering difference between the children of the island and the general population and it shows that these children were clearly high-risk kids as Werner and Smith supposed. But most surprising in their study was that in spite of their risk factors, many of them turned out relatively fine. As I discussed in chapter 4, there are three basic factors—risk factors, resiliency factors, and protective factors. What the Kauai study teaches us is the importance of protective factors. These children faced nearly all the risk factors I've addressed in other chapters and many of these children had few resiliency factors. But the nature of their community showed the dramatic effect protective factors can have in the face of increased risk and marginal resiliency.

Werner and Smith identified three major protective factors that helped children cope with their circumstances. These three protective factors were family, school, and community. These protective factors appeared to have an ability to interrupt negative outcomes and enable individuals to navigate life stressors. Most significant were family ties. In infancy, close contact with the primary caregiver was imperative and its effects extended into adulthood. The most resilient children in adulthood were those who had the fewest prolonged separations from primary caregivers in the first year of life. This close bond extended beyond infancy. The most resilient children were those who had lots of positive attention during infancy and childhood and that attention could also come from close friends or "a male family member who served as a role model." Even participation in extracurricular activities was related to resilience, apparently because it provided some of the same individualized attention that one might otherwise get from a primary caregiver.

The data showed interesting gender differences in the effects of poverty and parental caregiving deficits. During the first decade of life, the boys were more vulnerable than girls to the effects of poverty and poor parental care, but during the teen years the trend reversed. There was another interesting gender difference. The educational level of the parent had a differential effect on girls and boys. In general, resilient children are more likely to have educated parents, but this study demonstrated that educational level of the opposite-sex parent was most crucial—a mother's educational level for boys, and a father's educational level for girls.

In summary, strong, caring families that have high expectations of their children were very important. A loving family can be the saving grace for a child in the midst of trauma. Caring families teach children how to deal with difficulties and frustrations rather than leaving the child to fend for himself as he works through crises, and family serves as the front line for social support. In the absence of strong families, quality schools with caring teachers or close-knit communities where children can be mentored and where their emotional needs can be met by surrogates make up for family deficits. It has been repeatedly shown that teachers can be a very powerful influence on children who lack mentoring and direction at home. School also provides overt instruction in problem solving, conflict resolution, and critical thinking skills. Religious organizations can provide some of the same protective factors that schools provide. Youth ministers, pastors, priests, and rabbis can all be mentors, provide leadership, teach coping skills, and so forth. Boys' and girls' clubs, scouting, and other social clubs can also be lumped into this same category. They provide children with the opportunity to act upon their environment, take control over their own lives, be mentored, and they can see successes in their endeavors. Werner and Smith's study clearly demonstrates the importance of family and community involvement.

SEVEN LIES THAT PREVENT GROWTH

Protective factors provide children with the tools they need to take action in their lives and they provide the hope that is necessary to endure trauma. But the mind is a powerful tool. Even in the presence of protective factors, counterproductive voices in one's head can stunt the positive effect of protective factors. These voices, while not audible, are self-defeating. They come from many places such as the messages we've been given from friends or family or the negative thoughts we generate ourselves when our frail egos whisper negative thoughts in our ears. There are seven damaging lies, myths if you will, that people listen to that allow them to be defeated by their difficulties.

Lie #1: I am a helpless victim; I cannot act; and there are no solutions. This lie describes the person who is dominated by the feeling "I can't." I've been a college professor for more than 20 years and I've spent an equal number of years working with children in school settings. In both arenas, I come across learning disabilities with some regularity. I do not deny they exist. Some people clearly have learning disabilities that complicate their normal ability to function in the academic setting. What I have noticed, however, is that the students who cope most poorly with their learning disabilities are the ones who use their disability as a reason not to try. One student's mother demanded to meet with me as the campus psychologist one year. Her son, a freshman, had a series of learning disabilities and she provided a folder full of documents she had collected throughout his school career. It even included a letter she had written to the governor of her home state, petitioning his intervention in a school situation because of her son's disabilities. She wanted to meet with me to explain, as she had done with every teacher since the boy started grade school, why her son couldn't do a variety of academic tasks.

I met with the young man and his mother. I asked him what he thought about his disabilities. His mother answered for him. She told me that because of his learning disabilities he was unable to take notes effectively, distinguish important information in the reading from that which was less important, and concentrate well enough to study for tests. She added that he also had trouble taking tests because he got nervous. It was obvious to me that his life was dominated by a theme of "I can't."

"I don't doubt your difficulties," I said to the young man. "I will be happy to accommodate you if I can while you are a student here; however, you have to make a decision right now. You have four years of college to learn to overcome your deficits. When you graduate and eventually get a job, you cannot rely on your mother to go to your boss and explain why you don't get your work done, can't show up on time, or why you can't do a variety of things your job requires." He stared at me as if I was speaking French and he clearly had no idea what I was talking about. He had accepted his disability as synonymous with "I can't" and he was comfortable being helpless even though he was capable. Not surprising, this student dropped out after one semester.

Less resilient people accept their status as victims and do nothing to move beyond their present circumstances. I've seen this many times in homicide cases I've investigated. Victims believe that since their attackers are stronger than they are, they don't have a chance. Many of these victims simply put their heads down and prepare to die. In my book *Blind-Sided*, I describe the story of a young man in the library at the Columbine High School who survived that deadly shooting. Just days after the incident he was interviewed by a national network. He described hiding under a table when one of the shooters put a shotgun to his head. The boy said, "I just closed my eyes and waited to die." When I heard this I couldn't believe my ears. Even as he was retelling his story, this young man didn't see the obvious opportunity for action. The gun barrel was within inches of his head—well within his reach. He may have been hurt or even killed if he had tried to fight back, but at least he would have had a chance. Fortunately, the gun misfired and the shooter did not try a second time. Likewise, I've studied many hostages or kidnap victims who passed up golden opportunities to escape because they didn't believe they could.

This kind of learned helplessness differentiates resilient people from less resilient ones. The less resilient person doesn't bother to try—kind of like a college freshman waiting for mommy to fix it for him. In contrast, the resilient subjects in the Kauai study saw themselves as capable and determined. "The overwhelming majority of the resilient individuals considered their personal competence and determination to be their most effective resource in dealing with stressful life events. One of the resilient women, a daughter of an abusive mother, expressed her conviction succinctly: 'I am a fighter—I am determined—I will survive. I give 100 percent before I give up.'" Resilient people see solutions where others might see nothing. In the late 1970s I was a novice mountain climber. The first experience I had on a major technical climb was a 200-foot vertical wall in east Tennessee. My fellow climbers and I looked at the wall and saw a sheer cliff face. Yet our instructor helped us see that there were footholds and handholds everywhere. We just didn't know how to look for them. Solutions were right in front of us as clear as day when we knew how to look for them.

THINK INSTEAD: The voice resilient people hear in their heads is "I am powerful and can take control of my situation—I am a person of action. I am not a victim—I have power to take action and there are always solutions before me. Logic, intention, decisiveness, and action are my allies."

Lie #2—I am alone and I must do it on my own. There is a difference between being alone and being lonely. A person can easily be lonely in a room full of people. A person who feels he or she belongs can be alone without being lonely. Nobody wants to face life in isolation. It is antithetical to the human condition. We are social. When we see a great movie, hear a good joke, or enjoy a beautiful sunset, we want to share it with someone. That is why we take pictures, send postcards, and try to remember jokes. These events have the most meaning for us in the context of our relationships. One of the most important skills in counseling is being a good listener. People want to be *heard and understood by someone else.*

If one simply wanted to get a problem off of his chest, he could talk to his dog, the wall, or himself. Sharing who we are with each other and having others share with us helps us find a place in life.

But less resilient people feel like they must face life's troubles alone. When they are in distress, the time they need others the most, is the time when their loneliness overwhelms them. Every client I've ever had who was suicidal felt alone, yet each and every one of them was surrounded by loving friends and family. While many of their family systems were dysfunctional and some of their friendships were less than ideal, there were at least people there who were willing to help see them through their dark hours. Yet for some reason these suicidal patients were unwilling or unable to see them. On the other hand, resilient people see their experiences in the context of the world in which they belong. Remember Murray Lynn? His drive to survive was in part driven by his need to tell his story because he believed he had a place in the world that mattered. Minna Hong wanted to survive because of her children. Thoughts of her parents drove Tammy Legg when she might otherwise have given up. People matter and they give our lives meaning.

Messages that "we don't fit in" come from many directions. Parents who abuse or neglect their children are teaching them that they don't matter—that they have no place. Think of Dave Pelzer. An "It" has no place. But we get these messages from our culture as well. Western culture is highly materialistic. Materialism errantly teaches that happiness comes from possessions—high salaries, boats, big houses, and fancy cars. Yet none of these things have much meaning without someone with whom to share them. It isn't that possessions are bad in and of themselves, but too often people seek possessions in lieu of relationships. They spend their careers at work at the expense of their families. It is hard to balance both and the consequences are telling. Tim Kasser, author of *The High Price of Materialism*, provides an eye-opening look at American culture. He notes a direct relationship between nurturing mothers and teens who were materialistic. The more materialistic teens had mothers who were less nurturing. These teens apparently tried to replace the nurturance of family with possessions. On the other hand, teens who placed value on relationships, self-acceptance, and contributing to their community had more nurturing mothers. Possessions are never as satisfying as relationships. Kasser notes, "Materialistic values lead people into a style of life and way of experiencing that do a rather poor job of satisfying their needs." In his hierarchy of needs, Maslow identifies 16 characteristics of self-actualized people—those who are theoretically the most mature. One of those characteristics is that self-actualized people have relatively few friends, but those relationships are deep and meaningful. Perhaps this is why the children in the Kauai study were more resilient when they had caring parents, a caring teacher, or a caring mentor of some kind. There was someone who helped them find a place. Believing one has a place in community insulates him or her from feelings of isolation. As proof of the power of community, the resilient but high-risk subjects who had grown up in poverty still considered themselves "happy and satisfied with their adult accomplishments" even more so than their "affluent peers."

THINK INSTEAD: I am not alone. There is someone who cares about me and who makes life worth living.

Lie #3—The reality I perceive is the only possible reality. Vulnerable trauma victims see their circumstances from only one perspective. In effect, they see only one possible reality or interpretation of a situation. This is exceedingly limited as you will see in a moment, but first I need to address the concept of "reality." There are some interesting directions we could go with the issue of reality. Multiple realities, equality of realities, or even the existence of reality could all be a part of the philosophical discussion, but for the sake of simplicity I propose the importance of the concept of plurality of realities. In short, at any one moment there are a number of realities, or perhaps it is better to say "potential" realities. Consider this situation: in 1991, the Atlanta Braves were playing the Minnesota Twins in the World Series. In the second game of the series, Ron Gant crushed the ball into left field. The throw came to third where Lonnie Smith slid into the bag. The throw was high and the backup tried to catch Gant at first as he rounded the bag. Minnesota first baseman Kent Hrbek (pronounced Herbeck) awaited the throw as Gant rushed back to the bag. As he reached first base, it appeared that Hrbek actually pulled Gant off the bag and tagged him. A player cannot pull a base runner off of the bag, but the first-base official, Drew Coble, ruled Gant was out. He argued that Gant's momentum, not Hrbek, had caused him to be off the bag. Slow-motion replay made it clear that Hrbek almost certainly pulled Gant off the bag, but the call was made and it was a call that had a dramatic effect on the outcome of the game as well as the World Series. If Gant had not been called out, instead of losing the game by one, the Braves would likely have been up by one run at the end of the game. Instead, the Braves lost the World Series three games to four—a heartbreaking loss for Braves fans.

Set aside your biases for a minute if you are a Braves or Twins fan and ask yourself whether Gant was safe or out. The difficulty in answering the question demonstrates the plurality of realities. The replay clearly showed that the runner was pulled off the bag and was, by the rules of the game, safe. However, the official called him out. Therefore, by the rules of the game he was out. It is oxymoronic to say that Gant was definitely safe *and* definitely out, but this is what the plurality of realities is all about. The reality of "out" or "safe" is only a potential reality. There is no single "real" reality. If you don't believe me, sit and listen to two sports fans arguing such a call and you will quickly see that neither fan will concede because they are operating in different realities. In that game in 1991, once the call was made as all Braves fans found out that day, the only reality that mattered in regard to the outcome of the game was that Gant was out. The old umpire saying, "They ain't nothing 'til I call 'em" refers to a single reality, but it changes nothing about other realities that can clearly be seen in replays.

So what does this foray into baseball history have to do with trauma? The fact is that there are many ways an event can be perceived. There is no single reality. We choose the reality that serves us best. Twins fans are served by the reality that Gant was out so they are more likely to accept that reality. On the other hand, Braves fans are better served by arguing for a competing reality—that Gant was safe. For example, over the several years that I interviewed Minna Hong and other spinal-injury victims, I walked the halls of Shepherd Spinal Center in Atlanta many times. I've seen many spinal-injury patients. Some of them are paralyzed from the neck down and can only get around with the assistance of a wheelchair they control by puffing on a tube located near their mouth. Others with lower spinal injuries, like Minna, can get around in wheelchairs or sometimes even with a walker. Some of them were injured in car accidents; others were crime victims; some had falls from bicycles or all-terrain vehicles (ATVs), accidents in swimming pools, or accidental injury during medical procedures. Regardless of the causes of their injuries and regardless of the extent of their disabilities, these patients have to learn life over. Was the accident that caused the injury a bad thing? Common sense says of course it was. Yet that is only one possible reality and research tells us that many people in this situation are actually glad the accident happened. Remember Tedeschi's research from the preface of this book? As many as 25 percent of those who experienced trauma would not change anything if they could go back. That is an amazing figure. As odd as it seems, research is clear that a large portion of the people who have experienced a variety of forms of trauma experience change for the positive. In his book *Shocks to the System: Psychotherapy of Traumatic Disability Syndromes,* Laurence Miller calls trauma an "existential wake-up call," and Tedeschi and Calhoun, in their 1996 research, identify three major categories of benefits of trauma—positive changes in self, positive changes in relationships, and changed life philosophies. They grow from their experiences and, therefore, they can look back on their experiences as positive turning points in their lives.

As a therapist, it is important for me to differentiate between legitimate growth and illusionary growth. With legitimate growth, patients recognize the difficulties that face them, as did Minna Hong, but they do not let the truth of their difficulties defeat them and they are able to see the positive circumstances that have arisen because of their traumas. The illusion of growth occurs when patients deny the difficulties that they face altogether. For example, researchers Davis and McKearney note that "reminders of death in conjunction with a threat to one's benign view of the world lead people to exaggerate the extent to which their life seems meaningful. It is argued that in the context of loss, people may actively seek positives or gains to defend against mortality threats engendered by the experience, and, if found, serve to promote the belief that life is meaningful." In other words, these subjects appeared to experience growth when they were actually fooling themselves in an attempt to cope with their pain. It is almost certain that patients like these will experience relapse in their PTSD symptomology later because they have not dealt with the issues their traumas presented. Instead, they would have simply found a way to accommodate to their discomfort in something that writer John Preston calls the "zone of emotional tolerance."

In contrast to those who have posttraumatic growth, nonresilient people worry about events even before they happen. They create negative realities in advance. In his book of survivor stories, John Preston notes that less resilient people don't recognize that "'possible' doesn't mean probable." Worriers believe that "a bad outcome absolutely will happen, i.e., to see bad outcomes in terms of probabilities rather than possibilities." These nonresilient victims worry in advance and when something bad actually does happen, they accept a single reality, that the trauma was an awful thing, and refuse to look at it in any other way.

Resilient people do not enjoy their difficulties, but from many potential realities they choose a functional one. In therapy, we call this reframing. Patients who only have a single frame—or reality—through which they see their experience are limiting themselves to the consequences of that reality. Imagine if Coach Bobby Cox and the Braves could have had the power to choose their own reality in 1991. What would they have chosen? In fact, the reality of "out at first" was thrust upon them in terms of the outcome of the game, but we do not have such choices forced upon us like this very often. We can choose the frame through which we see life.

In the fall of 2008, my carpool partner and I made an agreement that we would both try to go a full week without complaining. My friend wasn't a complainer by nature so I don't know that our deal was much of a challenge for him, but I had to work pretty hard at it. That week made me aware of how often an observation was really a complaint and how much negative thinking could dominate my thoughts. As my friend and I drove to and from work, there were spans of time where nothing was said as we both realized we might otherwise have been complaining. At the end of the week I suggested we try another week. I liked the challenge and I wanted to be more positive. One week gave way to another and eventually we made it a permanent deal. I don't regret it. It not only makes me more fun to be around, but the attitude has shaped the way I see the circumstances of life. As "Garrison Keillor put it, 'Some luck lies in not getting what you thought you wanted but getting what you have, which once you have got it you may be smart enough to see is what you would have wanted had you known.'"

THINK INSTEAD: Even the most dismal situation holds possibilities. I will look for the best possibilities in events rather than the limitations they present.

Lie #4: The reality of the past is better than the present reality. Vulnerable victims are more comfortable living in the past than in the present. Their thoughts are possessed by "what ifs." They rue what is lost and dwell on things that cannot be changed. Suppose Joe Simpson had believed this lie. As he lay injured on an ice cliff in a crevasse in the cold air of the Peruvian Andes, he would have lamented his decision to climb that day, the decision to climb the west face, and his decision to descend by the north face. Perhaps he would have regretted his decision to attempt an ascent on the day he did with bad weather threatening or maybe he would have regretted selecting Simon Yates as his climbing partner. As he complained, rued, worried, and lamented his past decisions, he would have frozen to death or died of exposure and dehydration. But these questions, while they may have entered his mind, did not possess him.

One of the major criticisms of psychoanalysis as a mode of therapy is that it spends too much time dwelling on the past—things that cannot be changed. As a reaction to psychoanalytic theory, action-oriented theories like cognitive-behavioral therapy (CBT) have become quite popular and research indicates they are among the most effective treatments available. Action-oriented therapies work in part because the therapist doesn't allow patients to wallow in self-pity. The therapist forces patients into the here-and-now. They are forced even to use sentences in the present tense—"I am" instead of "I was." The past matters when it comes to understanding who you are, why you made the decisions you made, and how you might use that knowledge to make better decisions in the future, but we cannot remain stuck in the past.

THINK INSTEAD: The past is part of me, but it doesn't control me or determine my future.

Lie #5: I am injured so I am finished. During my firearms training course at the FBI Academy, our instructor made this statement: "You have to remember that just because you are shot, doesn't mean you are dead." He went on to describe several cases of law-enforcement officers who had been shot, some even blinded by their injuries, but who refused to quit and actually subdued their perpetrators despite their injuries. He was trying to teach us not to quit. If one's vision in damaged, rely more heavily on your other senses. If one's dominant hand is injured, shoot back with your weaker hand. Simpson portrayed this characteristic beautifully. His broken leg was completely useless, but he slid, hopped, and crawled instead of sitting and waiting for help that would never come. He used the assets he had rather than worrying about assets he had lost. This type of thinking is exceedingly challenging in the face of almost certain death. There were several times during Simpson's ordeal that he was certain he would die, but he continued to try. When he realized Simon had cut the rope, he thought he was going to die. When he realized he could not climb back up the crevasse, he thought he would die. Climbing downward, unable to see the bottom of the crevasse and with limited amount of rope, something that was completely counterintuitive, he assumed he would die. As he faced the rock field, he supposed he could never make it, but he tried anyway. As he approached base camp, he was almost certain no one would be there. Yet in all these situations, on top of pain, hunger, thirst, and delirium, he still kept going. His injury was a limitation, not a conclusion.

THINK INSTEAD: Injury doesn't mean death. I will find ways to function around the difficulties my injuries present.

Lie #6: The solution for my problem must be pain-free. A sad truth is that healing is often preceded by pain. Many times in my therapy room I've worked with patients who were functioning fairly well in their dysfunctional lives. Their marriages were a wreck; they were unhappy in their jobs, family lives, or other relationships; and many of them had serious traumas in their respective pasts, but they were able to put on a good front and make it through each day. In essence, they were faking it every day they got out of bed. In therapy, however, we can't fake it and as we started dredging up the causes of their troubles, it brought their pain to the surface. Many patients resist therapy at this point. In the early stages of therapy they wonder why they should go to therapy and end up feeling worse than they did before it started. But the answer is obvious. Facing pain is like excising an infected wound. Pain leads to growth and healing, but less resilient people unrealistically believe that the world should be pain-free. Resilient people, on the other hand, recognize that pain is preferable to death.

In 2003, the United States was stunned by the story of a 27-year-old man who was hiking alone in a desert area known as Bluejohn Canyon in Utah. While climbing between rocks in a gorge, a boulder rolled onto his arm trapping him. He was alone with minimal water and food. Nobody knew where he was and it was impossible to move the 800-pound rock. After seven days and nights of chipping away at the rock with a pocketknife in an attempt to free his arm, he realized his arm was hopelessly trapped. His tissue was decomposing and his only hope of escape was to cut off his own arm at the elbow. The knife was too dull to cut through bone so after severing the skin, he broke the bones of his forearm using the boulder as a lever. The very thing that imprisoned him was an asset he used to free himself. Once freed, he then had to hike out of the canyon, including a 60-foot rappel and a 5-mile hike, all with only one arm until he was discovered by other hikers. His story was broadcast worldwide. People could not understand how anyone could have the courage to do such a thing. I propose that such courage is present in many of us. We just don't tap into it.

Simpson displayed this same courage. He dragged, pushed, and hopped on his shattered leg for days. The pain must have been unbearable, but Simpson tapped into his survival instinct that taught him it was better to endure short-term pain and to live than to lie down and die. Fear of pain, the unknown, or loss of control is potentially paralyzing, but resilient people face their fears with courage. Many people choose to accept their current *known* situations, even when they are painful, unpleasant, or potentially fatal, rather than to risk stepping out into the unknown. The unknown is frightening. In a time of war, soldiers will sometimes shoot themselves or even commit suicide, because of their fear of battle. Ironic, isn't it? Fear of battle is the fear of pain, injury, or death, yet the individual risks all of these by doing it to himself. This demonstrates also the fear of being out of control. By taking control of the event oneself [shooting oneself], the individual at least has control over the type of injury and the timing of the injury. We've all experienced scary movies where we know the monster is going to jump out of the dark, but the scariest part is *waiting* for it to happen. Once we know when it's coming, such as if we've seen the movie before, it isn't as scary because our knowledge gives us control. Simpson faced his fears. He faced the fear of plunging further into the dark crevasse, the fear of reaching an empty base camp, and the fear of dying on the mountainside alone. Our fears lead us to believe that our current situation, even if it means death, is better than facing the unknown, and this in turn causes inaction.

THINK INSTEAD: Despite my pain, I will face my fears and act. I will not lie down and die and short-term pain is preferable to death. I will not let my fear of the unknown control me.

Lie #7: I can never forgive. Victoria Teague had a rough start in life. She was born into an emotionally distant family of substance abusers and from her early years she felt the need to perform to win attention and love. During her teen years she experienced the loss of her younger sister to cancer and her grandfather also passed away, the closest thing to a father-figure she had. Her emotional pain led her into a life of drugs and the culture that goes with it. For the next several years she drifted deeper and deeper into the drug culture, working as a stripper, and a prostitute. During this time she experienced several rapes, multiple abortions, and eventually found that her drug abuse was killing her. Her nose bled constantly and she weighed less than 90 pounds. Eventually she was fired as a stripper and she was on the street, homeless, addicted, and alone. A Christian couple took her into their home and helped her get her life back together. During those first months of recovery from drugs and her wild life of dancing and prostitution, she met a conservative Christian man who fell in love with her almost immediately despite her history. They married after only eight months together and for six months all was well, but soon Victoria found herself bored and unable to get a job. A chance meeting with a friend in Atlanta led to a drink together in a bar. That meeting led to cocaine use and a relapse into the drug culture and the sexually risky behavior she had known before. For six weeks she strayed, engaging in relationships with several men, using drugs, and often staying away from home for days. Instead of giving up on her and moving on with life as most people would have done in a similar situation, her husband came looking for her. He patiently waited at home when he couldn't find her and he prayed for her when she was absent. One night she came home late. The house was quiet and dark, but on the piano was a letter addressed to Diana, her dancing name. It was from her husband. He told her he loved her as Victoria and that he was committed to her; he would wait for her and he would be her husband and friend for life. This unconditional love and forgiveness was a turning point for her and she came home for good.

It may be that his motive for hunting for his straying wife had something to do with him being a needy person who could not bear to be alone, but I think his motive was something different. He was willing to forgive the unforgivable and his behavior had an incredible impact on Victoria. If a marriage can overcome that kind of difficulty, it came overcome anything. For 18 years since that time they have been happily married and Victoria runs a mission to strippers called Victoria's Friends.

Forgiveness is a powerful tool for both the forgiver and the forgiven. Forgiveness makes it possible for both to put the past behind them. Simpson had every right to be angry with Simon Yates for cutting him loose, but he held no grudge. Even on the mountainside, he was willing to let it go—one big step toward healing.

THINK INSTEAD: Letting go is up to me.

THE CASE OF THEO

Flip back to chapter 4 and find tables 4.1 through 4.3. Keep your finger there as we consider the case of Theo. I first met him when he was 13 years old. Theo had been sent to the residential care facility where I was working. In and out of trouble for much of his childhood, he had been convicted in juvenile court of breaking into a neighbor's house and for possession of marijuana. According to his documentation, his IQ was round 65—a range that is considered mild retardation. Theo was adopted by his parents when he was just a baby. No information was available about his birth parents, but we had lots of information about his adoptive family and his situation there. Theo was adopted at just a few weeks of age. There were no birth complications and everything seemed normal. His parents were eager to be good parents and to give their new baby the best of everything they could afford. In their zeal, they began pushing him into developmental milestones that he wasn't ready for. Some children, especially boys, just aren't ready to be potty trained by age two like many children and Theo was one of those kids. Often when children are forced into potty training, it actually takes longer to succeed than if their parents would simply have been more patient. As it was, Theo wasn't fully potty trained even at age four. By age three, his parents were pushing him to read and, again, he wasn't ready. He was physically and cognitively delayed in his development but still within the normal range for children his age, yet his eager parents were certain something was wrong so they had him tested by a psychologist.

It was discovered that Theo had an IQ of 65 and his parents were devastated. Their dreams of a future doctor, president, or Nobel laureate faded away as soon as they heard the diagnosis "mild retardation." All of this was unfortunate for Theo. His parents weren't aware, and the psychologist didn't tell them, that any IQ measure before age eight is highly unreliable. This is why most school systems begin standardized testing around third grade—when most children are around eight years of age and their IQs have stabilized. From the point of his diagnosis, Theo's parents began treating him as if he were mentally retarded and, perhaps more importantly, as if "mild retardation" meant "completely incompetent and oblivious to his surroundings." They talked about Theo as if he weren't there; they were condescending to him; and they had zero expectations from him. For example, in one interaction our staff had with his parents during his intake, we noticed his hair was poorly cut, his clothes were too small for him, and they didn't match. When we inquired about this with his parents, in Theo's presence they told us, "He's retarded, he doesn't know any difference." The few times when we saw them talk directly to Theo, they spoke to him almost as if they were addressing a family pet.

When Theo started kindergarten, he was automatically tracked as a special needs child and placed in special education classrooms with children who had profound learning disabilities, physical disabilities, behavior problems, and moderate and severe mental retardation. When children are slow to develop, they often begin catching up with their peers by grade three or four, but by placing Theo in special education, they set a standard of functioning significantly below his innate abilities. He was actually above average in a below-average classroom so nothing more was expected of him. Theo was capable of catching up with his peers developmentally, but his parents had already determined for him that he would never amount to much and that is exactly what they got. As he got older, he began to learn unproductive behavior patterns from the behavior-disordered children in his classroom. His misbehavior generalized outside the school setting and before he ever finished grade school he already had a juvenile record. By the time he reached middle school he was skipping school, smoking pot, and vandalizing homes in subdivisions under construction. Throughout his childhood it appears his parents were indifferent to his behavior. While they were good community members and professional people in the workplace, they supposed there was nothing they could do about their "little retarded boy" except pay fines and damages and to make apologies for him. By the time he came to us, he was pubescent, used to being ignored, and his behavior was out of control.

Now look back at table 4.1 from chapter 4. While his parents had no other children and their income was respectable, Theo saw none of the benefits of these two advantages. The benefit of a small family is unlimited personal interaction with caregivers, and a large income provides an academic advantage. Neither of these advantages worked in Theo's favor. His parents, while they were good human beings and they were in no way intentionally malicious, were indeed neglectful. They didn't see any point in spending too much time with Theo any more than one might feel obligated to spend time with a goldfish. Spending money on educational toys, puzzles, reading, or educational programming, things their affluence could easily have allowed, never crossed their minds. Theo was at risk in other ways, as well. His IQ was low; he spent hours entertaining himself sitting in front of a television, time that could have been spent reading books, going on walks with mom, and learning if his parents hadn't believed him to be mentally challenged. At least 6 of the 10 risk factors apply to Theo.

Now look at table 4.2. Space doesn't allow me to cover all 25 resiliency factors and it would be a little boring if I did, but I'll summarize by noting that Theo did not have a single resiliency factor. He had no coping or problem-solving skills, almost no motivation to help himself, few social skills, and understandably, his self-image was nearly nonexistent. For example, in one interchange with Theo at the group home where I worked, we were in a kitchen doing dishes together. Theo became agitated, grabbed a carving knife from the counter, and swung it at me. I easily took the knife away from him and neither of us was injured, but I said, "Theo, what were you thinking!" His response to me was, "I don't know any better. I'm retarded." Notice two things about his response. First, he quickly resorted to an excuse for his behavior that he had heard his entire life. He made no attempt to examine his behavior, introspect, or seek more productive options to deal with his frustrations. He simply said what his mother always said. Second, and equally chilling in terms of resiliency, he had no personal sense of efficacy—the belief that he could succeed at things he attempted. Even his weak attempt to cut me with a knife was half-hearted. He assumed before he ever picked it up that he wouldn't succeed and, fortunately for me, he didn't.

Now look at table 4.3 and let's look at what protective factors applied to Theo. Remember, even in the face of significant risk factors and with few resiliency factors, children still have a chance if they have protective factors in their environment. But as luck would have it, Theo didn't have any. While his parents were good people, they did not provide a loving and protective environment for Theo. Their expectations for Theo were not low—they were nonexistent. Theo was never allowed to engage in any social support system like boy scouts, church youth group, or athletics that might have mitigated his parents' negligence. If he had, Theo might have developed a social support network and he might have found successes in life, but as it was, he had neither. Of the 13 protective factors, at least 10 of them were absent for Theo.

From the point he was diagnosed as a mildly mentally challenged child, Theo didn't have a chance. He was faced with huge risk factors while at the same time his life was void of resiliency and protective factors. Given these facts, suppose it were Theo descending the north face of Siula Grande and suppose it were Theo who fell over a precipice and shattered his leg. Would he have survived? Almost certainly not. His response to his situation would be, "I'm retarded. I can't climb. I can't help myself." The seven lies would have been loud and clear in Theo's head. He would have seen himself as helpless (Lie #1) and alone (Lie #2). He would have seen the bleak chance for survival just as Joe Simpson did, but Theo would never have allowed his imagination to suppose there was any other way to look at the situation (Lie #3). He would have wondered why he was ever so stupid as to go mountain climbing (Lie #4) and he would have seen his injury as an impossible hurdle to overcome (Lie #5). He would never have pushed himself to endure pain for his own good and his fear would have paralyzed him (Lie #6). While he might have been forgiving (Lie #7), he never would have survived to forgive. He wouldn't have assessed his assets and most likely he would have died dangling from 150 feet of rope.

This sounds deterministic and I concede that it is possible that I'm wrong, but I doubt it. As I tell my statistics students, many things are *possible,* but few things are *likely.* Think about how safe air travel is, for example. You have probably heard the statistic that a person is more likely to die in a car crash on the way to the airport than to die in an airplane crash. While it is possible that we might die in a plane crash, it isn't statistically very likely unless we make a habit of flying with inexperienced pilots, unsafe aircraft, or in unsafe conditions. The conditions of air travel today predispose it to be relatively safe. In the same way, while it is possible Theo could have been as courageous as Joe Simpson, it just isn't very likely because the conditions predisposed him to fail. Sadly, Theo would never have the courage, adventuresome nature, or resources to be on Siula Grande in the first place. His world was much too small for that. He was faced with little traumas every day. He was incarcerated, away from his family; he had no friends; and he perceived himself as having no skills or abilities. Like all of us he had to face the troubles of life—wishes that don't come true, relationships that don't work out, and dreams that don't pan out as one might have hoped. Instead of facing these mini-traumas with courage, Theo faced them with the same tools he would have faced a trauma like Joe Simpson's in Peru. He gave up. If he had by some chance found himself injured on a mountainside, he would have metaphorically half-heartedly pulled a knife on a staff member. He would have lain down and died because he couldn't do any better since he was retarded.

Theo's story ends on a very sad note. Even though the staff of the facility where I worked tried to offset 13 years of negative messages and neglect, by the time he came to us we were very limited in what we could do. We tested him and found his IQ to actually be in the low 90s—on the lower end of average, but certainly not retarded—but neither his parents nor Theo would believe us. The social skills we attempted to teach Theo were undone each time he got a weekend pass and went home. By age 16 when he was released from our facility he went home but didn't finish high school. Instead, he spent his days in front of the television just as he had done in his childhood. With no self-regulation skills, few life skills, no mentor, and the hormones of a teenager, Theo quickly followed his sexual urges. He sexually molested several children before he was caught and sent to prison. He remains in prison today.

CONCLUDING COMMENTS

So why do some people survive despite seemingly insurmountable difficulties and others are derailed by what appear to be relatively minor setbacks? This may be the most important therapeutic question we can ask. In 2004, my dear friend of 20 years was arrested and eventually sent to prison for a crime of his own doing. He was guilty. He lost his family, nearly all of his friends, his career, and his reputation. He was financially ruined. For those first few years after his arrest I watched him in disbelief. He held his head up and accepted his fate, but he refused to be beaten. Today he is out of prison, remarried, and leading a very happy life. (This story is recounted in my book *Handcuffed: A Friendship Of Endurance.*) In the many years I've been a psychologist, I've seen people crumble under the weight of any one of these things—divorce, financial stress, loss of reputation, loss of a job. The difference between my friend and those clients I've seen fall and refuse to get up is that my clients believed the lies that prevent healing and growth. My friend did not believe these lies.

The research on resiliency is encouraging. As Bonnie Bernard notes, "While one in four children of alcoholic parents develops alcohol problems, three of four do not. Resiliency is more common than we might suppose." If more people would refuse to listen to the lies that prevent growth, we might find our lives a little easier to manage. Most of us don't experience the kind of trauma you've read about in this book, but these same skills for surviving trauma can help us in daily living. Resilient people will be just a little better in school; they might handle broken relationships just a little better; and perhaps resilient people will work through the normal, nontraumatic issues of life better.

REFERENCES

Bernard, B. (1991). *Fostering resiliency in kids: Protective factors in family, school, and community.* Portland, OR: Western Regional Center for Drug-Free

Schools and Communities, Retrieved December 3, 2009, from http://www.archive.org/stream/fosteringresilie00benarich/fosteringresilie00benarich_djvu.txt.

Boyum, R. (2008). Characteristics of a self-actualizing person. *Selfcounseling.com.* Retrieved December 3, 2009, from http://www.selfcounseling.com/help/personalsuccess/selfactualization.html.

Davis, C. G, & McKearney, J. M. (2003). How do people grow from their experience with trauma or loss? *Journal of Social & Clinical Psychology, 22,* 477–493, p. 477.

Kasser, T. (2002). *The high price of materialism.* Cambridge, MA: The MIT Press.

Krumboltz, J. D., & Levin, A. S. (2004). *Luck is no accident: Making the most of happenstance in your life and career.* Atascadero, CA: Impact Publishers, p. 44.

Livingston, G. (2004). *Too soon old, too late smart.* New York: Marlowe and Company, p. xvi.

Miller, L. (1998). *Shocks to the system: Psychotherapy of traumatic disability syndromes.* New York: W. W. Norton & Company, p. 284.

Powell, S., Rosner, R., Butolo, W., Tedeschi, R. G., & Calhoun, L. G. (2003). Posttraumatic growth after war: A study with former refugees and displaced people in Sarajevo. *Journal of Clinical Psychology, 59,* 72–83, p. 72.

Preston, J. (2002). *Survivors: Stories & strategies to heal the hurt.* Atascadero, CA: Impact Publishers.

Tedeschi, R. G. (2003, March). The paradox of trauma: Learning how to live well. Invited address, 26th Annual Convention of the Behavioral Sciences, University of Georgia, Athens, GA.

Werner, E. E., & Smith, R. S. (1992). *Overcoming the odds: High risk children from birth through adulthood.* Ithaca, NY: Cornell University Press.

8

———•◦•◦•———

HOPE FOR THE HURTING: CLINICAL INTERVENTION AND RECOVERY

Man is not upset by things, but instead it is what
he makes of the thing.

—Epictetus

There is nothing either good or bad,
but thinking makes it so.

—*Hamlet* (act 2, scene 2)

Chandrae was 14 when I first met her. She had been removed from her home by child protective services (CPS). Her mother left when she was a toddler and until CPS intervened, she had lived with her father, an alcoholic and a gambler. Chandrae was absolutely beautiful with an innocent face that concealed her hard life, yet she looked far more mature than her 14 years. She could easily have passed for 19, a fact that wasn't lost on her father and his friends, but despite her mature appearance she still had a developmental mind of an early adolescent. She regularly gained inappropriate male attention from her father's card buddies and even though it was never verified, at least two of them impregnated her—pregnancies that both ended in abortions before she was even 13 years old. She was a lonely girl who had no friends and no social life outside her father's weekend card games. Her self-image was nearly nonexistent. Each time she looked in the mirror, it was as if she were looking in a warped fun house mirror—her view of herself was so horribly distorted she truly couldn't see how lovely she was. She loved the attention from doting men, but at the same time she was repulsed by their sexual advances. More than once her father used her as a stake in one of his poker games. The winner shared her bed for the night.

Chandrae's life with dad came to an end late one Saturday night. The card game and drinking reached a fever pitch; two men argued over allegations of cheating; and weapons were drawn. A .38 caliber slug struck Chandrae in the thigh, barely missing her femoral artery. When she wore a swimsuit, you could see the scar where the bullet tore a hole in her upper leg. After a brief hospital stay, she was remanded into foster care where I met her.

Mary Beth was a 38-year-old mother of two girls ages 7 and 10. A real estate agent, Mary Beth had left her children with her husband for the weekend as she traveled to Chicago for a seminar. Her plan was to return home on Sunday night. She kissed her loving husband of 15 years good-bye at the airport curb and boarded her airplane. The weekend was not only informative for her career but a needed break from being a mom and full-time agent. But her break was short-lived when Sunday morning she saw the light flashing on her hotel room telephone. The message was from her father. She returned his call right away.

"There has been an accident. You need to come home," her father told her.

He explained that early that morning he had gotten a bad feeling. He hadn't heard from his grandchildren all weekend and he almost always talked to them on the phone on Saturday nights. Out of concern he dropped by the house. When he knocked on the front door of their house, the oldest girl came to the door. When she saw her grandfather, she leapt into his arms.

"Something is wrong with Daddy," she told her grandfather. He is in the basement.

Mary Beth's husband had apparently gone to the basement to run on an indoor treadmill on Friday night and died of a heart attack. The oldest girl had found him, but when she couldn't get a response from him, she panicked. The two children stayed alone in the house with their dead father the rest of the weekend until their grandfather arrived on Sunday morning. I worked with Mary Beth's youngest child as she tried to work through her fears, confusion, and worries about her experience. Anytime

I work with children, I try to also work with the parent. A healthy parent can often do much more for a child's progress than I can. In Mary Beth's case, she was a mess.

Although for very different reasons, both Chandrae and Mary Beth shared symptoms of posttraumatic stress. Both of them suffered normal grieving symptoms. Chandrae grieved the loss of her mother and father as well as the loss of her home. As dysfunctional as it was, home is still home and she was thrust into the sometimes cold and unforgiving foster-care system. Mary Beth's grief was obviously related to the loss of her husband, the loss of a father for her children, and fear regarding the effect the experience would have on her children. Compounding the trauma of losing her husband and her concern about her children's welfare, she had found disturbing evidence that her loving husband wasn't as faithful as she had always believed. On his computer she discovered numerous e-mail accounts under various names and in each of those accounts she found a number of e-mails from several women. "He had a great capacity to love," she explained to me, her eyes checking mine to see if I believed her interpretation of his straying behavior. She was angry, hurt, lonely, and afraid. She wasn't sleeping; her demeanor was agitated; and she was finding it difficult to eat. "I just start crying," she said to me. It would come with no warning. She would become overwhelmed when she thought of her children growing up without their father, and without her husband present to discuss the "capacity to love" issue, she was isolated and alone.

Both Chandrae and Mary Beth experienced something called "intrusive thinking" where they seemingly had no control over when, where, and how long thoughts of their respective experiences would invade their lives. Frequently, Chandrae would get in trouble at school for not paying attention when, in reality, she would much rather have been thinking about world history or algebra than the man who abused her the previous weekend. More than once Mary Beth sat through a green light at an intersection as thoughts of her husband's death and his apparent infidelity invaded her thinking. For both women, their intrusive thinking caused sleeplessness and bad dreams.

They both experienced episodes of depression, irritability, and hopelessness. This made it difficult for them to concentrate even on things that ordinarily brought them pleasure, and their depression and spacey behaviors interrupted their social relationship, making them even more isolated, alone, and depressed. Chandrae experimented with alcohol in an attempt to cope with her trauma, another symptom that is not uncommon in patients with PTSD. Mary Beth avoided the room where her husband's computer sat undisturbed after his death. She would not use the computer; she would not allow anyone else to use it; and she wouldn't even go into the room if she could avoid it. Chandrae also avoided reminders of her trauma. In therapy when we talked about what happened to her she would not say the words "rape," "sex," or "molestation." She only would say "it" in regard to her abuse. In fact, she couldn't even say her father's name. She referred to her father as "him." This kind of avoidance is understandable, but unhealthy.

People who experience trauma sometimes are hypersensitive to cues that remind them of their trauma. For example, Chandrae nearly became physically nauseated when she smelled tobacco on someone. The smoke itself wasn't a problem, but the smell of tobacco on someone's breath or clothes reminded her of painful hours lying in bed with men three times her age—all of whom were smokers. Mary Beth found herself confused that she became unusually agitated at the sight of any blinking light such as are common on microwave ovens and other appliances. Her agitation made sense when we discussed the conditioned response she must have experienced when she answered her telephone message at the Chicago hotel—a message indicated by a blinking red light.

It may seem odd, but both women also experienced guilt, another common PTSD symptom. Mary Beth felt guilty that she had taken her trip, that she hadn't picked up on her husband's behaviors before his death, and that she hadn't been what she called "a good enough wife" while he was alive. Chandrae felt guilty because her father, as well as several of the men who had molested her, ended up in jail. As horrible as their behaviors were, Chandrae still didn't want anything bad to happen to anyone and she felt responsible for their legal troubles and the financial devastation that followed. All of these guilt feelings are illogical, but not uncommon.

There are other symptoms of PTSD—anger, difficulty concentrating, numbness, hypervigilance, and even memory loss. A rape victim I once worked with had almost no memory at all of her attack. She suffered no head trauma and when depositions were being taken in preparation for her perpetrator's trial, his defense attorney made a major issue of the fact that she claimed she was raped but couldn't identify the man who attacked her in broad daylight. She wasn't even certain of the rapist's race. This normal

PTSD response concerned the district attorney enough that he chose not to take the case to trial.

But posttraumatic stress is only one of many threats to one's existence in the face of trauma. Victims like Chandrae and Mary Beth, if they fail to resolve their issues, face a number of psychological and social problems. Feelings of worthlessness, body-image problems, eating disorders, suicidal ideation, and sexual promiscuity as well as frigidity are not uncommon. Sleep disruption, bed wetting, anger and aggression, substance abuse, and high-risk behaviors (e.g., reckless driving) are also common symptoms of abuse and trauma. Confusion in future relationships and unwillingness to trust, a vital part of any healthy and satisfying relationship, could be permanently affected. Girls like Chandrae are also at greater risk for abusing her own children when they become mothers. A traumatized individual faces numerous other challenges, as well. Physical injury itself presents a number of challenges. Costs of recovery, physical therapy, doctor bills, modifications of the home when necessary, lost income, and the emotional stress that financial troubles bring can be overwhelming. Both the short- and long-term issues that trauma victims suffer give therapists plenty of work to do.

TREATMENT

The first time I met with Chandrae I could see guilt on her face. Even though she was the victim, she believed she was in trouble. After all, CPS took her away from home and forced her to live among strangers in a group-home situation; she had to share a room with a stranger; and she was required to meet with people like me—people she knew nothing about and whose motives or purpose she had no way of understanding. Like a five-year-old, she huddled in a chair across the room from me with her knees pulled up to her chin. Watching her big brown eyes, darkened with black eyeliner and green eye shadow, staring at me from behind her kneecaps, I realized the damage that her father and his cronies had done to her could take years to undo. I almost didn't know where to start. I was a young therapist, only an intern at the time, and nothing I had learned in school really prepared me for the situation I faced. I felt completely inadequate and I suspect Chandrae sensed my insecurity, but on the other hand, I was in my early twenties and to her I was an old man. She had no reason to trust me and I couldn't think of a good reason that she should trust me either. I did what I have learned to do many times since then when I am stuck. I was honest with her.

"I don't know what to say, Chandrae. You've had a tough time."

I left it at that. She watched me carefully. My hands were together in a prayer fashion, my fingertips gently pressing against my lower lip. She didn't say a word. For nearly 15 minutes we sat in silence. She was trying to wait me out. She was good at being stubborn and if I spoke first, not only would she win the battle (something of minimal importance to me), but more importantly I would have then set the pace for therapy—I'll talk and you respond. That is the last thing I wanted. Finally the quiet was too much for her and she spoke.

"So what are we supposed to do?"

"What would you like to do?" I asked.

"Smoke a cigarette."

She was testing me. She knew I couldn't allow that so she picked something that set me up to fail from the start—a common ploy among adolescents. Chandrae was angry at the world and I was part of it. This was the fastest way for her to prove that grown-ups don't really mean what they say. By being denied the one thing she asked for, she would then have ammunition to justify in her mind that I didn't really care about her.

"I didn't say you could do anything you wanted. I asked what you wanted to do."

"What difference does it make what I want. You'll just say no."

"Maybe so. You know the rules around here. What would you like to do that you know isn't against one of the rules? I want to let you choose."

Again she watched me. She wasn't sure what to do with my comments and she was trying to think of another way to make me fail.

"I want to talk to my dad," she said, looking confident that she had me in a corner.

"Great idea!" I said. I went to my lunch bag that was sitting one the floor in the corner and pulled out a banana. "Here, let's call him." I handed her the banana.

She looked at me with a combination of surprise and confusion, stifling a grin.

"We can't really call him, of course, but let's pretend," I said. "Here is your phone. Call him and say anything you want. This will work out great because you don't have to worry about what he might say back to you."

She took the banana and laughed at herself as she put it up to her head like a phone. She kept her eyes on me, waiting for me to tell her I was only joking, but I sat with a serious look on my face waiting earnestly for her to make the call. She chuckled and said it was stupid but she didn't put the banana down. Then the smile went away from her face and tears welled up in her eyes, which drifted off to some unseen distant place in the room.

"Daddy, you're an asshole," she said almost in a whisper and then she set the banana on the floor and turned away from me. Therapy had begun.

There are a number of approaches to treating patients like Chandrae and Mary Beth. But before I ever begin treatment, I have to ask myself if treatment is even necessary. The last thing I want to do is retraumatize a person through therapy if he/she is functioning well. I've seen a number of clients over the years whose symptoms were fairly mild and who appeared to be processing their experiences effectively with caregivers (i.e., parents), so I advised the parents to continue open communication with their children and, after giving them a number of warning signs to watch for, I suggested they call me if things changed for the worse. Numerous trauma studies have been conducted with refugee children. Refugee children are often studied because they are a quasi-captive audience, often living in refugee camps for years at a time, making tracking relatively easy. One such study showed that many PTSD symptoms in refugee children subsided over time without any professional intervention. In this study, these refugee children whose symptoms subsided were resettled. In other words, their lives were somewhat restored to normal. If I can help a trauma victim and the victim's family reestablish normalcy in life, formal therapeutic intervention may not be necessary. Stability of family life is essential. In fact, even professional intervention may be ineffective if the victim does not achieve some level of stability. In the refugee population, researchers have found that in the face of ongoing uncertainty (such as a threat of being deported), children do not respond well even when treated professionally. These studies are important to me and my decision-making, but I must also be aware that not all trauma is the same. Burn victims don't respond exactly the same as rape or assault victims, and children who witness violence do not respond the same as children who experience a natural disaster. Some research indicates that the type of trauma may have an effect on how people respond to it and how likely they are to suffer PTSD symptoms. For example, with everything else being relatively equal, refugee children whose parents were tortured and/or killed are at higher risk of developing long-term PTSD symptoms than refugee children whose parents were not killed. Again, the compounding loss of the parent most likely makes returning to a stable, predictable life more difficult. Therefore, researchers and clinicians must be careful about selecting treatment modalities given various forms of trauma.

In my initial intake interviews, I typically use the Global Assessment of Functioning Scale (GAFS) in the *Diagnostic and Statistical Manual IV— Text Revision* (DSM IV-TR) as a starting point to determine whether or not a child needs therapy. This scale, rated 0–100, gives the clinician a quick overview of how well a patient is functioning in life, regardless of diagnosis. The GAFS is important to me because if a person is functioning reasonably well, sometimes diagnosis doesn't matter and therapy may be unnecessary. However, clinicians must carefully search for PTSD symptoms despite apparent high levels of functioning. Some research has shown that people can function fairly well in spite of significant PTSD symptoms. An unskilled therapist could easily misinterpret high functioning as the lack of posttraumatic stress. For those victims that do need intervention, some may need medication to relieve symptoms of sleeplessness, agitation, and anxiety. Referral to a physician for medication is possible depending on how intrusive these symptoms are. However, medication will only treat the symptoms of PTSD, not the underlying causes.[1] The first step in the therapeutic process is to ensure that basic needs are met and ensure the safety of the home environment. This helps produce stability and reduces risk for retraumatization. Once that is done, the primary approach to treating PTSD is cognitive-behavioral therapy (CBT). CBT is a combination of behavioral intervention—exchanging unproductive behaviors and habits for more effective ones—and cognitive intervention—exchanging unproductive thinking patterns for more productive ones. Behaviorally, I want to help my clients identify habits and behaviors that are both helpful and hurtful to them. Removing the hurtful behaviors or replacing them with more productive habits is imperative. Cognitively, I help my clients think about their experiences in new ways. As you will see later in this chapter, *perspective* is everything. How we interpret what happens to us, in part, determines how we respond to it. Reframing as discussed below helps clients adopt a perspective that is more effective and functional. The third step in therapy is developing a strong social support system. The research is consistent that social support is a critical factor in healing and resilience. Fostering resiliency in traumatized individuals requires development of family support, such as a positive relationship with at least one parent and "environmental supports, including peers, teacher, nurse, and relatives." As much as possible, therefore, I include parents, spouses, siblings, and significant others in the therapeutic process. When they take ownership and participate, they are more likely to become a helpful part of the recovery process.

The sooner I can begin treating a person who has experienced trauma, especially children, the more positive the prognosis. In fact, I chose children as my clinical specialty while I was a graduate student. After seeing hundreds of adult clients in general mental-health settings who clearly were still suffering the effects of childhood trauma I realize that if I could have worked with them clinically when they were children, their lives very likely would have turned out very different. They may have chosen different careers, married different people, been more effective parents, and they probably would not have been sitting in a counselor's office at age 50.[2] Recent research confirms what I suspected more than two decades ago. It is recommended that intervention begin within 3–6 months of the trauma if possible and some research indicates that treatment should be "relatively short." Depending on the type of trauma and the client's motivation to work in therapy, 12 to 16 sessions are not uncommon. However, one form of CBT called "mindfulness-based cognitive therapy (MBCT)," may take half that time. The concept of this therapy, mainly meditation and/or prayer of some sort, may have the potential for treating various forms of PTSD. MBCT involves traditional CBT approaches, but also includes a form of meditation or prayer. It is relatively new and untested, but early indications are that MBCT is a good treatment for mild forms of depression and anxiety for those who are interested in a spiritual component to therapy. Spirituality is increasingly being studied in various areas of physical and psychological healing. Therapists are not pastors or priests, but early indications from the research are that spirituality provides victims with coping skills as well as strong social support.

Research is beginning to provide data on the effectiveness of Eye Movement Desensitization and Reprocessing (EMDR). This therapy, which requires specialized training by the clinician, involves eye movements, visual imagery, goal-setting, and journaling, as part of an eight-stage therapeutic process. However, this is a controversial form of therapy, not because of any harm it causes to clients, but because of disagreement among clinicians as to its effectiveness. Other treatments include support groups, hypnotherapy, and family intervention. Art, music, poetry, storytelling, behavioral-therapy programs combining relaxation techniques, and narrative therapy are also commonly used.

Almost certainly my clients and I will have to talk about their experiences. One reason therapy may not be useful is because talking about it may simply regenerate bad feelings that have been more effectively dealt with. For my clients who need therapy, part of their homework each week often involves thinking about their experiences. Thinking about what one has experienced is called "rumination." Thinking through the experience can be a therapeutic experience as long as the rumination is not intrusive, negative, or extensive. In other words, thinking through the process, processing details and looking for ways to avoid similar painful experiences can be helpful. Rumination also allows the patient to find a place for the experience. People want their lives to be coherent and meaningful. Trauma is unfair and unexpected. None of us really knows how we would feel if bad things happened to us. Rumination helps us find a place for the painful experience that gives meaning to the experience in the context of our worldview and belief system. Richard Tedeschi, one of the country's experts on posttraumatic growth, reasons that those who engage in "significant thinking about the event and its potential meaning and significances, are more likely to report experiencing posttraumatic growth." However, if rumination simply becomes a way of rehashing pain, it is destructive. Likewise, if it is consistently negative and intrusive, meaning the person is blindsided by ruminations at inopportune times, it is also unproductive. This type of rumination, in fact, is symptomatic of PTSD, a "strong need or impulse to repeat the tragic events in their minds over and over again." In fact, worry is a way of ineffectively ruminating before something bad has even happened. To plan for the worst is not necessarily a bad thing. It is when our worry possesses us, is consistently negative and intrusive, or creates inaction that we get into trouble. Gavin de Becker writes, "Worry is a way to rehearse dreaded outcomes so that if they occur, the worrier believes he will be more prepared . . . worry simply gives people some of the very same consequences they'd get if the dreaded outcome occurred—while doing nothing constructive to prevent anything bad from happening." Worry becomes anxiety, he says, when we attempt to predict things over which we have little control.

One of many problems of worry is that we overestimate danger in many situations by assuming the worst possible outcome as probable rather than possible. Under stress, obsessive individuals ruminate and worry, "paranoids spin conspiracy theories and plot revenge, hysterics emote histrionically or swoon with malaise, and implusives take action—immediately, planlessly, and often disastrously." My goal with my clients is to help them ruminate effectively, creating solutions for their problems and developing coping skills for their pain without inducing an impulsive need to relive the trauma or to worry. Russian writer Miroslav Volf calls this "remembering rightly."

As we talk about what happened, what preceded the event, and what followed, clients can see places where they can change their behaviors in the future. Feelings associated with each part of the trauma are explored. Working through each of those feelings (anger, resentment, sorrow, disgust, fear, etc.) and finding at least temporary resolution for those feelings is important. Sometimes resolution of emotions, especially anger, involves addressing the virtues I've addressed in previous chapters. For example, while I don't believe that forgiveness is absolutely necessary, my clients who learn to release their anger, vengeance, and regret tend to heal more quickly. Forgiveness aids in "redirecting memory toward reparative action and the affirmation of human rights." As Gordon Livingston observes, "The most secure prisons are those we construct for ourselves." Some researchers argue that there is no evidence that it is necessary to forgive in order to heal. However, *necessary* and *helpful* are not synonymous. Once again, research appears to support what I've known all along from the healing I've seen in my clients. Those who forgive have fewer PTSD symptoms. But I am dubious when clients tell me that they have forgiven their perpetrators, God, or whomever, and yet their conversations make it clear that they are still haunted by their pain and they haven't really let it go. Avoiding feelings is not forgiveness. They haven't forgiven. Instead, they are in denial because facing their emotions means also facing their pain head-on.

REFRAMING

My clients are reluctant to change their interpretations of events. "Memory is not, as many of us think, an accurate transcription of past experience. Rather it is a story we tell our selves about the past, full of distortions, wishful thinking, and unfulfilled dreams." Once we have interpreted our pasts and given meaning to what we believe occurred, we are "reluctant to revise our personal mythology." Reframing is a standard practice in therapy where clients are taught to see an issue from a different perspective. Consider this very simple example. The air conditioner in my home died the day before our daughter graduated from high school. It was Memorial Day weekend and very hot. We were expecting 50 people for a party with no air conditioning and no way to get it fixed until after the holiday. After opening the windows for air, I discovered termite damage to our house in the window sill. The broken air conditioner could have been seen as a problem, but after thinking about it I realized if it hadn't been for the air conditioner breaking, I might not have discovered the termite damage until it was too late to fix it without great expense. It was a good thing, not a bad thing. I reframed the event from a bad thing to a good one.

One of my former students was a man who nearly died in an automobile accident. At the time, he was driving while intoxicated and he had a friend's two children with him who died at the scene. My student suffered coma and traumatic brain injury that changed his life, wiped out his savings, and destroyed his successful business. Several years later he had recovered enough from his head injury to attend college and his life was getting back on track. He learned from his experience and he had become a better person. Then he found out he was going to be prosecuted for manslaughter for the accident that happened years before. He had become a changed person yet the law sought justice. It seemed very unfair and after his trial he ended up in jail. One might think that his mental limitations, memory problems, speech impairments, financial loss, guilt at causing the death of two innocent children, and loss of his freedom would be enough to destroy him, but it didn't. He faced his punishment and realized that in order to move on with life he had to accept things that he had no control over. He was a person of religious faith and his belief system taught him that there might be something to be learned even in tragedy. Instead of feeling sorry for himself, he reframed his tragedy and saw it as something that made him a better person. I asked him once if he could go back and change things, would he? Like many people that endure trauma, he said he would like to bring those two children back but despite all he lost, he personally wouldn't want anything to change. "I would never be the person I am today if it weren't for all the bad that has happened to me," he said. This is an amazing example of reframing.

A Lesson in Reframing

Reframing is most easy to see when one looks backward—way back—and examines the events of one's life in the context of the outcome. I've wondered many times how my own life turned out the way it did. If you had asked me 30 years ago what I'd be doing today, where I'd be living, and so forth, I wouldn't even have come close to guessing correctly. There have been too many turning points over the years that, had I been given a choice, would have gone differently, but in retrospect, those turning points, sometimes very unpleasant events, led to the life I have today—a life that is very satisfying. I was born into a home of modest means in the Midwest. I had no advantage of private education and my parents, well-intentioned as they were, spent little time training me in educational pursuits. Although they saw the value of a college degree, neither of my parents had a college education. I began working well before my teen years. By the time I graduated high school, I had worked more than a dozen regular jobs, including nearly full-time employment during my last year of high school. That year I got up at 3 AM and worked as a maintenance man for a restaurant until 7 AM when I came home, cleaned up, and headed for school. I was granted early release from high school at noon so I could return to the restaurant to work another shift until 11 PM. Throughout my last two years of high school I never participated in any social organizations, never went to a party, never attended a football game, and had few friends. I was in no college preparation courses and my high school had a marginal record for academic quality.

I considered skipping college. My parents had little money for college and the expense seemed out of reach. I had spent most of my high school years working and consequently my grades suffered. Scholarships were unlikely because of my mediocre grades. If I went to college, the money would come from loans, work-study, and marginal assistance from my family. But my father discouraged my decision to skip college so in 1979 I enrolled in a private college in the south that cost around $3,500 per year—a huge expense at the time. Looking back, my ignorance of how much $3,500 really was saved me. If I had really understood how much it would cost to attend this college, I would never have even applied. The likelihood of paying such an enormous bill would have seemed beyond my reach. Fortunately in 1979, business offices in private colleges often let students enroll without full payment. I finished registration that first week of my freshman year with a stop at the business office. I had only a few hundred dollars I had borrowed from a bank as a guaranteed student loan—only a fraction of the full bill, but I was allowed to enroll and begin classes. My plan was to work while I was in school and work I did. During my four years as a student I worked as a truck driver, steel worker, painter, carpenter, mechanic, and coal miner. I worked in the college recruiting office (a job I despised more than any other). I worked in a newspaper office, drove a bulldozer, worked in a sign company, and also worked as a janitor. I played guitar in nightclubs and dinner theaters, managed the Student Union on my small college campus, worked as a boat builder, telephone operator, and in a youth-detention facility. I was up by 6 AM every day, attended class in the morning, and worked in the afternoons and evenings. While working for the steel company, I would occasionally leave campus on Friday night and work all night, all day Saturday, all night Saturday night, and all day Sunday, returning to campus Sunday night with no sleep over 72 hours.

After a rough academic start during my first year of college, I learned to study and became an above-average student despite the long hours I spent working. By graduation, I had improved my performance from academic probation my freshman year to a grade point average of 3.4. Upon graduation I couldn't find a job in my academic area so to make ends meet I worked as a mechanic and mowed grass in a graveyard. Finally, I was offered a job in Atlanta as a youth director at a church where I was paid a salary below poverty level at the time, but more than twice what I was making at my job as a mechanic and grounds keeper. With aspirations for graduate school I applied to a prestigious graduate psychology program but was denied. I was discouraged, but in the meantime an Army recruiter I met through my church told me of a flight program I was qualified to apply for. I had always wanted to fly and the southeast region of the United States Army was accepting only two pilots into this new program. I applied. I received nearly a perfect score on the Armed Services Vocation Aptitude Battery (ASVAB) and was a top candidate for the position. After numerous interviews, my recruiter informed me that I was awarded one of the two positions and I was given my posttraining orders as a helicopter pilot. The Army had just introduced their new Apache helicopter and I was pursued by the Army as a potential trainee for this helicopter—the state-of-the-art in helicopter technology. It was a dream come true for me until just a few weeks before I was supposed to report for duty. I had numerous physicals during the process, but I was required one final flight physical. The examiner noted on my file that my eye-sight was 20/15 in one eye—better than perfect, but only 20/25 in the other. She looked at me and said, "They won't take you. I'm afraid you are out." The flight program required perfect uncorrected vision in both eyes and in seconds my officer's file was stamped "REJECTED." It was a devastating turn of events for me and for my wife of just one year. We had mentally prepared for a military career, but now that option had evaporated in front of us.

At the same time, the son of one of the members of my church had become the president of a small private college and asked me if I was interested in a job in recruiting. After working as a recruiter for my undergraduate college, I had sworn I would never do that again, but the president promised me a shot at other positions in the administration if I got my feet wet as the recruiter and we discussed financial assistance for graduate school that I would qualify for. I accepted the job and applied to a Georgia State clinical counseling graduate program. I was accepted into the program and just a few months following the disappointment with the military, I—a former probationary college student—started graduate school. I worked hard, studying full-time as a graduate student at the same time working as a full-time college recruiter. Two years later I graduated with a master's degree and, as the president had promised, I was hired as the dean of students. I realized academia was a career I might enjoy so even before finishing my master's program, I had applied to a doctoral program. While studying as a master's student I had become friends with a student who worked in the dean's office at GSU. When I applied for the PhD program, the dean wrote one of my recommendation letters.

Accepted into the PhD program, I simply had to complete my final quarter in the master's program, three classes, with at least two As. One class was easy for me; another was questionable; and the third, a class on neurophysiology, was also a question mark. The stress was high. One night around midterm, I came to the neurophysiology class and realized the midterm exam was that evening. I had mistakenly put it on my calendar for the following week. I hadn't even read all the material. One of my classmates advised me to leave and tell the professor I missed the exam because of an illness. In a panic I agreed and left class, but before I reached the train station on my way home my conscience got the better of me. I couldn't lie so I returned to the classroom expecting to see the professor at his desk. Instead what I saw stunned me. The professor wasn't there. His graduate assistant, someone

I had never met, was proctoring the exam and had, in fact, heard the entire conversation between my classmate and me. Our eyes met and the graduate assistant laughed. "What do I do?" I asked him. "Just take the exam and we'll talk to your professor if you really blow it." I did as he suggested and took the exam, but later the professor allowed me to do a makeup test. I passed the class with an A and was on the way to my PhD program.

For the next five years I continued to study full-time in my doctoral program while working as the dean of students. Toward the end of my PhD program, a student at the college where I worked began stalking another student. The president asked me if the student was a danger to the community. I said, "Yes, but I can't tell you why. I know in my gut there is something going on here that is dangerous, but I can't tell you why." At that time in history, only a few states had stalking laws and very little existed in the literature on assessing violence. I dealt with the student issue, but as a result I began studying the assessment of risk of violent behavior. I wanted to be more informed if this type of event happened again. After several months of research, I realized I had enough information for a research article so I wrote it up and submitted it to a journal for publication. It was accepted.

A couple of years after graduating I shifted my role at the college from administrator to full-time professor of psychology, continuing my research into violent behavior. One of my students was a single mother who was working full-time while trying to finish a college degree. I spent a great deal of time with her trying to help her graduate. I could relate with the difficulties she had trying to work while in school. She greatly appreciated my efforts and after reading (on her own) my article about assessing violent behavior she passed the article along to the corporate security director at Delta Airlines. The security director in turn called me to see if I would address corporate security on the psychology of violence and violence risk assessment. I agreed to do it for free. The corporate security director was impressed with the pragmatic nature of my approach to the subject and, as I later found out, he was also the former acting director of the Federal Bureau of Investigations—the very person who approved the first major serial killer research by Behavioral Science Unit (BSU) employees John Douglas, Roy Hazelwood, and Robert Ressler.

"This is just the kind of work the BSU does and they could use you," he told me. "Would you be interested in lecturing for them?" I jumped at the chance, not because I wanted to work at the BSU, but because I saw the BSU as a potential source for funding the research I wanted to do. For the next several years I lectured regularly at the FBI National Academy. During that time I made many contacts from all over the world and developed a good reputation in the field of violence risk assessment, homicide investigation, and violent behavior. I collaborated with friends in the BSU on research, including a rising interest in school shootings. Then, in 1999, a shooting happened at a high school near Atlanta. A friend from the BSU called me to see if I would be interested in sitting in on the investigation. It was the first time we would be able to be a part of a school shooting as it was being investigated as opposed to looking through case notes of old shootings. The lead investigator of the crime scene was an inspector from the Georgia Bureau of Investigation (GBI) and a graduate of the FBI National Academy. The GBI inspector had a monstrous ego and I suspect that his association with me as a quasi-representative of the BSU gave him prestige among his underlings even though I was not an FBI employee. I was given free access to the investigation, assistants to help me with anything I needed, and carte blanche freedom on the scene to talk to any witness I wanted. It was more than I could have asked for. During the day while interviews and investigations were continuing, I was fawned over by that other agents on the site. My academy connections and my expertise in a fairly new research area brought me a lot of attention and the attention threatened the ego of the GBI inspector. His attitude turned on me within just a few hours. He literally accused me of misrepresenting myself and I eventually found myself being interrogated in a small office by the inspector and one of his minions. After two hours of humiliating interrogation, I finally said, "That's enough. I'm leaving. If you want to arrest me, arrest me." I got up and left the crime scene utterly humiliated. Angry and hurt, I went home and sent a query letter to a publisher that same day. Within days a contract was presented to me and my first book was underway. Today I am still a college professor. I work as a regular profiler for Atlanta Cold Case Squad and I have had a thriving clinical practice with children for over two decades. I have published a half-dozen books on violent behavior and I am an expert in the field, having lectured on five continents and 18 countries.

Now let's look at these many events and see what was good and what wasn't. There were many turning points along the way, but I'll address 10. First, working early in life and especially working during high school conditioned me to work hard. Even though I had no social life in high school, I never would have gotten where I am without that. Not a bad trade in my opinion. My father instilled in me a work ethic that I value today and it has helped make me who I am. Without it I couldn't have paid for college and I wouldn't have had the "do what you have to do" mentality that allowed me to work in a graveyard after graduation. Without it I wouldn't have been accustomed to living a frugal life that was necessary when my wife and I moved to Atlanta making so little money; I wouldn't have taken the job as recruiter; and I would not have survived graduate school while also working full-time. Next, it may seem small, but again my father redirected my life. If he had not encouraged me to go on to college, I probably would have ended up working in a factory like may of my high school classmates. Who knows where I would be today. The third turning point was my ignorance of the expense of college. Ignorance is bliss and if I knew then what I know now about finances, I never would have gone to the private college I chose. Fourth, I had help from my college. If they had required full payment in advance, or even proof that I would be able to pay, I wouldn't have been admitted. Fifth, I was devastated when I was denied admission to the first graduate program I applied to, but it was a nonclinical program and if I'd been accepted, I know I wouldn't have been happy. Being denied opened the door for me to pursue what I know now really makes me happy. Likewise, being denied my commission in the Army to fly was a blessing in disguise. I may have loved the Army, but the Apache became the front line assault helicopter in numerous conflicts since that time—the first was just a few months after my rejection. (Ironically, the Army called me and offered me a commission as a pilot during this conflict, but I had already started graduate school and my life was on a different path so I turned down their offer.)

The next turning point again came because I had help. When I applied to my PhD program, the dean at GSU who wrote one of my recommendation letters was, by chance, a good friend of a member of the admissions committee of the program to which I was applying. This admissions committee member later became my graduate mentor and one of my favorite teachers, but he confided in me that he was skeptical of my application. He talked it over with his friend, the dean, who vouched for me. If I hadn't spent two years sitting in her office studying with my classmate, her student secretary, I would have been denied admission to my PhD program. The next turning point, number seven, was also because I had help, not to mention my conscience. If I had left that neurophysiology classroom and lied to my professor about missing the exam because I was "sick," not only would I have failed the exam, but I might have been expelled from school and lost even my master's work. The professor's willingness to help me saved my career.[3]

Turning point number eight was the stalker. He made my life miserable and I nearly quit my job as the dean because of it. He was mentally ill and, looking retrospectively, one of the most vicious stalkers I've ever worked with in my career. Yet because of that painful time, I started my research in violent behavior and published my first article that was the launching point of the rest of my career. That article led to my student helping me (once again I had help) by giving a copy of my article to Delta Airlines, and, subsequently, my decision to work for Delta for free in those early years has earned me thousands of dollars since then. Even my decision to lecture at the FBI Academy was a turning point because it wasn't what I thought it would be. I wanted a research outlet, but instead it became the foundation on which my future publications and the strength of my credentials rested in my early career. If they had just offered me a research partnership I would have taken it, but I would have missed the thing that has really been most meaningful in my work—consulting, writing, and homicide investigation. Finally, one of the most painful and humiliating experiences of my life was my interrogation by the GBI. I was totally abased in front of dozens of agents from a half dozen different agencies that day, all because of one man's frail ego. I was so humiliated I didn't even tell my wife about it for months. Yet that event caused me to pursue a publisher for what became my first book. I hadn't even written it yet, but the publisher was impressed with my history, other publications, and my connection with the FBI Academy. In some ways I owe my whole career to two of my greatest enemies—a stalker and a GBI Inspector.[4]

Keep in mind, we could look back even further in my history. We could look at the events in my parents' experiences and how those experiences created them to be who they are and, in turn, how they treated me as a child that made me who I am. But for the sake of simplicity, you can see that each of these turning points was a place where I could have seen the event as awful, wonderful, or neutral. But each of them together set the stage for what has become a very fulfilling life for me. As you will see in the next chapter in the case of Viktor Frankl, this is why I try to help my clients take events one at a time and frame them in the best possible light. There is always something good that can come of even the most devastating experiences. This doesn't mean that we sit back and let life happen to us, but instead we seize opportunities when they arise, even when they seem like problems.

One of the men I greatly admire is the founder of Chick-fil-A restaurants, Truett Cathy. I agree with his sentiments that he shared in one of his many books about his success in the food industry. "Some people look at what has happened and say we were lucky. There may be some luck involved, but I'm not sure how much. If you examine 'luck,' you will usually find that the people who have been lucky have also worked hard, understood the value of a dollar, and taken advantage of unexpected opportunities."

CONCLUDING COMMENTS

In his book *Shocks to the System,* Laurence Miller summarizes what we need to do in therapy with victims of trauma. He writes: "(1) listen to your patient's story and let it emerge at its own pace . . . (2) people are different—assess and respect your patient's strengths and weaknesses in the cognitive, emotional, temperamental, and relational spheres . . . (3) utilize therapeutic strategies that encourage the use of reflection, planning, and active problem-solving. Teach your patient how to take care of himself and exert some control . . . (4) encourage healthy human relationships . . . (5) help your patient find some meaning in what's happened to him." This isn't a simple process and there are other considerations. For example, there are gender differences in response to trauma, numerous assessment instruments that may be helpful in assessment and treatment planning, and there is even research that indicates there are different types of PTSD. But a trained therapist and a highly motivated client create a combination for successful therapy. Miller concisely outlines the things that help people transcend their traumas.

> Transcendent copers described a healthy, secure upbringing characterized by a supportive relationship with their families, friends, and others. After the incident, they were able to either freely express and cathartically talk out their trauma or, alternatively, suppress and deny the traumatic experience, simply putting it out of their minds and moving on. They typically enjoyed favorable, restorative circumstances following the trauma. They did not "dwell on" the trauma. They characteristically lived hard-working, productive lifestyles with self-determination and self-reliance. They were able to accept and learn from the traumatic experience and face life's future challenges. They found a way to do for themselves and/or for others what was needed but lacking. They described personal religious or philosophical faith and hope. They were not embittered or cynical but kept a sense of humor.

As a therapist I want to draw on these transcendent qualities that may be present in my clients and foster them where they are absent. In science there is a concept called "emergence." Emergence is the theory that complex systems are developed by the introduction of smaller parts. From these systems emerge new outcomes or structures that were not a part of the original smaller parts. A very simple example of emergence is a pistol. Suppose you have a pistol that you can disassemble into 15 separate parts. The "pistol" doesn't exist until all the minor parts are assembled together.[5] In other words, the pistol *emerges* from the smaller parts that together create something that did not exist within any of the individual parts. Resiliency is like that. One isn't resilient if he or she has one or two components of resiliency. Resiliency is what emerges when enough of the components appear at the same time in the same individual. My therapeutic job is to help put as many of those parts together as I can.

None of us live in a vacuum; none of us, no matter how hard we work, are truly self-made; and none of us can truly do it alone. In his amazing book *Outliers,* Malcolm Gladwell examines the reasons exceptional people have found success. The bottom line in his research is this—"we know that outliers will always have help along the way . . ." As I demonstrated in my own story, I had help from my parents, my undergraduate college, and even my students. Even though, as Gordon Livingston notes, "we are responsible for most of what happens to us," both good and bad, those who succeed are those who make the best of opportunities when they arise. One major difference between those who succeed and those who do not is that successful people seize opportunities when they arise. Vulnerable, less-than-resilient people don't open the door no matter how loud opportunity knocks and they are likely to be traumatized by all the noise.

I wish I could give you an update on Chandrae, but I can't. I lost track of her after she left our facility and I've haven't heard from her in years. The last time I met with her she was doing very well. She trusted me, a huge step in her recovery. She still had a hard time making eye contact for very long—a sure sign of continued insecurity, but she would at least briefly look me in the eye. We walked across the athletic field beside the unit where she lived and talked for one last time. She was due to be released into the custody of relatives in just a few days.

"So what do you think your future holds, Chandrae?" I asked her.

"I don't know. I guess I'll finish school."

"But what do you want beyond that?" I asked. I wanted her to think further into the future.

"Maybe get married someday."

"And what kind of man do you think you want as a husband?" Our spousal choices are often a reflection of how we see ourselves. If she was looking for a loser, she would certainly find one, but it would mean to me that she saw herself no better than a "loser" as well.

"I guess I want someone who will treat me with respect," she said thoughtfully. Her answer sounded like a "therapy" answer.

"And what does a respectful person do?"

"Maybe he will see inside me, not just take me." She said this very matter-of-factly. She knew what it was to be used and fortunately, she had enough of that. I have high hopes for her and even though I don't know where she is today, I like to think she has found a respectful husband, has 2.5 children, and is living a life far better than the way it started out for her.

Mary Beth did very well in therapy. Through our weeks together, she worked through her anger, jealousy, resentment, and sorrow. She was able to see her husband for the good man he was, despite his unfaithfulness, and her children adjusted to the loss of their father as well as could be expected. There will be hard times ahead for both Mary Beth and Chandrae, but that is life and they've both learned to roll with the punches. They have the tools they need to face new traumas should they arise and they have the internal strength and social networks to help them stand when they can't do it themselves. That is about all we could hope for.

NOTES

1. There are numerous articles that validate this claim. Here are a sampling: Hobfoll, S. E., Canetti-Nisim, D., Johnson, R.J. (2006). Exposure to terrorism, stress-related mental health symptoms, and defensive coping among Jews and Arabs in Israel. *Journal of Consulting and Clinical Psychology, 74*(2), 207–218.

Hobfoll, S. E., Canetti-Nisim, D., Johnson, R. J., Palmieri, P. A., Varley, J. D., & Galea, S. (2008). The association of exposure, risk, and resiliency factors with PTSD among Jews and Arabs exposed to repeated acts of terrorism in Israel. *Journal of Traumatic Stress, 21*(1), 9–21.

Brady, K. L., Acierno, R. E., Resnick, H. S., Kilpatrick, D. G., & Saunders, B. E. (2003). PTSD symptoms in widowed women with lifetime trauma experiences. *Journal of Loss and Trauma, 9*, 35–43.

Schumm, J. A., Briggs-Phillips, M., & Hobfoll, S. E. (2006). Cumulative interpersonal traumas and social support as risk and resiliency factors in predicting PTSD and depression among inner-city women. *Journal of Traumatic Stress, 19*(6), 825–836.

Vanderweker, L. C., & Prigerson, H. G. (2003). Social support and technological connectedness as protective factors in bereavement. *Journal of Loss and Trauma, 9,* 45–57.

Johnson, D. M., Palmieri, P. A., Jackson, A. P., & Hobfoll, S. E. (2007). Emotional numbing weakens abused inner-city women's resiliency resources. *Journal of Traumatic Stress 20*(2), 197–206.

2. This is called simple and complex trauma. For more information, see Schottenbauer, M. A., Glass, C. R., Arnkoff, D. B., & Gray, S. H. (2008). Contributions of psychodynamic approaches to treatment of PTSD and trauma: A review of the empirical treatment and psychopathology literature. *Psychiatry, 71*(1), 13–34.

3. His graduate assistant and I are still in contact today. He teaches at another university in Atlanta and we sometimes joke about this event.

4. I honestly hold no grudges against either man and I've thought many times about sending the inspector, now retired, copies of my books with a thank-you note, but I have never been able to figure out how to do that without it sounding sarcastic.

5. Don't try to use this as an excuse to carry pistol parts through airport screening. I doubt the TSA would have this sort of philosophical perspective on firearms.

REFERENCES

Berman, H. (2001). Children and war: Current understandings and future directions. *Public Health Nursing, 18*(4), 243–252. Retrieved September 13, 2008, from research database Ebscohost.

Cathy, T. (2007). *How did you do it, Truett?* Decatur, GA: Looking Glass Books, p. 10.

Connor, K. M., Davidson, J.R.T., & Lee, L. (2003). Spirituality, resilience, and anger in survivors of violent trauma: A community survey. *Journal of Traumatic Stress, 16*(5), 487–494.

de Becker, G. (2002). *Fear Less.* Boston, MA: Little, Brown and Company.

Ferren, P. M. (1999). Comparing perceived self-efficacy among adolescent Bosnian and Croatian refugees with and without posttraumatic stress disorder. *Journal of Traumatic Stress, 12*(3), 405–420. Retrieved September 13, 2008, from research database Ebscohost.

Gladwell, M. (2009). *Outliers: The story of success.* New York: Little, Brown, and Company, p. 120.

Hjern, A,. & Angel, B. (2000). Organized violence and mental health of refugee children in exile: A six-year follow-up. *Acta Paediatrica, 89,* 722–727.

Lee, J., Semple, R.J., Rosa, D., & Miller, L. (2008). Mindfulness-based cognitive therapy for children: Results of a pilot study. *Journal of Cognitive Psychotherapy: An International Quarterly, 22*(1), 15–27.

Livingston, G. (2004). *Too soon old, too late smart.* New York: Marlowe and Company, p. 55.

McCloskey, L. A., & Southwick, K. (1996). Psychosocial problems in refugee children exposed to war. *Pediatrics, 97*(3), 394–397. Retrieved September 13, 2008, from research database Ebscohost.

McKnight, A. N. (n.d.). Historical trauma, the persistence of memory and the pedagogical problems of forgiveness, justice and peace. *Educational Studies 36,* 140–158.

Miller, L. (1998). *Shocks to the system: Psychotherapy of traumatic disability syndromes.* New York: W.W. Norton & Company.

Oras, R., Cancela de Ezpeleta, S., & Ahmad, A. (2004). Treatment of traumatized refugee children with eye movement desensitization and reprocessing in a psychodynamic context. *Nord J Psychiatry, 58*(3), 199–203.

Orcutt, H.K., Pickett, S.M., & Pope, E.B. (2005). Experiential avoidance and forgiveness as mediators in the relation between traumatic interpersonal events and posttraumatic stress disorder symptoms. *Journal of Social and Clinical Psychology, 24*(7), 1003–1029.

Patel, N., & Hodes, M. (2006). Violent deliberate self-harm amongst adolescent refugees. *European Child Adolescent Psychiatry, 15,* 367–370. Retrieved September 13, 2008, from research database Ebscohost.

Preston, J. (2002). *Survivors: Stories & strategies to heal the hurt.* Atascadero, CA: Impact Publishers.

Schwarz, R. A., & Prout, M. F. (1991). Integrative approaches in the treatment of post-traumatic stress disorder. *Psychotherapy, 28*(2), 364–373.

Segal, Z.V., Teasdale, J.D., Williams, J.M., & Gemar, M.C. (2002). The mindfulness-based cognitive therapy adherence scale: Inter-rater reliability, adherence to protocol and treatment distinctiveness. *Clinical Psychology and Psychotherapy, 9,* 131–138.

Tedeschi, R. G., & McMillan, J. (2000). A correlational test of the relationship between posttraumatic growth, religion, and cognitive processing. *Journal of Traumatic Stress, 13,* 521–527, p. 526.

Volf, M. (2006). *The end of memory: Remembering rightly in a violent world.* Grand Rapids, MI: William B. Eerdmans Publishing Company, p. 12.

9

———◦◦◦———

THE MEANING OF LIFE

I do not intend to tiptoe through life only to arrive safely at death.

—Unknown

He who has a why to live can bear with almost any how.

—Nietzsche

One of the most influential books I've ever read as a therapist is Viktor Frankl's book *Man's Search for Meaning*. Frankl was captive in a concentration camp during World War II and his experiences are recounted in this book. But his book is more than a chronology of his experiences as a prisoner in a concentration camp. Frankl provides an account of his experience, but he also juxtaposes his experiences against the context of why some of his fellow inmates survived and some did not. He notes that the strongest inmates were not necessarily the physically strong. Instead, the strongest were those who "were able to retreat from their terrible surroundings to a life of inner riches and spiritual freedom. Only in this way can one explain the apparent paradox that some prisoners of a less hardy make-up often seemed to survive camp life better than did those of a robust nature." This is consistent with what we have known for years about the training practices of elite groups like the Navy Seals. The men and women who are most muscular or physically fit are not necessarily the ones who succeed in the Seals program, but instead those who have the strongest mental capacity to endure their struggles are the ones most likely to succeed. As his resilient fellow inmates survived amid the tragedy of the camps, Frankl found meaning in their endurance and he discovered meaning for his own life in the camp. One's meaning, he writes, comes from relationships with loved ones. These relationships give one the inner strength to endure trauma. "The salvation of man is through love and in love. I understood how a man who has nothing left in this world still may know bliss, be it only for a brief moment, in the contemplation of his beloved." As I have said numerous times throughout this book, social relationships give our lives meaning and those relationships sustain us when we face life's challenges.

But amid his philosophical reflections on loving, Frankl also acknowledged the pain of his experience. In fact he embraced it. He continues: "When man finds that it is his destiny to suffer, he will have to accept his suffering as his task; his single and unique task. He will have to acknowledge the fact that even in suffering he is unique and alone in the universe. No one can relieve him of his suffering or suffer in his place. His unique opportunity lies in the way in which he bears his burdens." Through his experience in the camps, Frankl learned to accept what fate brought to him rather than trying to force his future to be something he thought he might have wanted. In *Murder on the Orient Express,* the story is told of a famous actress named Armstrong whose three-year-old daughter is kidnapped. The ransom is paid, but the child's dead body is later found. This dialogue regarding the tragedy is exchanged between Agatha Christie's detective Hercule Poirot and "the Italian":

"You remember the Armstrong case?"

"I do not quite remember. The name, yes? It was a little girl, a baby, was it not?"

"Yes, a very tragic affair."

The Italian seemed the first person to demur to this view.

"Ah! well, these things happen," he said philosophically . . ."

"Ah, well, these things happen . . ." In a way this sounds like a tragically jaded response to life's misfortunes, but from a therapeutic perspective, some of this attitude is actually helpful. Events happen—both good and bad. Frankl understood that life inevitably brings pain, no matter what we do to try to avoid it and his "ah, well, these things happen" attitude helped him to take life as it came. Many of my clients over the years suffered a great deal not only because of their traumatic experiences, but because of their anger that they should have any pain in life at all. To them, their trauma seems unfair and they search diligently for someone to blame. In a worldview where one believes life should be pain-free, any pain is traumatic and unfair. A dose of "ah, well, these things happen" can help them let go of their anger and resentment. Once my clients grasp the truth that pain will eventually find them no matter where they hide, they begin to heal. Frankl recounts a Persian fable that encapsulates this thought.

> A rich and mighty Persian once walked in his garden with one of his servants. The servant cried that he had just encountered Death, who had threatened him. He begged his master to give him his fastest horse so that he could make haste and flee to Teheran, which he could reach that same evening. The master consented and the servant galloped off on the horse. On returning to his house the master himself met Death, and questioned him, "Why did you terrify and threaten my servant?" "I did not threaten him; I only showed surprise in still finding him here when I planned to meet him tonight in Teheran," said Death.

My healthiest clients learn to change what they can but also to accept what they cannot change.

But Frankl doesn't only express the inevitability of pain. Happiness, too, is a by-product of our existence when we change the focus from ourselves to the needs and interests of others. Pursing happiness brings discouragement because it ultimately leads to boredom. And it is boredom, Frankl writes, that "brings more problems to psychiatrists than distress." He goes on, "happiness, cannot be pursued; it must ensue, and it only does so as the unintended side-effect of one's personal dedication to a cause greater than oneself or as the by-product of one's surrender to a person other than oneself." Again, my clinical practice confirms Frankl's words. My clients who look for a way to focus their energies outside of themselves, investing energy in improving the lives of others, are the ones who heal most quickly. Those who wallow in their sorrow may not heal at all. I am interested in helping my clients find some way to give some of their energy to others. Mark Katz, in his book *On Playing a Poor Hand Well,* writes that trauma victims may experience positive changes when they are "required to perform actions that significantly help others in their personal times of need." He notes that during the bombings of London in World War II, doctors discovered that citizens who worked to help others not only experienced "fewer than anticipated adverse psychological reactions," but one "observer even noted that individuals who were of poor mental health prior to the air raids were actually faring much better following the raids if they had a personally satisfying job to perform that others saw as socially necessary."

But this doesn't mean they have no weaknesses. No one is invincible and the most resilient people I've studied over the years have weaknesses. George Harris, in his book *Dignity and Vulnerability: Strength and Quality of Character,* argues that the virtue of strength of character is also balanced by the virtue of vulnerability of character. As an analogy, he suggests that the character of good wine is its vulnerability—its weakness. Wine reaches its peak boldness at some point in its life, after which it begins to break down. Wine is fragile and it can be bruised. Without its vulnerability it would not be great wine. It is great precisely *because* it is vulnerable. Ironically, as Harris eloquently points out, human character can be both incredibly strong and yet incredibly vulnerable because of the same thing. Our "value for the intimacy of personal love" is what makes us vulnerable, but it is also these same powerful and intimate relationships that give us enduring strength. He continues, "There is overwhelming evidence that those who cope best with tragedy befalling loved ones are those who are involved in healthy personal relationships that are deeply intimate, even though it is this kind of intimacy that made the tragedy possible in the first place."

Some people believe that abandoning one's self-interests also means abandoning the self. I have often heard scoffers ridicule the monks and priests who have taken a vow of poverty, celibacy, and isolation in order to get closer to their gods. What these critics fail to understand is that abandoning one's own interests can give life intense meaning and, in return, help define oneself. When people lie on their deathbeds they rarely wish for more money or possessions. When people face death, and I have walked the path to death with many people, they more likely wish for more time with family and friends. They wish for one last conversation with a loved one or one last look at a spouse, a child, or a grandchild. As long as the self is dependent upon external objects for definition (money, power, position, etc.) then one cannot be free to dig deeper into the purpose of one's life. By abandoning the self, we abandon the *how* in favor of the *why*. Thereby, we find purpose—happiness. How else can you explain the incredible level of unhappiness among some of the world's most wealthy and powerful individuals? They have enough money to buy anything in the world they might want and yet they spend thousands of dollars on therapy and drugs to simply help them tolerate another day of existence. "Nietzsche proposed that to be truly happy requires some such disregard of the past accompanied by deep immersion in the present. For him, the child is a symbol of happiness undisturbed by the burdens of the past." Living in the moment with all it brings is where reality resides. Livingston adds, "We have effective treatments for the symptoms of depression; the bad news is that medication will not make you happy. Happiness is not simply the absence of despair. It is an affirmative state in which our lives have both meaning and pleasure." In summation, the most easygoing clients, the ones who heal most quickly, are those who take life as it comes—both the good and they bad—and they divest themselves of the burden of trying to force their own fate. They look at ways to invest energy in others—their families, friends, and community—rather than drowning in self-pity.

In an interesting irony, one day while I was working on this book, I was especially busy. I had to take two of my three children to school early in the morning. Just after that—too long to hang around the school, but not enough time to make the 30-minute round-trip home—I had to be back at my daughter's school for a contest where she was reciting a poem, thus killing another hour of my already busy day. A friend's father had died and I needed to go to the funeral around midday in a nearby town. Then in the afternoon after the funeral I had to hurry back to my children's schools to pick up all three of them—each school was 20 minutes apart. That evening I then had to take my son to a Boy Scout meeting. Even before I was out of bed that morning I could see that by the time I was done with all of my errands for other people, it would be late in the evening before I was home, leaving me no time to work on this book. My attitude probably wasn't the best as I started out the day. About mid-morning as I sat in the media center of my daughter's middle school awaiting the start of the recitations, I rehearsed thoughts and ideas in my head about what I wanted to write for the day and I held a copy of Frankl's book *Man's Search For Meaning* in my hand. Then it struck me. How odd it was that I was busy organizing thoughts in my mind about the meaning of life when the meaning of life was right in front of me. My meaning, my purpose, is not in books I write, my contributions to the field of psychology, or speeches that I give. It isn't in how much money I make, how many television shows I've been on, or how many people know my name. Meaning is in the seemingly mundane—chauffeuring children to and from school, supporting my daughter as she recites *Maybe Dats Your Pwoblem Too* at her middle school library, attending a scout meeting with my son, and supporting my friend by attending the funeral of his father. My guess is by the time this book is published most of the events of that day will have been forgotten—even by me. None of these events had earth-shattering impact by themselves, but in the bigger picture of life, they have far more meaning than the words I might have pecked out on my word processor that day. The meaning of life is found in living life as it comes—whether pleasant or not—not in rushing through it. My frustrations early that day were self-created because of what I *wanted* to do and because of that, I nearly missed what I *needed* to do.

I started this book with the intentions of impressing the reader at the amazing things people have survived. I wanted people to read each story, each case study, and at the conclusion of the story say, "Wow! That is amazing!" Maybe you have done that a time or two as you read through these pages. My original goal was to show how people could survive and to learn the secrets of their survival. But by talking to these survivors I have learned a lot. I have learned from Minna, Murray, Tammy, and Pius. They've taught me that life is more than breathing for another day. Surviving trauma is entwined in the meaning of relationships and investment in those relationships.

It was not my initial intention to write any kind of existential or philosophical work, but it has happened nonetheless. Survival isn't just about psychology and it isn't a recipe that one can easily mix together after collecting a few ingredients. Rather it is a way of looking at the world—a way of living that must be embraced. I would have liked to think that I was wise enough to have recognized this from the beginning, but I wasn't. Having spent two decades studying psychology and researching behavior, I have grown accustomed to breaking down systems into their subcomponents and analyzing those components. Yet understanding how people successfully survive the traumas of life is not like fixing a broken toaster. People are complex and there are no easy answers. But maybe part of the answer involves understanding something that was there all along—a meaning that is found amid the family and friends that make up one's social world. As Frankl says, "No man can tell another what [his] purpose is. He must find this out for himself." I hope that in reading you have also developed some clarity in your own purpose in life.

I don't know what you were seeking when you picked this book up, but whatever you were looking for, I hope you have found it. I suspect that what you have found is closely tied to what motivated you to read the book in the first place. As Frederick Buechner says, "The conflict between science and religion . . . is like the conflict between a podiatrist and a poet. One says that Susie Smith has fallen arches. The other says she walks in beauty like the night. In his own way each is speaking the truth. What is at issue is the kind of truth you are after." If you were looking for confirmation that religion is an answer to healing and recovery, you may believe you have found that confirmation. If, on the other hand, you are more of a social constructionist, you undoubtedly have found confirmation of the importance of parenting, social groups, and upbringing. But what I've tried to show is that both are important. Successfully navigating the dangerous waters of life requires one to have many tools at his or her disposal—a strong hull and steady mast, good navigational charts, and a competent crew. One without the other weakens the ship. When we have the right tools, we can face the challenges that inevitably confront us. As noted by Gordon Livingston, "Life is a gamble in which we don't get to deal the cards, but we are nevertheless obligated to play them to the best of our ability."

So where can we go from here? What have I contributed in these pages other than a collection of fascinating stories? Each of the subjects I've written about in this book has proven to me the following truths about life:

1. Life is full of ups and downs, just like your mother probably taught you.
2. Life is a journey, not a destination. Focus too hard on the goal and you will miss the process, and it is the process that ultimately makes life meaningful.
3. There are social issues and protective factors that can make resiliency more likely.
4. Surviving trauma is partially in the will, but the will to survive can be fostered through relationships with others and strength of community.
5. Resiliency isn't a formula. It is a way of life.

6. Our courage can only be tested when we experience what we think we could not endure and we can almost always endure more than we thought we could.

7. Endurance and hard work can compensate for weaknesses in protective and resiliency factors.

CONCLUDING COMMENTS

Trauma doesn't dictate how we cope. We cannot control our pasts nor can we always control what occurs in our present, but our response to trauma is our choice—100 percent—and it can either destroy us or make us stronger. Dick Hoyt and his wife knew something was wrong as soon as their son Rick was born. The child was born with cerebral palsy. He was bound to a wheelchair throughout his childhood and early adult years, and all of the exciting milestones most parents look forward to in raising their children were absent from their lives. But Dick and his wife were committed to helping Rick live the fullest life possible. For years he scarcely could communicate with them and doctors told them he was incapable of any meaningful communication. However, computer technology eventually gave Rick a voice. His first words, "Go Bruins," were reflective of his love of sports. The father-son bond through sports was powerful and Dick was so committed to his son that he began pushing his son's wheelchair as he ran road races. That hobby led to a string of more than 20 Boston Marathons and eventually one of the most incredible stories of athletic endurance you will ever hear.

The Iron Man Triathlon run each fall on the Big Island of Hawaii is in my opinion the most impressive test of athletic endurance on the planet. This grueling event begins at seven in the morning with a 2.5-mile swim in the ocean waters off the Kona coast. Then participants bike for 112 miles. Finally, the event concludes with a full marathon—26.2 miles. Athletes in top condition would have a hard time completing any one of these three events, but Iron Man participants do all three back-to-back in one day. The race officially ends at midnight, but some participants continue into the wee hours of the morning, pushing themselves to the very end of their endurance.

In 1989, Dick Hoyt decided to give his son the experience of the Iron Man. In order to accommodate his son, he pulled his son on a raft during the swim, carried him on a specially built platform on the front of his bicycle for the bike portion of the race, and pushed his racing wheelchair for the final leg. This first year Dick was unable to complete the course, stopping somewhere in the middle of the marathon. Ten years later, however, they competed again. This time it appeared their luck would not be any better than in 1989. The course was windy and their bike broke down in the middle of the bike leg. They repaired the bike, but at the transition between the bike and run, they were an hour and a half past their self-imposed cut-off time. It looked as if they would not be able to complete the marathon by midnight. However, through the dark hours Dick pushed on. Incredibly, they crossed the finish line almost an hour ahead of the midnight deadline. One last detail that makes this story even more amazing. Dick Hoyt was almost 60 years old when he ran the Iron Man in 1999. Iron Man athletes do everything they can to cut down their weight—light racing shoes, ultra-light bicycles, even shaving their body hair to be more streamlined for the swim. Yet 60-year-old Dick Hoyt completed all three legs carrying the extra weight of his son.

I watch the Iron Man every year and I watched the Hoyt team in 1999. The endurance and determination of this team brought tears to my eyes. Dick Hoyt was asked by a reporter what he would do if he fell. "I'd get up again and keep running." When asked what if he fell again, he responded, "I'd keep getting up no matter how many times I fell." Dick Hoyt embodies the many strengths of resiliency that I have addressed in this book. One has to wonder what the world would be like if all of us were this dedicated to success.

Joseph J. Ellis, in his volume *Founding Brothers,* comments on the likes of John Adams, Alexander Hamilton, Thomas Jefferson, and their contemporaries. "If they sometimes behave like actors in a historical drama, that is often how they regarded themselves. In a very real sense, we are complicitous in their achievement, since we are the audience for which they were performing; knowing we would be watching helped to keep them on their best behavior." While the ramifications of our observations of the survivors in this book may not be as historically significant as the observations of our founding fathers, watching the actors in the dramas that have played out successfully before us allows us not only to participate in their drama, but also to learn from it. We are, in a very real sense, complicitous in their dramas because their dramas represent the very best that we can be. Our observations of these survivors may not answer all the questions about trauma, resiliency, and recovery, but I believe we have at least made a start.

Sir Isaac Newton once said, "I don't know what I may seem to the world, but as to myself, I seem to have been only like a boy, playing on the seashore, and diverting myself in now and then finding a smoother pebble or a prettier shell than ordinary, whilst the great ocean of truth lay all undiscovered before me." Newton was one of history's greatest scientists and yet he realized that despite all the discoveries and answers he had provided for the world, he had scarcely made a dent in the work that needed to be done. This is where we are. While we have answers, there is an ocean of knowledge still before us waiting to be discovered. Until I have answers for all of those questions, I will have to be satisfied with Dick Hoyt's answer. When trauma happens to me, I'll get up again—and again and again—as many times as it takes.

In closing I quote Gordon Livingston one last time. "When we think about the things that alter our lives in a moment, nearly all of them are bad: phone calls in the middle of the night, accidents, loss of jobs or loved ones, conversations with doctors bearing awful news . . . Virtually all the happiness producing processes in our lives take time, usually a long time: learning new things, changing old behaviors, building satisfying relationships, raising children. That is why patience and determination are among life's primary virtues." Easy to say, but hard to practice. Nonetheless, as for my clients and me, this is the mantra we will pursue as we look for a life that is more satisfying and more meaningful. I wish the same for you.

REFERENCES

Buechner, F. (2004). *Beyond Words: A word a day to keep the demons at bay.* San Francisco: HarperCollins, p. 362.

Christie, A. (1934/2004). *Murder on the orient express.* New York: Berkley Books, p. 175.

Ellis, J. J. (2000). *Founding brothers: The revolutionary generation.* New York: Vintage Books, p. 18.

Frankl, V. E. (1984). *Man's search for meaning.* New York: Pocket Books.

Harris, G. W. (1997). *Dignity and vulnerability: Strength and quality of character.* Berkley: University of California Press.

Katz, M. (1997). *On playing a poor hand well.* New York: W. W. Norton & Company, p. 142.

Livingston, G. (2004). *Too soon old, too late smart.* New York: Marlowe and Company.

Volf, M. (2006). *The end of memory: Remembering rightly in a violent world.* Grand Rapids, MI: William B. Eerdmans Publishing Company, p. 72.

BIBLIOGRAPHY

Amanpour, Christiane. (December 4, 2008). Scream bloody murder. *CNN* broadcast.

Barker, Greg. (Writer, Producer, and Director). (2004). *Ghosts of Rwanda. Frontline,* coproduction with BBC.

Bennett, William. (1995). *The book of virtues.* New York: Simon and Schuster.

Berman, H. (2001). Children and war: Current understandings and future directions. *Public Health Nursing, 18*(4), 243–252. Retrieved September 13, 2008, from research database Ebscohost.

Bernard, Bonnie. (1991). *Fostering resiliency in kids: Protective factors in family, school, and community.* Portland, OR: Western Regional Center for Drug-Free Schools and Communities.

Boyum, Richard. (2008). Characteristics of a self-actualizing person. *Selfcoun seling.com.* Retrieved December 3, 2008, from http://www.selfcounseling. com/help/personalsuccess/selfactualization.html.

Brady, K. L., Acierno, R. E., Resnick, H. S., Kilpatrick, D. G., & Saunders, B. E. (2003). PTSD symptoms in widowed women with lifetime trauma experiences. *Journal of Loss and Trauma, 9,* 35–43.

Buechner, Frederick. (2004). *Beyond Words: A word a day to keep the demons at bay.* San Francisco: HarperCollins.

Burch, J. M. (1984). *They cage the animals at night.* New York: Signet Books.

Burns, Melanie O., & Seligman, Martin E. P. (1989). Explanatory style across the life span: Evidence for stability over 52 years. *Journal of Personality and Social Psychology, 56,* 471–477.

Buss, David M. (2000). The evolution of happiness. *American Psychologist, 55,* 15–23.

Byzek, Josie. (October 2003). Bring it on. *New Mobility.* Retrieved from http://www.newmobility.com/articleView.cfm?id=758&srch=minna%20hong.

Cathy, Truett. (2007). *How did you do it, Truett?* Decatur, GA: Looking Glass Books.

Christie, Agatha. (1934/2004). *Murder on the Orient Express.* New York: Berkley Books.

Connor, K. M., Davidson, J.R.T., & Lee, L. (2003). Spirituality, resilience, and anger in survivors of violent trauma: A community survey. *Journal of Traumatic Stress, 16*(5), 487–494.

Conroy, Pat. (2002). *My losing season.* New York: Doubleday.

Davis, C. G, & McKearney, J. M. (2003). How do people grow from their experience with trauma or loss? *Journal of Social & Clinical Psychology, 22,* 477–493.

de Becker, G. (2002). *Fear Less.* Boston: Little, Brown and Company.

Diener, Ed. (2000). Subjective well-being: The science of happiness and a proposal for a national index. *American Psychologist, 55,* 34–43.

Dixon, Andrea L., Scheidegger, Corey, & McWhirter, J. Jeffries. (2009). The adolescent mattering experience: Gender variations in perceived mattering, anxiety, and depression. *Journal of Counseling & Development, 87,* 302–310.

Ellis, Joseph J. (2000). *Founding brothers: The revolutionary generation.* New York: Vintage Books.

Emmons, Robert A., & Crumpler, Cheryl A. (2000). Gratitude as a human strength: Appraising the evidence. *Journal of Social & Clinical Psychology, 19,* 55–69.

Engler, Barbara. (2001). *Theories of personality* (4th ed.). New York: Houghton Mifflin.

Ferren, P. M. (1999). Comparing perceived self-efficacy among adolescent Bosnian and Croatian refugees with and without posttraumatic stress disorder. *Journal of Traumatic Stress, 12*(3), 405–420. Retrieved September 13, 2008, from research database Ebscohost.

Frankl, V. E. (1984). *Man's search for meaning.* New York: Pocket Books.

Gettleman, Jeffrey. (2008, October 30). Many flee as Congo rebels approach eastern city. *New York Times.* Retrieved October 30, 2008, from http://www.nytimes.com/2008/10/30/world/africa/30congo.html.

Gettleman, Jeffrey. (2008, November 3). In Congo, a little fighting brings a lot of fear. *New York Times.* Retrieved from nytimes.com.

Gil, Eliana. (1991). *The healing power of play: Working with abused children.* New York: The Guilford Press.

Gladwell, Malcolm. (2009). *Outliers: The story of success.* New York: Little, Brown, and Company.

Harris, G. W. (1997). *Dignity and vulnerability: Strength and quality of character.* Berkley: University of California Press.

Hjern, A., & Angel, B. (2000). Organized violence and mental health of refugee children in exile: A six-year follow-up. *Acta Paediatrica, 89,* 722–727.

Hobfoll, S. E., Canetti-Nisim, D., & Johnson, R. J. (2006). Exposure to terrorism, stress-related mental health symptoms, and defensive coping among Jews and Arabs in Israel. *Journal of Consulting and Clinical Psychology, 74*(2), 207–218.

Hobfoll, S. E., Canetti-Nisim, D., Johnson, R. J., Palmieri, P. A., Varley, J. D., & Galea, S. (2008). The association of exposure, risk, and resiliency factors with PTSD among Jews and Arabs exposed to repeated acts of terrorism in Israel. *Journal of Traumatic Stress, 21*(1), 9–21.

Hosen, Ron, Solovey-Hosen, Dina, & Stern, Louis. (2002). The acquisition of beliefs that promote subjective well-being. *Journal of Instructional Psychology, 29,* 231–244.

Howard, S., Dryden, J., & Johnson, B. (1999). Childhood resilience: Review and critique of literature. *Oxford Review of Education, 25,* 307–324.

Howard, S., & Johnson, B. (2000). What makes the difference? Children and teachers talk about resilient outcomes for children "at risk." *Educational Studies, 26,* 321–337. ERIC Document: ED419214, p. 334 in Dryden, J., Johnson, B., Howard, S., & McGuire, A. (1998). Resiliency: A comparison of construct definitions arising from conversations with 9–12 year old children and their teachers. Proceedings of the American Educational Research Association Meeting, San Diego, April 13–17.

Ilibagiza, Immaculée. Immaculée. Retrieved January 6, 2009, from http://www.immaculee.com/story.html.

Johnson, D. M., Palmieri, P. A., Jackson, A. P., & Hobfoll, S. E. (2007). Emotional numbing weakens abused inner-city women's resiliency resources. *Journal of Traumatic Stress 20*(2), 197–206.

Kalafer, Steve (Producer), & LeDonne, Peter (Director). (2006). *The diary of Immaculée* [Motion Picture]. United States: New Jersey Studios, Hay House.

Kasser, T. (2002). *The high price of materialism.* Cambridge, MA: The MIT Press.

Katz, Mark. (1997). *On playing a poor hand well.* New York: W. W. Norton & Company.

King, David C. (2006). *Cultures of the world: Rwanda.* New York: Marshall Cavendish Benchmark.

Krumboltz, J. D., & Levin, A. S. (2004). *Luck is no accident: Making the most of happenstance in your life and career.* Atascadero, CA: Impact Publishers.

Lacey, Marc. (2006, December 14). Rwandan priest sentenced to 15 years for allowing deaths of Tutsi in church. *New York Times*. Retrieved from http://www.nytimes.com/2006/12/14/world/africa/14rwanda.htm.

Lee, J., Semple, R. J., Rosa, D., & Miller, L. (2008). Mindfulness-based cognitive therapy for children: Results of a pilot study. *Journal of Cognitive Psychotherapy: An International Quarterly, 22*(1), 15–27.

McCloskey, L. A. & Southwick, K. (1996). Psychosocial problems in refugee children exposed to war. *Pediatrics, 97*(3). Retrieved April 22, 2009, from research database Ebscohost.

McCullough, M. E. (2000). Forgiveness as a human strength: Theory, measurement, and links to well-being. *Journal of Social & Clinical Psychology, 19*, 43–55.

McKnight, A. N. (n.d.). Historical trauma, the persistence of memory and the pedagogical problems of forgiveness, justice and peace. *Educational Studies, 36*, 140–158.

McWhirter, J. Jeffries, McWhirter, Benedict T., McWhirter, Anna M., & McWhirter, Ellen Hawley. (1998). *At-risk youth: A comprehensive response*. New York: Brooks/Cole Publishing Company.

Miller, Laurence. (1998). *Shocks to the system: Psychotherapy of traumatic disability syndromes*. New York: W. W. Norton & Company.

Moffatt, G. (2005, February). One quiet hour. This article first appeared in my newspaper column in *The Citizen*, Fayette County, GA.

Myers, David G. (2000). The funds, friends, and faith of happy people. *American Psychologist, 55*, 56–67.

Oras, R., Cancela de Ezpeleta, S., & Ahmad, A. (2004). Treatment of traumatized refugee children with eye movement desensitization and reprocessing in a psychodynamic context. *Nord J Psychiatry, 58*(3), 199–203.

Orcutt, H. K., Pickett, S. M., & Pope, E. B. (2005). Experiential avoidance and forgiveness as mediators in the relation between traumatic interpersonal events and posttraumatic stress disorder symptoms. *Journal of Social and Clinical Psychology, 24*(7), 1003–1029.

Patel, N., & Hodes, M. (2006). Violent deliberate self-harm amongst adolescent refugees. *European Child Adolescent Psychiatry, 15*, 367–370. Retrieved September 13, 2008, from research database Ebscohost.

Pelzer, Dave. (1995). *A child called It*. New York: HCI.

Pelzer, Dave. (2000). *A man named Dave*. New York: Plume.

Percy, Walker. (1983). *Lost in the Cosmos: The last self-help book*. New York: The Noonday Press.

Perry, Bruce D. (1997). Incubated in terror: Neurodevelopmental factors in the "cycle of violence." In J. D. Osofsky (Ed.), *Children in a violent society* (pp. 124–129). New York: Guilford Press, p. 124.

Perry, Bruce D. & Szalavitz, Maia. (2006). *The boy who was raised by a dog*. New York: Basic Books.

Peterson, Christopher. (2000). The future of optimism. *American Psychologist, 55*, 44–55.

Powell, S., Rosner, R., Butolo, W., Tedeschi, R. G., & Calhoun, L. G. (2003). Post-traumatic growth after war: A study with former refugees and displaced people in Sarajevo. *Journal of Clinical Psychology, 59*, 72–83.

Power, Samantha. (2002). *A problem from hell: America and the age of genocide*. New York: HarperCollins.

Preston, J. (2002). *Survivors: Stories & strategies to heal the hurt*. Atascadero, CA: Impact Publishers.

Reuters Foundation. (2004, April 6). Eyewitness: Word games in Washington as blood flowed in Rwanda. Retrieved from http://www.alertnet.org/thefacts/reliefresources/108124945499.htm.

Richardson, Glenn E., & Waite, Phillip J. (2002). Mental health promotion through resilience and resiliency education. *International Journal of Emergency Mental Health, 4*, 65–76.

Schottenbauer, M. A., Glass, C. R., Arnkoff, D. B., & Gray, S. H. (2008). Contributions of psychodynamic approaches to treatment of PTSD and trauma: A review of the empirical treatment and psychopathology literature. *Psychiatry, 71*(1), 13–34.

Schroeder, Carolyn S., & Gordon, Betty N. (2002). *Assessment and treatment of childhood problems: A clinician's guide* (2nd ed.). New York: The Guilford Press.

Schumm, J. A., Briggs-Phillips, M., & Hobfoll, S. E. (2006). Cumulative interpersonal traumas and social support as risk and resiliency factors in predicting PTSD and depression among inner-city women. *Journal of Traumatic Stress, 19*(6), 825–836.

Schwarz, R. A. & Prout, M. F. (1991). Integrative approaches in the treatment of post-traumatic stress disorder. *Psychotherapy, 28*(2), 364–373.

Segal, Z. V., Teasdale, J. D., Williams, J. M., & Gemar, M. C. (2002). The mindfulness-based cognitive therapy adherence scale: Inter-rater reliability, adherence to protocol and treatment distinctiveness. *Clinical Psychology and Psychotherapy, 9*, 131–138.

Seligman, Martin E. P. (2006). *Learned optimism: How to change your mind and your life*. New York: Vintage Books.

Seligman, M.E.P., & Maier, S. F. (1967). Failure to escape traumatic shock. *Journal of Experimental Psychology, 74*, 1–9.

Sue, D. W., & Sue, D. (2008). *Counseling the culturally diverse: Theory and practice* (5th ed.). New York: John Wiley, and Sons.

Suh, Eunkook M. (2002). Culture, identity consistency, and subjective well-being. *Journal of Personality & Social Psychology, 83,* 1378–1391.

Tangney, June Price. (2000). Humility: Theoretical perspectives, empirical findings and directions for future research. *Journal of Social & Clinical Psychology, 19,* 70–82.

Tedeschi, R. G., & McMillan, J. (2000). A correlational test of the relationship between posttraumatic growth, religion, and cognitive processing. *Journal of Traumatic Stress, 13,* 521–527.

ten Boom, Corrie. (1971). *The hiding place.* Old Tappan, NJ: Fleming H. Revell Company.

Terr, L. (1976). *Too scared to cry.* New York: HarperCollins.

Thompson, Charles L., & Rudolph, Linda B. (1996). *Counseling children* (4th ed.). New York: Brooks/Cole Publishing Company.

Trieschmann, Roberta. (1988). *Spinal cord injuries: Psychological, social, and vocational rehabilitation* (2nd ed.). New York: Demos Medical Publishing.

Vanderweker, L. C. & Prigerson, H. G. (2003). Social support and technological connectedness as protective factors in bereavement. *Journal of Loss and Trauma, 9,* 45–57.

Volf, Miroslav. (2006). *The end of memory: Remembering rightly in a violent world.* Grand Rapids, MI: William B. Eerdmans Publishing Company.

Werner, Emmy E., & Smith, Ruth S. (1992). *Overcoming the odds: High risk children from birth through adulthood.* Ithaca, NY: Cornell University Press.

Young, William P. (2008). *The shack.* Los Angeles: Windblown Media.

INDEX

About the Author

GREGORY K. MOFFATT, PhD, is professor of psychology and the chair of the Counseling and Human Services Department at Atlanta Christian College in Atlanta, GA, where he has served for 25 years. He is the author of numerous articles and books, including the Praeger titles *A Violent Heart: Understanding Aggressive Individuals, Blind-Sided: Homicide Where it is Least Expected, Wounded Innocents and Fallen Angels: Child Abuse and Child Aggression,* and *Stone Cold Souls: History's Most Vicious Killers.*